Drugs and Mo

The phenomenon of psychoactive drugs and our reactions to them is one of the most fascinating topics of the social history of humankind. Starting with an analysis of the 'policy of fear' in which law enforcement is 'haunted' by drug money, or its fearsome image, *Drugs and Money: Managing the drug trade and crime-money in Europe* offers a radical reconsideration of this highly contentious issue.

In this intriguing book, Petrus C. van Duyne and Michael Levi expose an ever-unfolding series of problems:

- the proliferation of mind-influencing substances;
- the complications of international drug regulation;
- the interaction between markets and economic actors, with the consequent amassing of huge amounts of crime-money.

The social, cultural and economic aspects of this crime-money are explored, alongside the ongoing threat it poses to the legitimate economy and the state.

Petrus C. van Duyne is a Professor of Empirical Penal Science at the University of Tilburg. **Michael Levi** is Professor of Criminology at Cardiff University.

Organizational Crime
Editor: Professor Vincenzo Ruggiero
Middlesex University, UK

The extraordinary variety of forms displayed by white collar and corporate crime, along with the array of offences committed by states and other institutional agencies, renders attempts to coin comprehensive definitions very difficult. **Organizational Crime** is a term normally utilised to identify some of the criminal acts performed by powerful groups of offenders.

This new Routledge series expands the meaning of **Organizational Crime** to include all criminality that can be analysed through the lenses of organization theory and the theory of the firm, thus encompassing old and new forms of organized crime.

Its themes will centre on 'business as crime', therefore focusing on both respectable and conventional offenders, on deviant business groups as well as criminal organizations, and finally on partnerships between the two.

Drugs and Money
Managing the drug trade and crime-money in Europe
Petrus C. van Duyne and Michael Levi

Drugs and Money

Managing the drug trade and crime-money in Europe

Petrus C. van Duyne
and Michael Levi

LONDON AND NEW YORK

First published 2005
by Routledge
2 Park Square, Milton Park, Abingdon, Oxon OX14 4RN

Simultaneously published in the USA and Canada
by Routledge
270 Madison Ave, New York, NY 10016

Routledge is an imprint of the Taylor & Francis Group

Typeset in Garamond by
Keystroke, Jacaranda Lodge, Wolverhampton
Printed and bound in Great Britain by
Cromwell Press, Trowbridge, Wiltshire

British Library Cataloguing in Publication Data
A catalogue record for this book is available from the British Library

Library of Congress Cataloging in Publication Data
A catalog record for this book has been requested

ISBN 0-415-34176-0 (hbk)
ISBN 0-415-35475-7 (pbk)

Contents

Tables and figures

For the figures in this book, the European continental annotation has been adopted. That means that the comma has been used for decimals, and the point to indicate the thousands. Hence: 1.200.345,87 instead of 1,200,345.87.

Tables

Figures

Preface

The phenomenon of psychoactive drugs and our reactions to them is one of the most fascinating topics of the social history of humankind. This is not simply because of the nature of the substances involved, or because of the criminal markets which developed after the putting into place of a global prohibition regime. After all, the organization of the drug market has many features in common with other clandestine markets, and when one has analysed a number of organized smuggling cases, one discerns much repetition. What is more fascinating is the various ways in which societies have tried to control drug-related behaviour, whether consumption or trafficking. For good reasons, potentially addictive and/or cognitively distorting substances are considered a threat to health, and some are considered to make users 'uncontrollable' as soon as they come under their influence. This evokes public fear and a need for control by the authorities, who have sought to reduce harm to others, and more contestedly, to reduce harm to the users themselves even when the latter do not agree that what they are doing is harmful to them. The historical conditioned reflex in industrialized countries has been to respond to these alarms by means of penal law and enforcement thereof. This penal law enforcement has unfolded in an increasingly international way, both within and (especially) outwith the European Union. The fact that we understand the term 'drugs' in this context as a signifier of harmful substances is a reflection of this. Otherwise it would merely be a neutral term indicating substances with chemical effects.

Nowadays, it is not drug-related behaviour alone which is the subject of control: drug *finances* are ever more vigorously subject to official scrutiny. This concerns not only law enforcement and intelligence agencies, but also the private sector who have increasingly been mandated (or coerced) to act as the conscripted intermediaries of public policy. Therefore this book addresses not just drug markets and related policy, but also the financial aspects of these markets. These financial aspects do not only concern *money-laundering*, which is a derivative of the criminal underground economy (and other profit-motivated law breaking). The finances connected to the drugs economy relate also to broader aspects, like the financial role of drug money in the licit economy and in war zones, like Southeast Asia, Afghanistan or Latin America.

From its onset, much of the policy around the control of drugs originated in the United States, so although this is a book about drugs and money in *Europe* – principally western Europe – and most of the empirical material about drug money in it comes from the member states of the European Union, it cannot stop at the (widening) borders of the EU. The same applies to the developments of drug policy within the United Nations, which were heavily influenced by the dominant role of successive US delegations.

In casting our eyes over other jurisdictions for comparison, we became increasingly puzzled about the nature of these drug profits, or rather more generally, 'drugs finances', about which so much is written and spoken, but so little stands up to rigorous scrutiny. This applies particularly to the question of the whereabouts of the many hundreds of billions of euros annually stealthily passing by worldwide. Why do so many industrious and vigilant law enforcement agencies working with growing if still modest resources and equipment, a global financial reporting regime, and broad support of private industry notice so little of this drug money, while they believe there is so much of it? The reader may share our puzzlement, which means that many questions remain unanswered, partly due to lack of basic data. Perhaps these unanswered questions form the most fascinating side of the drugs and money connection. We hope that future readers in the academic, policy and practitioner communities will be stimulated to ask and try to answer harder questions than have often been posed hitherto.

We have sought to situate the more empirically oriented central chapters on European drug markets and money-handling within a broader historical and policy context. Drugs policies are an arena in which there is seldom scope for the meeting of minds, and (values not being empirically derivable) we ourselves do not hold the same views on what principles should guide the control of illicit drug-taking for all age groups. However this work aims to be a dispassionate analysis of currently available evidence about European drug markets and the underlying money-handling aspects thereof, whatever views readers and we personally may have about what regulatory policies and practices are 'appropriate' in this highly contentious area.

1 The mind, drugs and the policy of fear

Trust and fear are important components in the development of modern state building. Granted, being 'soft' components, they have received less attention than battles and revolutions. Nevertheless, they are important underlying currents, driving subjects and rulers to these very battles and revolutions often resulting in new forms of government. The content of most constitutions, beginning with that of the US and in Europe, after the French Revolution, can be viewed as codifications of distrust on the part of the citizens – usually the better-off – towards the state, personalized in the arbitrariness of the absolute monarchies of the *anciens régimes*. This applied particularly to the area of finances, taxation and the judiciary. The emerging liberal bourgeoisie preferred a state acting as a night watchman, but this aloof role did not last long, if it ever existed in its pure form (Mosse, 1974). Gradually the authorities were empowered to design laws to further societal aims and to protect the citizens against new threats to their acquired interests. Depending on the social and economic backgrounds, such interests concerned small landholders, as in France, the 'Junker-estates' in Prussia, the powerfully developed industrial entrepreneurs as in Britain or Belgium, or the staggering merchant classes in the Netherlands.

It is interesting to investigate to what extent fear as a society-shaping motive contributed to the changing, mainly increasing role of the state and its institutions. It depends on who fears what. In 1848, fear of the mob drove many autocratic thinking monarchs in the German Länder and the King of the Netherlands to seek an alliance with the bourgeoisie and allow liberal constitutions. In the Netherlands this led to the present form of parliamentary monarchy, while in the German states the fear waned and authoritarian rule was in most cases restored. This implies that the explanatory power of the factor 'fear' is not one-dimensional. It depends how it is managed (Chambliss, 1994). Fear is a state of mind which can be aroused, strengthened, nursed and maintained, not as a self-propelling autonomous process, but by interested parties, like the church, the bureaucracy and the ruling elites (if any) which are their main stakeholders. An example is fear of deviant or non-conforming behaviour or attitudes, which do not directly victimize other people, but are nevertheless considered a subversive challenge to social stability. The fear of enlightened revolutionary ideas and 'mob rule' in the era of Restoration (1815–1848) requested a tough stance from the authorities. Later in the century, the rising working class held the nineteenth-century elites in Europe as much in its grip as did the fear of communism in Europe after 1945 (Hamerow, 1983). However, the states differed in their reactions: repression of labour movements, partial reform to take the wind out of the socialist sails, as in Germany (Gall, 1997), or allowing a gradual emancipation as in the Netherlands (as long as the rule of the elite and the monarchy were not jeopardized).

As the English political philosopher Hobbes recognised in his construct of Leviathan, to soothe fears, many citizens are willing to trust the authorities to take strong measures, which may encroach on their liberties. Whether such fears have any foundation is of little importance. What counts politically is the belief in the projected threat, to which the authorities will only rarely respond by playing it down, at least in the contemporary era of media-fuelled populist 'law and order'.[1] Except where this might reflect badly on their stewardship, either for political popularity or in pursuit of some other objective, they usually will respond by strengthening the 'security apparatus'. In the beginning of the nineteenth-century, the security apparatus consisted mainly of the army, which was deployed to quench the frequent riots, often directed against the economic pressures arising from industrialization (Hamerow, 1983; Stearns, 1975). Gradually, due to the extension of professional policing and the penal law system, the response was directed to enhance procedural and substantive law and penal sanctions. This has been the usual dominant response to religious, social or nationalistic unrest. Of course, this is not an explanation of all criminal law developments, nor an equal driving force in all jurisdictions. Parallel to strengthening the law enforcement system was the development of penal reform, leading (for a while) to more humanity and leniency. But in times of unrest, as with socialist agitation, separatist movements or even suffragette activism, the authorities' response was to resort to strengthening law enforcement powers.

In this chapter we will elaborate the hypothesis of an intriguing penal law interaction concerning the supposed threat emanating from the use of mind-influencing substances, which the authorities worldwide (and sections of the public) have considered to be a major and a serious threat. The chosen response has been the prohibition of these substances, maintained by penal

1 Though reactions to threats do not proceed at the same speed in all societies. In some countries such as the UK, for example, there is disagreement between law enforcement bodies, many of whom are suspicious of allegations about the pervasiveness and impact of 'organized crime', 'cyber crime' and such-like phenomena, for the combating of which the government and specialist units seek to 'top-slice' their budgets.

law enforcement. A part of this interaction concerns the consequence of this penalizing in the circumstance of a continued and even increasing demand, namely the subsequent development of an underground market of illicit production, traffic *and* the ensuing proceeds and profits of crime.[2] We will see that these criminal finances have evoked an independent fear. As the word 'psychoactive' denotes, such substances affect the mind in a way that is judged negatively. The justification of authorities to meddle in the individual's choice to consume these substances rests in its assumed right to have some say over the 'correct state of mind' of its adult and juvenile citizens. This is not a 'blessing' characteristic of modern times or the result of evil dictatorship, but a concern which has long historical roots.

1.1 The concern for the 'correct' state of mind

The human being may be the only animal species that displays an intrinsic preoccupation with its own mind. Not in a deep metaphysical or philosophical sense, but in the more mundane meaning of busying themselves with how they feel and experience things. In this regard, humankind represents an exceptional species, which is highly susceptible to a state of mind called boredom. In fact, humans are perhaps the only bored animals. That state of mind is addressed by a restless stimulus seeking (Zuckerman, 1980). Whether one values this drive as positive or negative, it has driven humankind to conquer (or ruin) this planet, creating art as well as war. Since time immemorial, this explorative conduct satisfied the need for stimuli to some extent. But alongside these ventures, people discovered, by trial and error, other stimuli derived from the products of nature. Yeasted grapes and other fruits proved to be alcoholic, which came to be highly appreciated.[3]

Since their discovery, mind-influencing substances have continued to play a particular role in stimulus-seeking conduct. Depending on cultural values or interests of the state, many societies have tried and succeeded in socializing or regulating their consumption. The most widespread mind-influencing substance, alcohol, has evoked very diverse responses, like most other drugs. It has been prohibited in the Muslim territories, while in most other states the authorities have made the best of its consumption by taxing it. Other substances like cannabis, coca, opium, tobacco and all caffeinated beverages were known for ages, albeit in their weak, raw forms. For a long time their use appeared to be too limited, for example restricted to religious ceremonies,

2 Proceeds are what the drugs are sold for; profits are proceeds net of business costs. As we will see, many drug profits are spent in the course of daily maintenance and lifestyle.

3 Interestingly, not only people enjoyed this arousing substance: elephants and monkeys are reported to like to taste the yeasted fruits of some African fruit trees too. However, only humans discovered the skills to organize production and the technology to preserve and store such agricultural products to be consumed at a later moment (Gerritsen, 1993).

or sufficiently socialized, to attract the disapproval of the authorities. If sufficiently popular they are bound to attract the greed of the authorities, who will tax them. As most substances are not inherently good for the human body, their use may also be prohibited or made unattractive by imposing prohibitive taxes. That is a matter of policy choice. In this regard, western society at first imported or invented a variety of mind-influencing substances, like brandy, opium or tobacco. In a later stage the social and political appreciation of some of those substances changed, leading subsequently to political decisions to restrict their use, with far reaching consequences (Courtwright, 2001).

For centuries the correlation between the mind-influencing substances and the state of mind did not bother the authorities of the slowly unfolding European nation states: the economy was too frugal and primary living conditions too meagre to allow for more than mere survival of the masses (Slicher van Bath, 1987). However, this does not mean that the authorities were indifferent to the mental states of their subjects, even if they were starving. The Christian territories, and emerging nation states especially, developed an obsessive desire to eliminate wrong, 'devilish' beliefs, which were supposed to have taken possession of the soul of a person. In fact, before and during the Age of the Reformation, Europe felt the ironclad fist of the first 'thought police', whose task was to detect and suppress religious deviations: the Inquisition (Baigent and Leigh, 1999). True, this bloody mind-control was just a malicious peak in an ongoing church–state alliance to keep spiritually deviating subjects down.[4] This was not an exclusive Roman Catholic policy. Even in the Protestant states, where the inquisition itself was abolished, the concern for the correct religious state of mind remained a concern for the authorities.[5] Many dissenting, more 'fundamental' (or 'pure') Protestants felt compelled to leave and migrated to the North American continent, where they added their flavour of spiritual intolerance, till the present day.

Being preoccupied with religious deviations, the ecclesiastical and secular authorities showed few interests in the (ab)use of the most prevalent psychoactive substance: alcohol. Why should they? Even if the abuse was chronic and widespread, there was no interest in developing an 'anti-alcohol'

4 This alliance, stemming from the beginning of the Carolingian rule, was soon affected by two other usual state preoccupations: power and money. Spiritually deviating subjects not only found themselves on the stake, but they and their families found their assets confiscated as well. Conversely, when it suited the Prince, he changed sides and confiscated the church lands.

5 The Reformation did not lead to the abolition of the witch trials in all the Protestant territories. For example Cromwell retained his 'Witch-finder General' and in the Puritan colonies of New England, the witch-hunt continued till the end of the seventeenth century (Baigent and Leigh, 1999).

policy in pre-industrial society. As a taxed commodity, it was (and remains) a valuable source of income, while the impurity of most water supplies at that time induced many consumers to drink alcoholic beverages from dawn to sunset. The salty quality of virtually all foodstuffs increased this universal and 'oceanic thirst' (Slicher van Bath, 1987). Lacking cold storage and preservatives other than salt, everything was salted: butter, porridge, fish and meat, to mention just a few daily commodities.[6] The poor could quench their thirst with diluted beer, the rich with wine. After the sixteenth century, Dutch genever, gin, schnapps and other spirits were added to the alcoholic menu. Even if this led to widespread drunkenness, landed interests, which benefited from the growing grain-for-gin production, did not further effective measures to stem this state of national alcoholism. In the beginning of the eighteenth century, gin shops advertised: 'drunk for a penny, dead drunk for twopence, and straw for nothing'. After a petition in 1736 by the Middlesex justices to restrict the excessive sales of spirits, Parliament adopted measures to restrict the sales of gin and other 'spirituous liquors'. The Gin Act was followed by riots, while the aimed reduction in the number of small gin shops was met with wholesale evasion (Rudé, 1970).

Despite this indifference, various social and economic developments provided increasing counterweights to this phenomenon. The most important counterweight may have come from the change in life rhythm imposed by industrialization since its take-off in the last quarter of the eighteenth century in Britain and in North Western Europe during the nineteenth century (Dillard, 1967). Factories with their expensive machinery required a regular working rhythm, which deviated strongly from the rural, semi-planned plodding of farmers and artisans. One could no longer turn up late, let alone turn up unstable with a hangover on the mechanized work floor. The safety of the machines (and, perhaps secondarily, of the workers) required discipline, which was incompatible with the taste for gin.[7]

Alongside, but usually following, this economic development was the Christian moral crusading against 'bad habits' in general and bad substances in particular. In the Christian framework of the nineteenth century, one may summarize this as a fight against wicked godlessness, gambling and drinking. To this trio may be added sexual laxity. Did this moral crusade have an effect in reducing the 'sinful' abuse of alcohol? Comparing the declining trend in the use of alcohol during the whole of the nineteenth century and the moments of the emergence of these moral initiatives, it appears that the

6 Slowly other forms of preserving developed: pickling, smoking (together with salting) and, in the nineteenth century, canning. See Shephard (2000).

7 Industrialization was not the only disciplining force at work in the modernization of society. The slowly developing school system and the ever-growing armies in the eighteenth century, required an elaborate system of discipline and punishment (Foucault, 1977).

latter *followed* rather than anticipated this reduction (Gerritsen, 1993). The moral crusading was most effective in creating an ethical framework in which already ongoing behavioural changes could be moulded and furthered. However, it seems more likely that apart from the industrial working rhythm, additional economic and material changes provided a more important drive to the reduction of alcoholic abuse. Water works began to provide clean water, and beverages like coffee and tea became cheaper and more widely available, though still a luxury for the poor. Also the appalling housing conditions improved gradually (Gauldie, 1974). Instead of fleeing a damp and cramped house to find comfort with a brandy in the alehouse, there was an alternative now and the lamentation 'father please, oh drink no more', started to make sense. The housewife could serve tea or coffee instead (Gerritsen, 1993). This sounds idyllic, but these material conditions and educational pressure from the enlightened bourgeoisie *and* 'elite' workers' circles contributed to Christian sobriety and a more homely life.

Industrial, social and political developments, particularly the division between state and church, furthered the relaxation of the official religious mind control, a trend which had begun in the eighteenth century Enlightenment. This did not imply an indifference to the moral state of citizens. Fear of riotous and anarchic behaviour stemming from seditious, immoral ideas was too deeply rooted in the consciousness of the aristocracy and propertied classes to let developments take their own course. Apart from that, not only fear, but also philanthropy moved part of the industrial elite to further improvements in the public domain. On the one hand, during the nineteenth century most industrializing states assumed responsibility (a) for national schooling, regularly conflicting with the Catholic church (Droz, 1971), and – very important – (b) for public health and housing (Hamerow, 1983). On the other hand, many of the moral and educational tasks (for the lower classes) were carried out by charity institutions. The well-off classes developed a broad network for the improvement of the material and moral state of the labouring classes and those who fell into sin, either because of licentiousness or because of alcohol. The gradual emancipation of the working classes entailed that they did not remain the object of paternalistic concern. Depending on the speed of industrialization, the growth of the urban population and the political system, labour cooperatives, associations and later unions developed, which took over many of the aims of philanthropists, apart from economic and political emancipation. It is interesting to observe that the movement against alcohol abuse did not become a major issue within the labour movement in Europe. Attempts were made to put it on the agenda, but it led to much disagreement: was working-class poverty the result of alcoholism or did the poor workers resort to alcohol to escape the depression of poverty? Fighting alcohol abuse remained a moral mission of individuals and individual associations in France, Germany and Belgium (Sournia, 1990, ch. 8).

The role of the churches in fighting alcoholism, rather considered a sin than an illness, varied. In general, the Catholic Church's attitude towards alcoholic abuse, or sin in general, was (and is) less strict. The temperance societies found a more fertile soil in the Protestant regions, particularly in the US, than in the Catholic ones (Sournia, 1990, ch. 8). Though official 'mind control' had practically stopped,[8] and political secularization had become the norm in most industrialising countries, the concern for the moral (i.e. Christian) state of mind and soul did not wane. It would set the interpretative framework for assessing 'bad habits', i.e. the display of unwanted conduct like gambling or the use of psychoactive substances. This moral framework cast its shadow on the coming policy regarding these substances and the continued use and ensuing traffic. But first we will discuss the growing importance of the professional medical class in the area of public health in general and the development of the drug issue.

1.2 Drugs, public health and the modern state

There was a continued concern not only for the moral state of mind and soul. The state of the health of the population at large moved gradually, but unavoidably within the orbit of the responsibilities of the authorities. The onset of an organized concern for the health of the (common) people was to a large extent determined by worried benefactors, some of them industrialists aiming to relieve the sorry plight of the working classes. Being men of influence, they did not restrict their actions to improving local conditions, like housing, schools, fresh water supply and sewerage, but tried to translate their philosophies into legislation. In the heyday of the liberal state they, together with the rising medical profession, succeeded in extending the responsibility of the state to the health of its citizens. In this endeavour they found spiritual support in the evangelical revival and its new humanitarianism towards the poor, as well as more earthly awareness that the recurrent cholera epidemics did not stop at the poor man's door. The sanitary movement in western Europe led to the introduction of officers of health, as in Liverpool in 1847 (Parry and Parry, 1976). At the end of the nineteenth century, a fully fledged public health policy had been developed in the industrialized states of Europe and North America.

An important component of this public health policy concerned the regulation of the administration of medicines. Part of medication always consisted of all sorts of painkillers, of which the most prominent in that time span was opium. Here our story begins in real earnest.

8 This was only a gradual development: during the era of Restoration (1815–1848) many states (Austria, Prussia, Russia) still maintained a kind of mind control to protect their subjects against seditious liberal literature (Mann, 1995; Palmer and Coltin, 1995).

At the turn of the eighteenth and nineteenth centuries, when pharmaceutical knowledge was still in its infancy, opium was widely used as a magical healer. It was used against pain, cholera, sleeplessness, rumbling stomachs and running bowels, or to keep children quiet. It was widely available, prescribed by doctors (and quacks), who prepared their own medicines, as well as at the local chemists for as little as a penny (Parssinen, 1983). The consumption of all sorts of beverages and pills, containing an often unpredictable amount of opium of uncertain purity, raised concern, but in the absence of other therapeutic agencies, it was an invaluable cheap medicine. In the absence of an affordable medical service, it was the 'Victorian aspirin' for the self-medication of the working classes.

Given its widespread availability, opium was also used for non-therapeutic purposes. This non-therapeutic use ranged from overworked mothers and baby-minders putting children to sleep, suppressing appetite (preferred to a crying hungry child), to a cheap replacement for alcohol. In other words, it became a euphoric agent, to forget the misery of industrial life in the slums (Berridge and Edwards, 1987; Parssinen, 1983) or to fight the boredom to which many of the better-off ladies were condemned (Courtwright, 1982). In the UK the escapist or, as it was called at the time, 'stimulant' use of opium was widespread in certain depressed areas like the Fen district, the marshy, damp areas of Lincolnshire, Norfolk and Cambridgeshire. This stimulant use by the working class, rather than the casualties caused by impure or too strong opium tincture (laudanum), raised serious concerns. The opinion that drugs should not be for recreational consumption contributed to the *Poisons and Pharmacy Act* of 1868, which first regulated opium and most other poisons. It was a compromise Act with limited impact, but for the pharmacists, who were designated exclusively to dispense the drugs, it was a milestone of recognition as a profession (Parssinen, 1983). Parliament showed a temporary willingness to set aside its distrust of government intervention and, as *The Times* once put it, 'to be bullied into health'. The anxiety subsided till some decades later, when a few Chinese opium smokers in the London dockyards would fan the fear of drugs again (Berridge and Edwards, 1987).

Though beginning hesitantly, as far as psychoactive substances are concerned, the 'bullying into health' would become a repeated pattern of persuasion, and develop into a legalized, strong-arm supported policy. Although starting with concern about the working-class stimulant use, this variety of abuse soon lost the attention of the new medical profession. This was no accidental neglect, given the low likelihood that a working-class addict (if he recognized his addiction at all) could afford the fee to visit a medical practice.[9] Medical consultation remained the privilege of the better-

9 There was an inter-relationship between private and public medical assistance, regulated under the Poor Law of 1834, according to which medicine and other medical care was

off, a few of whom developed another addiction pattern: hypodermic injection of morphine prescribed by the family doctor. Like the addiction to opium tincture or pills, the subcutaneous injection of morphine, introduced in the second half of the nineteenth century after the perfection of the hypodermic syringe, started as a new panacea. However, uncontrolled administration contained a high risk of leading to an 'uncontrollable desire . . . as a stimulant and a tonic' (Parssinen, 1983, p. 86).

Within decades, the professional attitude towards morphine (as well as other psychoactive substances) would change. The 'sin' of addiction was transformed into a 'disease'. It was not just a physical disease, but a *moral* one, a lack of will-power (Berridge and Edwards, 1987). But it was also a *sin*, a *vice*. Diseases have to be cured and vices have to be fought. Different interpretations started to emerge, inaugurating different approaches to the newly recognized problem: European treatment and the US 'war against' approach, of which more in the next section. But irrespective of the choice between them (some considered addiction both a disease *and* a vice), there was a clear task for the state and the medical profession. Meanwhile, the latter had established itself firmly, improving the quality of education, formulating professional standards and supervision, while the administration had increasingly assumed a more active policy in matters of cure and prevention (Parry and Parry, 1976).

In this historic framework, it is not surprising that the medical profession became a cornerstone in the debate on this (still small) drug problem (often induced by liberally prescribing doctors) and its solutions. Meanwhile one solution was developing quite naturally: better living standards and new and better medicine and palliatives like aspirin reduced the habit of popular 'opium eating'. The addiction to the syringe was not a matter of the common people, though the fear of opium and morphine addiction remained. In literature and in press reports, the place of the desperate worker was taken by the innocent young woman seduced into vice by Chinese opium mongers in their filthy opium dens. Fantasy and stereotypes, including the brave police inspector who broke the ring of vice and rescued the misled woman from the clutches of the vile seducers, began replacing facts to fan the fear.

1.3 Zero tolerance and prohibition

At this point, an interesting difference between Europe and the United States became visible. In most of the emerging democracies on the European continent in the nineteenth century, the movements for the moral and physical improvement of the working class became embedded or even

dispensed to the poor (Parry and Parry, 1976). Its effect on the treatment of lower-class addicts remains unclear, however.

integrated in the various socialist parties fighting for the material welfare and emancipation of the workers. In the decades before the First World War, in many Western European countries the labour movement became also more reformist, though much of the militant rhetoric remained. In addition, in some countries, like the Netherlands, Christian political parties, Catholic as well as Protestant, adopted social care as a moral task and strove to draw the labourers within their orbit, lest they would be seduced by the godless socialists.[10] This implies that many social and moral issues and concerns were incorporated in political programmes of various parties. Without necessarily becoming diluted as far as their contents and aims were concerned, they obtained a role within the pragmatics of reformist politics (Hamerov, 1983). As a consequence they became less the targets of single-issue moral 'crusading' programmes.

In the US, a similar labour movement to incorporate such moral programmes into the moderating pragmatics of social(ist) politics was absent. Socialism did not find fertile soil in a country in which belief in freedom and individualism constituted a kind of 'civil religion'. Collective socialist emancipatory movements did not develop as they did in Europe. This may partly explain why in the US, the moral reform movements during the 'progressive era' (1895–1920) did not flow into major political parties, but were scattered over many issues and spheres of material and especially *moral* interest (Toebes, 1995). The reform-oriented middle class, in which women played an important role, was focused on fighting 'vice' per se and not as a social abuse, a disease or personal tragedy. They retained strong 'fundamentalist' moral crusading traits. One may say they inherited and (still) display(ed) the righteousness of the Founding Fathers, including inherent intolerance. The nature and orientation of this drive cast its shadow over the policy developments concerning virtually all sin-inducing matters, well beyond the twentieth century. The basic philosophy was and remained: 'Just say no'. It started with the US alcohol issue of the nineteenth century, driven by powerful associations like the Women's Christian Temperance Union and the Anti-Saloon League. They exerted directly political pressure on political candidates and in the name of virtue and morality, did not shy away from attacking bars and their owners (Sournia, 1990). It is unsurprising that from this attitude towards 'vice', 'wars' against all other recreationally consumed varieties of drugs could be launched. The means by which these

10 Elsewhere, many Christian Democratic parties, and even conservative anti-socialist politicians like Bismarck, also adopted social welfare issues and enacted advanced social laws in order to take the wind out of their sails (Gall, 1997). On the other hand, socialist parties (or moderate sections) became more reformist, though their rhetoric often retained the tough nineteenth century radical ring (Mann, 1995).

wars were fought invariably included zero tolerance, prohibition and total control, preferably by means of the penal law.[11]

The US fight against alcoholic consumption contained a number of components, which have made themselves felt to the present day. Without representing them in a rank order of importance (which may differ according to the time span), the following elements manifest themselves regularly. In the first place the aim is a *total* one: full prohibition, buttressed by the force of law. No reduction by socialization of 'bad' habits, but demonization and criminalization of 'wicked' habits. In the second place there is an element of racism and xenophobia, which may vary from time to time in its intensity, but which hardly ever fails to manifest itself. There is always the fear that the bad habits of 'non-Americans' might infect the good (white) American citizens. A pamphlet of the Anti-Saloon League made this fear of (in this case, non-racial) contamination clear: Europe sends its drunkards with their un-American ideas about morality to the US – 'they dominate in large parts of the country our Sabbath, the sacred Sunday' (Toebes, 1995, p. 85). As virtually all popular drugs (apart from alcohol and, increasingly if less often acknowledged officially, marijuana) are produced abroad, the associative connection with a threat 'from outside' is easily made.[12] It goes without saying that this 'threat to the minds and health of our youth' has to be faced head on. The enemy has to be fought not only by a tough internal policy, but particularly by an active, if not aggressive foreign policy where the substances or the perpetrators may be foreign (Bewley-Taylor, 1999; Friman, 1996).

The fight against alcohol and the saloon was fought with increasing intensity in an era in which its consumption actually had already declined. As mentioned before, this was due more to the process of industrialization than to the moral influence of the Anti-Saloon League. Nevertheless, the usually Anglo-Saxon, rural Protestant middle class considered the saloon to be the very place of vice: the source of drunkenness and the location for

11 This is not just history. After a fascinating commercial career for most of the twentieth century, the approach to nicotine as an addictive drug appears to be following the same course. As the crisis of obesity hits Western medical care costs, the unhealthy addictive 'fatteners' as provided by 'junk food' outlets are also becoming targets (Courtwright, 2001). The difference in these cases is the countervailing commercial lobbies, and that the conduct is not yet associated in the public mind with disreputable behaviour by consumers.

12 Depending on the time span, this is not always true: during the 1970s/80s the production of cannabis in California increased dramatically, due to the success of the eradication programme in Colombia (Perkins and Gilbert, 1987). LSD and other stimulants were also US home-produced, although at the turn of the century the Netherlands became an important supplier of stimulants like XTC. Schlosser (2003) discusses the role of illicit labour in the contemporary American labour market, including the importance played by domestic drug cultivation as well as the underground economy, better analysed by Naylor (2002).

gambling, prostitution and (dirty) politics. It also looked with misgivings upon the influx of wine- or beer-drinking Catholic Italian, German and Polish immigrants, who settled in the cramped housings of the densely populated industrialized cities of the east coast (Krabbendam, 1995).

In the end, the Anti-Saloon League and related associations succeeded with the Vollstead Act of 1919. Its historic outcome is well known. After fourteen years of apparently ineffective enforcement, the rise of wholesale crime-enterprises and widespread corruption, the law was repealed. The US prohibition experiment provided a unique sociological 'open air' experiment. However, its lessons were better learned by behavioural scientists than by policy makers.

Meanwhile, another prohibition development, also originating in the nineteenth century, resulted just before the First World War in the first international anti-drug legislation. This heralded the war against (psychoactive) drugs, which would drag on until the present day. It has proven to be a remarkable *non-territorial* war *against* drugs, being preceded rather paradoxically by two wars *on behalf of* drugs: the first and second Opium Wars against China in the 1840s and 1850s. After the Chinese imperial authorities closed their harbours against the importation of opium, the colonial powers safeguarded their interests by force of gunships.[13] After the second Opium War, opium-trading countries such as Britain, France, the Netherlands and American skippers (who were soon out-competed) no longer found obstacles to draining China of her silver while keeping millions of Chinese addicted (Gerritsen, 1993; McCoy, 2003).

Why has the war on behalf of drugs been converted into a global war *against* drugs? After all, this trade did more than any other traffic to turn the usual colonial trade deficit – especially with British India – into a surplus. Despite this commercial success, a stand against this trade was emerging from various angles. In the first place there was a sincere ethical concern for the dire fate of the addicted native population. Missionaries began to agitate against this state-supported addiction. This was not without self-interest: some claimed to make fewer converts due to the local addiction to opium (Beeching, 1975). As we have seen in the previous section, the medical professions began to feel worried about opium consumption in their own countries as well. Like the ethical movement against alcohol, this 'ethical'

13 As a matter of fact only the first Opium War (1839–1842) was related to the attempts of the Chinese imperial authorities to halt the import of opium, whereupon Britain occupied Canton and other harbours. The second Opium war (1856–1860) was caused by an incident with a coaster, provoking new unrest. This time France joined England (Napoleon the III grasped every opportunity to profile himself, certainly after a French missionary had been crucified). After having occupied Beijing they imposed onerous peace terms on China (Beeching, 1975).

concern towards the colonial populations was directed at the abolition of the abuse, alongside raising the natives to a better moral (i.e. Christian) and material state. But unlike the domestic policy reformers at home, strict prohibition was not the aim of the colonial reformers.

This 'gradualistic' European approach towards (colonial) drug consumption, which persisted well into the 1930s, was internationally brushed aside from another angle: the aggressive foreign policy of the US. Having no longer any stake in the opium traffic with China, the US became China's ally when the latter asked for its support to halt this 'blood-letting'. The US government was happy to out-manoeuvre the colonial powers, redressing its previously aggressive policy towards China in a relatively easy and cheap way (Musto, 1973). Fighting the social and economic disruption caused by widespread opium consumption, China needed the support of the Americans. For the Americans, this counterbalanced their racist reputation in China concerning the bad treatment of their compatriots in the US, where there was little sympathy for the cheap Chinese labourers in the first place. This combined with an outright disgust for their opium-smoking habit (Gerritsen, 1993). This policy was not directed at a 'soft' reduction of abuse, but at a straight international prohibition, which was bound to affect negatively the interests of colonial powers like the Netherlands, France and Britain (McCoy, 2003; Gerritsen, 1993). Finally the US succeeded in its prohibition drive, but not without fraud and deceit. By deliberately inflating the number of addicts, the influential Hamilton Wright, one of the three US international delegates to the Shanghai Opium Commission in 1908, tried to achieve results at home to obtain a moral leverage abroad. Perhaps as a form of 'noble-cause corruption' in his mind, he created a statistical illusion of a sustained increase reaching one million addicts, despite having been advised that opiates consumption per capita had *decreased* in the previous decade (Courtwright, 1982, p. 29). The fraudulent figures had their (long-term) effect. In the short term, Wright achieved international success: the Opium Treaty of The Hague, banning all opiates and cocaine was signed in 1912, coming into force with the Treaty of Versailles in 1919.

We have seen that the anti-drug stand was strengthened by medical concern about the liberal dispensing of opium and later morphine. To this can be added the relative newcomer, cocaine, in the second half of the nineteenth century. It also became a popular panacea, particularly after being applied in coca-extract wine in 1863 in Europe. In 1886 the American Pemberton followed with the introduction of coca-cola as a medicine against headaches and a stimulant against depression (Verbeek, 2001). The enthusiastic reception of all sorts of coca products resulted in a widespread abuse, if not addiction, which had to be countered as severely as alcoholism. There were also alarming reports about increased cocaine-induced violence, particularly among the lower (black) classes. Under the influence of cocaine, blacks were reported to have become invulnerable to a standard .32 police revolver, causing some Southern police departments to increase the calibre of their guns (Adler, 1995). Even if the evidence for such wild stories was lacking, they were believed, and tolerance turned into fear and a call for prohibition. This was realized by the Pure Food Act of 1906, prohibiting the application of cocaine in commercial products. In 1914 this was followed by the Federal Harrison Narcotics Act, prohibiting all free sale of all opiates and narcotics: only general physicians were licensed to prescribe such substances.

The failure of Prohibition from 1919 till 1933 should have taught the lesson that penal law enforcement is not a self-evidently sensible remedy against bad habits. However, as the British historian A.J.P. Taylor remarked, policy makers just repeat past mistakes in new forms. The next variety of rehearsing past mistakes appeared to be the anti-marijuana policy. During the 1930s, reports mentioned a relation between violence and the use of this substance by Mexican labourers. This gave it the qualification 'killer weed'. However, it seems more likely that the aggressive weekend behaviour of the Mexican labourers was due more to their favourite tequila than to smoking pot. Nevertheless, here was another scare, underpinned by official reports, while medical reports contradicting them remained unmentioned (Himmelstein, 1983). Though the Federal Bureau of Narcotics (the successor of the Bureau of Alcohol and Drugs) was at first reluctant to endorse a new prohibition, its director Anslinger finally lent his support. In 1937 the fear of this 'killer weed' was converted into law: the Marijuana Tax Act.

Looking back at the roots of the present-day anti-drug policy, one may conclude that they are firmly planted in the soil of fear. This fear may be motivated by the genuine belief in the damage caused by substances to the physical and mental well-being of citizens. However, the evidence for harm was and is often episodic and based on poor science as well as on taken-for-granted beliefs about the right to impose on others one's vision of 'the good society'.[14] This does not exclude other rational considerations and interests, like foreign trade and policy, nor the rational management of such fear for political agenda purposes. In Western societies, there has always been a fear of mental or spiritual deviation as a kind of internal psychological corruption. In liberal nineteenth century states, this fear for the corruption of the mind did not wane, but to a large extent was taken over by private moral initiatives and movements. Some of these were reformist; others were characterized by a zealous militancy, particularly in the US. If the medieval corruption of the

14 As the contemporary debates over ecstasy (XTC) and marijuana illustrate, there continue to be serious disagreements about medical effects, quite apart from social dilemmas – seldom aired in popular discussions and the media – about the 'rights' of people to use substances that may damage 'only' a modest proportion of them.

mind was caused by the devil and heresy, the modern corruption is brought about by substances and a lack of moral will. To soothe these fears, the authorities had to demonstrate that such corruption deserved no tolerance, but total prohibition. This did not entail a one-formula approach: depending on the philosophy about human nature, the lack of moral will can be treated as a disease or punished as a vice.

The conclusion that this policy was 'planted in the soil of fear' does not exclude other perspectives, like foreign policy, trade and institutional interests. Fear is a vague and 'fluid' (collective) state of mind, which needs to be directed by rational political management, as is described concerning the organized crime fear in the 1990s by Chambliss (1994) and Van Duyne (2004).

1.4 The fear of the fruits of crime: money

Historically, the fear of drugs, which after eight decades was followed by that of drug money as a major threat, retained a self-propelling force similar to the nineteenth-century drive of the Anti-Saloon League against alcohol. Irrespective of the level of drug consumption, the fight went on. If consumption was low, as was the case shortly after the Second World War, there was a *potentially* looming threat. If consumption was high, previously stern measures had not been severe enough, and the 'war' had to be stepped up. A convincing combination was always the projection of drug trafficking onto the conceptual framework of *organized crime*. In this projection we meet similar ingredients, reinforced within and by the organized crime framework. The recurring fear-arousing component in this framework is the 'alien conspiracy' representation, starting with the American-Italian Mafia, later renamed as Cosa Nostra (Albanese, 1983). It was first officially reported by the Kefauver Committee of 1950. Later congressional and presidential commissions hardly deviated from this popular imagery. They merely added new 'Mafias', like the cocaine 'cartels' operating out of Colombia (Abadinsky, 1991; Zaitch, 2002). Not surprisingly, after 1989 the 'Russian Mafiya' was conveniently added to this organized crime threat too (Rawlinson, 1998; Varese, 2001). Such imagery was only partly adopted in Europe where, Italy excepted, there was greater scepticism about the existence of organized crime as a hierarchical model. However, the availability of the *term* routinely conjured up images of *The Godfather* among the public, police and politicians.

To this mixture of threats, the components of which are mutually enforcing, was added a new candidate: the looming threat of *crime-money*. Organized crime was not only poisoning youths by selling psychoactive substances. Even worse, it was also supposed to be 'on the march' to the vital financial control chambers of society, by laundering its ill-gotten profits and reinvesting it in the upperworld. Whether this threat was a real one is sociologically less important than the belief that the accumulated crime-moneys (or, in the felicitous phrase of Sir David Omand, then Permanent Secretary at the UK Home Office, 'mutant capital') constituted a tremendous capacity for corruption. There is actually little new about this threat. The history of the sordid relationship between organized crime and local US elections indicates that the corruptive tradition did not commence with drugs money (Peterson, 1983; Chambliss, 1978; Schoenberg, 1993). In some jurisdictions though, like Latin America, the volume of drug money intensified the corruption problem, giving it a broader dimension.

Irrespective of the seriousness of this threat, the US legislature eventually enacted Draconian laws to 'hit the criminal where it hurts him most', in his wallet, commencing with the Comprehensive Forfeiture Act of 1984, which was directed at forfeiture of the tools of crime, the proceeds or both. The motivation appeared to be partly fear of what the money might fund and partly a belief that stripping criminals financially might deter them. From the point of view of civil liberties and 'equality of arms', the new legislation did not display much subtlety in balancing the interests of the state against those of its citizens. Moreover the police ability to retain a portion of the forfeiture procedures generated an incentive to act improperly (Rasmussen and Benson, 1994; Levy, 1996). Eager to increase their budget and to lay their hands on coveted property like cars and real estate, in some regions the policy degenerated into 'legal street robberies', as one of the sheriffs regretfully admitted (Blumenson and Nilsen, 1997, footnote 176).[15] The forfeiture law not only created much undeserved hardship; it also created a new commercial enterprise: informing for profit, which may yield up to 25 per cent of forfeited profits (Woodiwiss, 2001, pp. 354–361). This outcome is not surprising given the attitude which filtered top-down: already in 1990 the Attorney General warned the local attorneys against a 'failure to achieve the $470 million projection [as this would] expose [us] to criticism and undermine confidence in our budget projections' (Blumenson and Nilsen, 1997, note 102).

As has happened with the War on Drugs, the war against crime-money, or rather money-laundering, has been exported to the rest of the world. As has been done in the War on Drugs (Bruun *et al.*, 1975; Bewley-Taylor, 1999), the US used its political leverage in the United Nations as it did with the passing of the Single Convention on Narcotic Drugs (1961) and the Convention on Psychotropic Substances (1971). The United Nations Vienna

15 In Volusia County, Florida, the Sheriff's Department drug squad seized over $8 million from motorists between 1989 and 1992, justified as a part of the War on Drugs. In over 75 per cent of cases no charges were filed. To fend off the enraged citizens who wanted their money back, the sheriff employed a forfeiture attorney at $44.000 per year. Only four people got their money back; the rest settled for 50–90 per cent of their money if they promised not to sue the Department (Rasmussen and Benson, 1994, p. 137).

Convention of 1988 obliged in Article 5 the 'deeply concerned' parties to adopt measures to confiscate proceeds derived from drug offences. In 1989, the heads of the governments of the G-7 countries established the Financial Action Task Force on money-laundering. The report of that working group formed a real watershed, not because of the validity of its evidence, which was dubious, according to recalculation by Van Duyne (1994), but because of the belief in the global threat of the crime-money it conveyed. Its huge figures of crime-proceeds of $300 billion dollars *yearly* were later augmented to one trillion by the United Nations: political figures for political believers (Naylor, 1999). In 1990, the Council of Europe produced the first significant European Convention, its *Convention on Laundering, Search, Seizure and Confiscation of the Proceeds from Crime (Treaty No. 141).*

Fear has many faces and effects, also in foreign politics. The FATF, an independent body with no obvious accountability except to its constituent member states, has relentlessly exploited the fear of crime-money. Its reviews are feared, especially among those non-members which do not comply with its 'recommendations' (actually demands). Once it has gone through the initial and Plenary meetings, there is no appeal against being put on the list of 'non-cooperative countries and territories'. This may have grave consequences for the stigmatized countries' economies (though there are now procedures for applying to get off the list). In the light of this, every country which wants to avoid being blacklisted has adopted anti-laundering legislation and organizational measures (Stessens, 2001; Levi, 2003a). One may wonder whether this obedience has been caused by the fear of crime-money or by the fear of sanctions for being considered 'non-cooperative'. Nevertheless, irrespective of the nature of the fear, it has worked as intended, at least in formal institutional terms. The legal 'fishing net', defining the concept of money-laundering, has been broadened to such an extent that virtually every consequential act of a crime for profit can legally be considered laundering (Stessens, 2000; Van Duyne, 2002). In addition, though the dogma still is 'to prevent the corruption of the financial system', increasingly more non-banking professions (lawyers, accountants, car dealers, art and precious-metal dealers) have become obliged to report unusual or suspicious transactions. And those who suspect (or, in some cases, ought to suspect) that funds are proceeds of crime or are intended to finance terrorism but do not make reports are liable to be prosecuted for being an accomplice to the act of laundering. After 11 September 2001, the financing of terrorism and related moneys were added (though these are outside our brief here).

Fear of crime has been converted into fear of not reporting a fellow citizen, irrespective of the costs to the financial sector and other enterprises obliged to report (Harvey, 2003). One may wonder whether we have not somehow returned to a variety of the social control situation during the state–church alliance in the Middle Ages and beyond. At that time, the fear of a religiously deviating state of mind induced people to report on their fellow citizens, or else they faced the consequences of not having reported it. Now the fear of crime-money has obliged increasingly more private parties to report unusual, deviating transactions.[16] All for the common good.

In the next chapters, we will investigate the empirical foundations of this fear-induced control policy as far as the drug markets in Europe are concerned. How did the drug markets develop and consolidate? What kind of market conditions and criminal entrepreneurs do we meet and what does the extent and nature of the criminal money-management really look like?

16 We find a related intermediate form in the system of Czar Peter the Great, who encouraged his subjects to report on corruption. If successful, the informants were entitled to (part of) the assets of the wrongdoers. However, he threatened his subjects with harsh punishments in case they failed to report (Holm, 2003, pp. 95–98).

2 The unfolding of illegal drug markets in Europe

2.1 Eurodrug markets and the United States

The development of the illegal drug markets in Europe is not a geographically distinct phenomenon. From its beginning, it was embedded in an international landscape, which requires a broadening of the scope of our story. Part of that broadening is directed to the US, which may wrongly give the reader the impression of an insertion of a subsidiary theme: 'US and drugs', with other countries following as mere puppets. As social surveys indicate, most illegal drugs are viewed as harmful in many countries, and their use attracts widespread disapproval.[1] However, as we will see, there is no 'subsidiary theme', but an interwoven pattern of policy threads, in which the US component has traditionally but not universally been very strong, as the real or apparent formulator of the drugs policy. Indeed, many brands of drug, like cocaine, heroin and MDMA, were discovered or invented in Europe during the nineteenth and early twentieth centuries, but the impact of their consumption was first felt and disapproved of in the US, after which there followed international prohibition. As the illicit drug market is mainly shaped by the nature of its prohibition regime, which also started in the US, a description of its development in Europe should therefore be projected against the nature and reach of the US prohibition policy and its huge impact on the European drug markets. The reasons for this impact are very diverse and cannot be fully elaborated here. Nevertheless, a few aspects of this broader policy landscape have to be indicated. Two clusters can be discerned: the carry-over of domestic drug issues into foreign policy; and the extent of the presence of military, customs and police officers abroad.

In the first place, the US administration has always addressed its domestic drug issue as a *global* problem, which from its beginning led to 'exporting

1 This observation may contain some circularity: as soon as a substance has been declared illegal or harmful, more people will express their disapproval even if the only thing they know about it is the official stance.

the War on Drugs' (Friman, 1996). This approach is based on rational choice as well as prejudice. Most drugs do stem from other countries, for which reason it can be defined as a threat from abroad, namely from producing and exporting countries. Hence one can justifiably argue that the drug problem must be solved by the countries where the commodity is produced and exported. This approach is at odds with the principle of national sovereignty, which may be felt as an impediment to be overcome by all means. The willingness to overcome national sovereignty was furthered by xenophobic and racist prejudice. This prejudice was unambiguously expressed by Richmond Hobson, an anti-narcotic campaigner in the 1920s: 'Like the invasions and plagues of history, the scourge of the narcotic drug addiction came out of Asia' (Bewley-Taylor, 1999). This was not an isolated, exceptional remark. Later anti-drug crusaders in high places, like Anslinger, the Commissioner of the US Federal Bureau of Narcotics, did little to wrap such sentiments in more politically correct wording. Therefore, developing a 'narco-diplomacy' entailed international diplomatic initiatives and pressure, which can be documented from the first decade of the twentieth century onward. This narco-policy exportation gathered pace after the Second World War under the relentless drive of Anslinger who, as representative on the United Nations Commission on Narcotic Drugs, used this body successfully as a platform to further the US drug policy conception (Bewley-Taylor, 1999).

Behind this global perspective and rhetoric, many domestic law enforcement 'turf' issues played a role. One was the relation between *federal* and *state* law enforcement. As the drug problem was considered to be a *federal* issue in the US, it was endorsed by the federal administration, which enabled it to strengthen its powers towards the states in an uncontested policy area. (This effect is also a factor in marshalling support for measures to deal with 'organized crime' in many federal and even non-federal jurisdictions.) This was not only a top (federal)-down movement. Bottom-up, there was pressure as well. Through their concerned representatives, constituencies could bring local drug problems in Congress to the attention of the federal administration. Because most drugs are imported and are therefore considered to be a *foreign* threat, local concerns expressed in Congress are easily carried over into foreign policy. This happened with the policy of (de)certifying South American drug-exporting countries, in which Congress has an important say (Crandall, 2002, pp. 42–44).[2] Another interaction between federal anti-drug legislation and foreign policy concerned the need of US delegates to demonstrate to the often not very energetic European countries

2 In concrete terms it means that if a local constituency is concerned about local drug problems, its representatives in Congress may be under pressure to vote for the decertifying of a country which is blamed for the export of the drugs.

that the US had already put the prohibitionist legislation into place (Courtwright, 1982; Bewley-Taylor, 1999).

In the second place, the US has a tradition of policing abroad: first in its own 'back yard', Central and South America, and after the Second World War, in the occupied territories of Germany and Japan. In addition, the US administration lent much police support to Third World (anti-communist) countries, such as training police officers for civil as well as counter-insurgency tasks. In this role, foreign aid became tainted because of torture practices by the trainees. After criticism, the training programme was (temporarily) abandoned, whereupon many police officers stepped over to the expanding DEA presence abroad, continuing with much of their personal law enforcement network in another policy area (Nadelmann, 1993).

In the third place, after the Second World War, the US had a large military presence in many countries surrounding the USSR. These troops were policed by the military police, who had to cooperate with the local police forces, certainly where it concerned the sensitive point of drug trafficking related to the military bases. Particularly in drug investigations, an intimate cooperation between the military police and the local crime-squads developed (Nadelmann, 1993, ch. 3). Cooperating or intervening – a thin or purely semantic dividing line – in foreign jurisdictions was therefore a 'natural' way of furthering US interests.

In the last place, one should not underestimate the enormous foreign policy leverage in international matters which the US acquired after the Second World War. A military superpower, economically overawing and with an unrivalled international moral prestige, it could dominate law enforcement issues, in which fighting drugs was always one among the dominant issues. The leverage could be observed in the UN's drug committees as well as in jurisdictions which were in an economically dependent position. How this produced the desired results can best be summarized by a quote from a field officer of the Federal Bureau of Narcotics (the forerunner of the DEA), stationed in Europe during the 1960s. When his local police partners, willing to cooperate, were restrained by their superior officers or politicians, he 'found that a casual mention of shutting off our foreign-aid programme, dropped in the proper quarters, brought grudging permission for our operations almost immediately' (Nadelmann, 1993, p. 134). This leverage, or coercion, increased with the gradual proliferation of US law enforcement offices abroad. It did not only concern operational police activities. The delegated agents were also expected to push for 'structural changes' in law enforcement, to lobby for tougher laws and to contribute to 'institution building' (Nadelmann, 1993, pp. 145–146). In the end these zealous missionary activities resulted in a common belief in the correctness of the tough prohibition policy (or at least an outward compliance with it), which at internationally decisive levels numbed an open debate about alternatives (Woodiwiss, 2001).

From this brief summing-up one should not deduce that all foreign jurisdictions were unwillingly 'dragged' into US drug policy, though there was little room for free manoeuvring. Weighing the advantages of compliance and economic support against following a dissident policy, Europe stepped into line. Since prior to the 1960s, Europe experienced no major drug problems, there were no stimuli to think about an alternative policy, thereby opposing the US prohibition regime and risking a negative pay-off. It is uncertain whether delegates shared the British awareness that the requested international cooperation served primarily the mitigation of the US domestic drug problem.[3] France, for example, became as 'hawkish' as the US (Boekhout van Solinge, 2002).[4] It would therefore be incorrect to qualify the US-disseminated drug policy as a kind of 'drugs imperialism', at least from an American point of view. They rather felt they had a mission towards the 'opium bloc' of some European countries before the Second World War, which had to be completed after 1945. Nevertheless, the end result appeared to be a far reaching 'Americanization of European drug enforcement', particularly regarding the changes demanded or incited by the Americans (Nadelmann, 1993, ch. 4).

Against this broader horizon, we can describe in more detail the international backgrounds and the unfolding of the drugs markets in the twentieth century.

2.2 Some international developments

Looking back is easier than looking forward. Few policy makers in the last decades of the nineteenth century, who were concerned about the evil of opium consumption and traffic would have surmised that a century later, that evil would still be with us. Worse, the evil more than survived, and had grown into a 'global' illicit drug market. In hindsight the policy makers' designed international regime of prohibiting psychoactive substances, with the exception of scientific, medical and therapeutic applications, turned out to grow into the eventual worldwide 'War on Drugs'. At the beginning of the twentieth century it did not start as such, but rather (ominously) with an outright fraud as to its scale (Courtwright, 1982). It was not a one-dimensional development. On the way towards prohibition, many influences and interests as well as zealous moral crusaders came together and

3 The British delegate, Hutson, added if it had not been '*for the white drug problem in the USA* . . . the suppression of the raw material and their indigenous consumption in a relatively harmless form [in the production countries] would not have carried on as far as it has' (quoted in Bewley-Taylor, 1999; emphasis by Hutson).

4 France maintained already a strict control policy at home and a lenient opium policy in its colonies, particularly in Indo-China.

prevailed over powerful 'contra-interests', for example from the pharmaceutical industry (Nadelmann, 1990).

We have already observed in section 1.2 that in the course of the nineteenth century there was a growing concern in the industrialized countries (and China) about the consumption of medicinal substances. These comprised opium and later morphine and cocaine, either prescribed by doctors or taken as self-medication (Parssinen, 1983). This concern was supported by the administration, which was increasingly regarded as the guardian of the public health, sometimes vigorously driven by moral entrepreneurs. Alongside we find the interests of the rising medical profession, which was naturally against self-medication and the free dispensing of these panacea drugs.

In section 1.3 we showed that in the colonial era, opium played an important but disputed role in the foreign trade in South and East Asia. Reformers acting against the consumption of opium at home equally condemned the commercial profits made at the expense of the Chinese or the colonial natives. But internationally in the anti-colonial opium trade policy on behalf of China (the 'victim' country), the US took the lead in forging a new international anti-narcotic order. After much pressure, particularly by missionary moral entrepreneurs like Hamilton Wright, the new policy began to unfold during and after the opium conferences in The Hague, 1912–1914. Its aim was to control and reduce the production and the colonial trade of opium products, particularly by the British and the Dutch (Gerritsen, 1993).[5] After the First World War, this initial objective shifted gradually towards a full international system of control of opium products and other 'dangerous substances' to reduce the supply and consumption in the western countries as well as in the colonies.

The International Opium Convention of The Hague was adopted by the League of Nations in 1919 and extended in 1925, 1931 and 1936. The armed conflict in Europe after 1939 made the work of the League's control agencies difficult and the US invited the Permanent Central Opium Board and the Drug Supervisory Board to move to Washington DC. It heralded a new era of US dominance in the drug portfolio and the policy of the League's successor (Bewley-Taylor, 1999). After the Second World War, the policy against psychoactive substances was inherited and intensified by the United Nations. In 1946 the agreements and conventions were amended, and the United Nations took over the whole bureaucratic machinery, which had developed in the League of Nations era. As time passed by it added a considerable number of new agencies to handle various drug problems (Bruun *et al.*, 1975).This resulted in an organizational tree with many branches and

5 Britain, trying to stall the conference, insisted that cocaine was added to the agenda, much to the dislike of Germany, which was the main producer of cocaine.

secretariats: whatever the magnitude of the global drug problem or the related crime-market, the drug bureaucracy had become a vested interest in itself.[6]

As is the case with any organization established to deal with a problem, the anti-drug bureaucracy thrived and flourished with the growth of 'their' problem. With the development of the pharmaceutical industry many new dangerous, 'addictive' drugs were detected and added to the ever growing perimeter of prohibited substances. Patterns of consumption (or abuse) also changed over time, becoming more extensive as well as diverse. The morally driven 'problem owners' grew accordingly in importance and pressed increasingly for 'adequate' (= tough, severe) measures to stem the tide. Indeed, they tried to beat an expanding informal market, which after the Second World War became more extensive and commercial. Finally the protagonists and antagonists became inextricably intertwined in a protracted deadlock (Wisotsky, 1986). The illegal drug economy has become an enduring global commercial and political phenomenon, providing a profitable market for the prohibited drug traders and moral entrepreneurs alike.

2.3 The onset of the illegal drug market

It is common to speak of a 'market' as soon as there is a demand and a supply. In this sense the Western countries had their illegal 'drug market' as soon as the prohibition regime was put into place in the first decades of the twentieth century. However, from a commercial perspective the market was still small and not very professional. The authorities' worry and the gradual extension of the international control organizations therefore reflect no commensurate growth of the market for illegal drugs. As a matter of fact, the objectives of the anti-drug 'system' and changes in the market circumstances are not simply correlated. The initial objective was the elimination of the 'evil' colonial opium traffic from British India and the Dutch East Indies to China. This objective was gradually reached: the Dutch income from opium sales halved between 1914 and 1932 from *f*35 million (Dutch Guilders) to *f*17 million; for Britain in the same period, income fell two-thirds from £7,5 to £2,5 million (Gerritsen, 1993).

This reduction of the colonial traffic did not entail an end of the narcotic trade of the West with China, however. Between the World Wars, drugs,

6 It is interesting to observe that while the staff of drug-control secretariats increased, the attention to alcoholism diminished relative to drug dependency. The number of pages in the World Health Organization Director General's report devoted to the drug problem far outreached the number of pages for alcoholism (Bruun *et al.*, 1975). Only gradually and less universally has interest in alcoholism increased again, in the case of the UK with the rise of the night-time economy and rowdy behaviour in town centres from the late 1990s.

especially opium, morphine and heroin, were available as an overflow from the overproduction of the Western pharmaceutical industry, a large part of which found its way to China. In the US and Europe, users of opium, morphine and heroin (hardly known in Europe) obtained their illegal supply mainly from general physicians, though it had become illegal to give prescriptions without strict medical reasons. And prescribing 'maintenance doses' for addicts was not considered a medical, therapeutic reason.[7] However, despite the concern of the professionals in the committees of the League of Nations, there was little drug demand in Europe (perhaps with the exception of post-war Germany) or in the United States, and no commercial market.

In absolute numbers, the US market outnumbered the European, and much use was made of the appearance of an epidemic. However, though the American political rapporteurs to the Senate estimated the number of addicts at 1 million, Courtwright (1982) demonstrated that the most plausible estimate was 250.000 between 1900 and 1914, a number which further declined between 1919 and 1940 to approximately 100.000. As mentioned already in section 1.3 this was not an inaccuracy but a fraud. The rapporteurs, like Wright in 1910, who first suggested the 1 million addict figure as well as the rapporteurs of the Treasury Department's *Traffic in Narcotic Drugs* of 1919 jumped willingly to conclusions. Realizing their mistakes they persisted, for fear of or out of deference to other committee members.[8] Once taken for true, the imaginary figures, subsequently inflated to 1,5 million, continued to scare legislators into action. It would not be the last fraud in the drug policy portfolio.

A new feature was the introduction of heroin after 1898, a new medicine to treat respiratory ailments. Soon it became clear that the cure had a high risk of leading to dependence. After the ban on (smoking) opium in 1909 and the increased scarcity of cocaine, due to various informal controls of retailers and doctors before the 1914 Harrison Narcotics Act (criminalizing the sale of narcotics), persistent users resorted increasingly to heroin. This commodity was more effective, cheaper and more available than the other substances.

Compared to morphine and opium addiction, it is interesting to observe a new class distinction. While morphine addicts were often older, female

7 Till the late 1960s the policy of maintenance doses remained the medical practice in Britain before pressure towards increasing restrictions was exerted. In the US this medical approach was already outlawed after the First World War in favour of a penal law enforcement approach.

8 The author of the 1918 report *Some Facts Concerning Drug Addiction*, DuMetz, repudiated his work in a 1924 article by lowering the number of addicts to 246.000. Later he dismissed the 1.000.000 estimate as arrived at by ignoring facts already 'discovered when the report was made'. The matter was never discussed in print, however (see Courtwright, 1982, p. 32).

and had a history of chronic illness and pain, heroin users were younger, male and more often from the lower working class. The heroin addicts were mainly second-generation Irish and Italian immigrants, living in the slums of the eastern industrial cities (Gerritsen, 1993). This difference expressed itself in the institutions to which convicted addicts were allocated: morphine users found themselves more frequently admitted to hospitals and asylums, while heroin addicts were referred to jails and prisons (Courtwright, 2002).

In England the population of registered morphine addicts was much smaller, comprising many middle-aged women (often nurses) and doctors charged with violating the Dangerous Drugs Act by prescribing narcotics. The consumption of *cocaine* appeared to be more restricted to the (lower-class) West End nightlife in London. Arrested cocaine users were younger, frequently women in the low-wage female economy: chorus girls, prostitutes or a mixture of both. Following waves of moral panics during the First World War (the fighting power of soldiers might be undermined by drug dealers), a new regulation issued in 1916 outlawed the possession of drugs for everybody except doctors. Drug cases got much, sometimes hysterical, media attention (Kohn, 1999).[9] Despite all this panic, the informal drug market was still small and hardly professionally or commercially organized. The absolute numbers of convicts remained small, till the 1960s.

In Germany and Austria, the attitude of the authorities had already changed towards the control of dispensing drugs before the Hague conferences. This change towards drug control was brought about through a bureaucratic process in the Imperial Reich and subsequently the Weimar Republic, not by moral crusaders or media sensationalism, and was little thwarted by the fragmented chemical industry. In addition to higher opium prices than in England or the US, another important circumstance which reduced the market was the absence of a tradition of self-medication. To relieve their misery, industrial workers compensated for the lack of opiate drugs by widespread alcohol abuse (Selling, 1989). During the chaotic years after the First World War, the problem of uncontrolled use of morphine and particularly cocaine increased sharply. In artistic and the psychoanalytical Freudian circles, morphine and cocaine were already broadly used before the war, partly as a 'protest-attitude' against the authoritarian structure of the 'Wilhelmian' Germany. After 1919, cocaine consumption became a 'wave' and spread to broader layers of the population (Springer, 1989). In Berlin a public cocaine

9 Stimulated by sensationalist drug films from the US, the press seems to have taken over its shrieking tones with headlines like: 'Vicious Drug Powder – Cocaine Driving Hundreds Mad – Women and Aliens Prey on Soldiers. London in the Grip of the Drug Craze'. The fact that some actresses had become 'victims' of their usage added a personal touch to the press stories: the problem got a 'face'.

scene developed, which was considered a threat to public order (Gunkelmann, 1989). By the late 1920s, an estimated 10–20.000 addicts were recorded in Berlin alone (Kohn, 1999). After the Nazis came to power the consumption of such drugs was declared a 'French decadence', not befitting a German, and was considered a serious threat against the public health of the newly purified *Deutsches Volk*. No surprise that a police commissar interpreted a case of drug trafficking also as a 'Jewish plot' (by the 'Jüdisches Kapital') against the German 'Volk', because of the 'greed' behind the trade (Mach and Scheerer, 1998). Soon the German people and Europe had greater threats than morphine and cocaine abuse to worry about.

In the Netherlands, with its East Indies colony being an important producer of Java crude coca, partly for the German cocaine industry, the illegal market was not very conspicuous. As in many other countries, after the First World War 'household medicines' for self-medication, if containing opiates or cocaine, were prohibited and restricted to the professional medical class (Dutch Opium Law, 1919). Addiction to opium and cocaine was not unknown in the Netherlands, but the situation was smoothed (or kept under control) by the medical practice of prescribing maintenance doses. There were some excesses of over-prescription, but in general this practice succeeded in keeping addicts from the illegal market (De Kort, 1999). Whether this was an intentional policy from the start is difficult to tell, but until the 1960s it was successful in keeping the underground market of illegal drugs small. The small 'Chinatowns' in Amsterdam and Rotterdam were centres of opium smoking by Chinese residents. In general, possession of small quantities of opium of less than 2 grams for personal use was not punished (De Kort, 1999). Otherwise addicts were considered patients, who had to be treated by professional doctors. In this benign climate of tolerance, recreational consumption of drugs did not get much attention. Moral panic and sensational reports about cocaine abuse were considered a matter of the 'decadent world capitals' like Paris, London or New York. The Calvinist inward-looking Dutch society was still far from becoming a staple market for the international drug traffic.

It is difficult to provide an estimate of the inter-war volume of the illegal drug markets in Europe, the US and China, which were the main consumption areas. The League of Nations was dependent on member countries to provide statistics, which was no guarantee of their accuracy. Despite this flaw, the few statistics assembled by the Commission on Narcotic Drugs showed an increase in the amount of seized raw and prepared opium: in 1931 an amount of 48.000 kilos of raw opium was seized, jumping up to 124.000 kilos in 1936. For the same years the figures for prepared opium were 7.000 and 18.000 kilos. As far as the 'underground' economy is concerned, as indicated in the previous section, initially most of the illicit traffic originated from the Western pharmaceutical industry, which was all too happy to get rid of its overproduction. Part of this surplus found its way to China. The Swiss firm

Hoffmann-La Roche and the Dutch firm Naarden were involved in massive smuggling operations of morphine, heroin and cocaine to China in 1927/28. The implementation of the 1931 Convention for limiting the manufacture and regulating the distribution of narcotic drugs did have effect on the licit industry, however. At the same time the continuous demand gave a stimulus to the emergence of underground manufacturing laboratories, which became particularly important for the production of heroin in Turkey as well as the Far East (Bruun *et al.*, 1975; Meyer, 2002).

The Second World War entailed a general reduction of the international trade and strict controls on all shipments. Seizures of illicit shipments of opium products fell by 80 per cent; heroin was down to 3 per cent of its pre-war level. This did not mean that the traffic infrastructure was destroyed or that the market conditions had disappeared. As a matter of fact, in China opium traffic had revived. During the Chinese struggle against Japan till the end of the Second World War and subsequently during the civil war between the communists and the Guomindan, opium and heroin were becoming the illegal currency with which the war efforts were partly sustained. None of the belligerents were exempt from this form of fund raising, even if all acknowledged the magnitude and seriousness of the Chinese drug addiction. After its victory in 1949, the new Communist regime in China clamped down on all things related to narcotics consumption as 'bourgeois' and 'decadent'. The mainland Chinese market closed down until it revived in the last decade of the twentieth century.

In French Indochina, the production capacity of the poppy regions at the border of China remained intact. After the Guomindan was routed, the Indochina border region and Northern Burma became important safe-havens for itinerant Guomindan remnants of the Nationalist army. On various occasions they tried to penetrate southern China in the hope of staging a revolt, but these attempts failed dismally. For years to come, the Guomindan groups would dabble in an unsuccessful guerrilla warfare, sustaining their efforts by their revenues from the opium trade with the hill tribes (McCoy, 2003). As the southern provinces of China were closed, the contraband had to find its way through the north of French Indochina to reach the refineries in Taiwan and Hong Kong.

In this phase, at the beginning of the 1950s, one can discern a gradual transition from the pre-war at most semi-professional international drug market to an ever expanding, more 'professional' crime-market.[10] It is an interesting

10 The quotation marks indicate that the professionalism of this market can in many cases be doubted. As described by Reuter (1983), Van Duyne *et al.* (1990) and Van Duyne (1995), the organizational level of underground markets is more characterized by cunning and good luck than sophistication. This does not exclude professionalism in some of the links of the trading chain between production and consumption.

hypothesis that this expansion was fanned by the relationship to a military struggle. Does it signify a clear milestone in drug history? True, history knows few clearly cut dividing lines, especially in the area of socio-economic developments, let alone unregulated markets. The Middle Ages did not end with the fall of Constantinople in 1453, nor did modern history begin with the destruction of the Bastille. These are just milestones of convenience. Our drug history, being an underground phenomenon, has even vaguer milestones, though the connection of drugs and war efforts heralded an important development. Applying drug revenues as a policy to fill the war chest, was not restricted to the Guomindan. As Southeast Asia was also in turmoil, the contraband served not only the Chinese nationalists, but also drug entrepreneurs and other warring parties, the insurgent Viet Minh as well as the French army. This developing entanglement of drugs revenues in the war against the Viet Minh and later against the Vietcong, which we discuss in section 2.4, may be considered an important milestone after all. It demonstrates that the story about drugs and money is not merely one of the vile greed of ruthless drug entrepreneurs, the 'merchants of death'. It is the story of a scarce commodity, which may serve anybody stealthily looking for quick money, villains as well as secret services denied other sources of operational funding. However, irrespective of the exploits of the villains or secret services (and their sometimes opportunistic symbiosis), they could not benefit as fully as they did without a demand, which at that time was expanding, first gradually, to 'explode' in the 1960s and thereafter.

2.4 Freedom and indulgence

Compared to the First World War, the end of the Second World War brought no 'crazy epoch' in its wake. The worldwide devastation was followed by a decade of recovery, reconstruction, restoration and a fear of a new war against the 'Red Menace'. In this social climate people were discouraged from deviating from socially accepted patterns and roles. Fifteen years of hard work, fifteen years of investing in material well-being and safety brought freedom as well as democratized affluence. In the 1960s, old threats were beginning to lack conviction for the new affluent generation of baby boomers. Despite all rhetoric after the Russian Cuba fiasco of 1962, the 'Red Menace' had become something like stable 'furniture' in the international political landscape, though it still flared up in various remote regions such as Indochina and later in Central and South America. There was no threat of real poverty (in the industrialized 'Free World'): the purchasing power and the free time to spend it had increased tremendously. With the introduction of the new contraceptive pill, another 'threat' was removed: women needed no longer to be afraid of sex because of unwanted pregnancy. Small wonder that in many Western European countries, the 'stuffy' norms and lifestyles

Table 1 World (licit) production of dependence-producing drugs, 1959–1970

	1959	*1970*	*% increase*
Morphine (kg)	108,2	177	64
Codeine (kg)	98	169	72
Heroin (kg)	80	100	25
Coca leaves (tons)	11,3	18,6	64
Distilled spirits (1.000 hectolitre)	21.224	44.457	109
Wine (1,000 hectolitre)	219.017	286.149	31
Beer (1,000 hectolitre)	382.707	630.157	65

Source: Adapted from Bruun *et al.* (1975). The rows for morphine and codeine show an overlap, as most morphine is converted into codeine.

of the 'old guard' of ruling elites[11] and of the 'older generation' became utterly boring and unpersuasive as a role model to 'careless' youngsters used to affluence, leisure, sexual freedom and craving for new sensations. New musical styles and psychoactive substances, like cannabis, already increasingly consumed, offered such new sensations (Whitaker, 1987).

These new developments appeared to have had a long-lasting impact on the old market for psychoactive substances, licit as well as illicit. The whole consumption pattern of the whole range of mind-influencing substances showed an upward trend in the 1960s. If we look at the *licit* production of opiates, cocaine and spirits, wine and beer, we observe a tremendous increase in the general world figures between 1959 and 1970.

The figures illustrate a general consumption increase in whatever could be swallowed legally, whether prescribed as medical drug or for recreational purposes, like alcohol. This general trend remains the same for the US, the UK and the Netherlands if we adjust for the increase in population (Gerritsen, 1993). The increasing consumption of licit psychoactive substances also reflected new developments in the public health system. The pharmaceutical industry discovered new psychoactive medicines, while the general prescription rate kept pace naturally with the ever growing public health system. The number of prescriptions of psychoactive substances in Britain jumped from 26,2 million in 1961 to 45,1 million in 1971. However, as a percentage of the total prescription the increase is less steep: from 12,6 per cent to 18,2 per cent (Bruun *et al.*, 1975). It does not seem too speculative to state that while the adults swallowed their legally prescribed drugs, the youngsters did so illegally and perhaps with more fun (though the latter could be an artefact of their youth).

11 The concept of 'ruling elites' did not only indicate conservatives of various denominations (liberals, Christian democrats) but, in countries with a tradition of coalition governments, also extended to social democrats.

The cultural and economic changes outlined somewhat crudely above provided the susceptibility to new sensations, which were offered in the form of an exciting mixture of new music, dress, sex and drugs. Authors like Aldous Huxley and Timothy Leary added some tinge of respectability to drug consumption, particularly concerning the new hallucinogenic drug LSD (Whitaker, 1987). In the new wave of hippiesque anarchic counterculture, drug consumption was reinforced by the deep rift caused by the Vietnam War as well as by the returning GIs, who brought a solid heroin problem in their wake (though both incidence and prevalence fell compared with their use in Vietnam). When sons and daughters of the respectable classes also embraced the new drug culture, the socially conservative middle classes became really frightened. Politicians such as Goldwater and Rockefeller, eager for votes, responded to this fear by outbidding each other with tough measures against the new 'plague', which could only be subdued by an 'all-out war'. In order not to be outdone, Nixon had to up this rhetoric by making his own 'War on Drugs' the cornerstone of his 1968 election campaign.

In terms of market conditions, the new repressive law enforcement wave had important consequences which, though intended for electoral 'internal consumption', went far beyond the US drug market. Even if the 'War on Drugs' policy did not stem the new drug tide, it affected the composition of the market players in many ways. As far as the US was concerned, the already conspicuous involvement of crime-entrepreneurs from '*La Cosa Nostra*' as wholesale importers grew at the expense of the amateur trader (Bruun *et al.*, 1975; Lupsha, 1987). The latter was not only more easily targeted by the police, but also more risk averse. However, contrary to the general image disseminated by the police forces, the amateur smuggler with his one or two kilo contraband in his Volkswagen van or rucksack never really deserted the scene (Bruun *et al.*, 1975): the small flows from amateur peddlers continued alongside those of 'organized crime'. Another important consequence of the US drug war was the displacement of some addicts as well as traffickers to the more lenient European jurisdictions, beginning with Britain (still lenient in the 1960s). However, the addicts and traffickers brought not only cannabis or acid (LSD), already popular in the youth culture and shocking enough to the establishment to provide some rebellious satisfaction, but also, especially, heroin. The number of known *new* heroin addicts in the UK, already gradually rising since 1960 (a mere 24!), jumped to 1.306 in 1968. For the media it provided an inexhaustible source for horror stories, for politicians a cheap vote-raising issue, which required just a minimum of mental capacity and effort to call successfully for tough action and severe legislation (Whitaker, 1987; Young, 1971).

As the 1970s passed, the wave of hedonism and indulgence levelled off, but did not disappear. An expanded market for illicit psychoactive substances remained. Part of the illicit market expansion was a product of legislation: as soon as a new mind-influencing substance became popular or got media attention, legislators intervened. The relationship between these interventions and market developments is ambiguous though. Was it law enforcement that was responsible for the decline of LSD consumption? Was the drug scare justified by the prevalence figures? In Chapter 6 we will elaborate the prevalence of these substances. Suffice it to indicate that for the US, the high school drug-prevalence figures meandered, but in general declined. A thirty days prevalence rate of heroin of 0,2 per cent was observed in 1980, just at the height of the heroin scare. As the history of this market and its law enforcement war reveal, its movements frequently do not meet the general expectations and imagery.

2.5 Market movements, hot money and Cold War

Observing the tenacious continuity of the illicit market for psychoactive substances, one may wonder whether they function autonomously, irrespective of whatever the authorities try to do to repress them. An affirmative answer would be to jump to conclusions based on outward appearances. Looking at historical evidence, long before the recent alarm flag about 'transnational' crime was raised, the illicit drug market has always been a multinational system of communicating vessels. A telling example of this communication or interactive system is given by the history of the US cannabis policy in Latin America during the 1980s. The policy of interception and eradication with pesticides in the production countries like Colombia had the desired effects: the Colombian export of cannabis products decreased significantly from 77 per cent to 7 per cent.[12] However, the unpredicted, unintended and unwanted side effects were considerable. The export of Mexican cannabis increased, while Colombia replaced its lost trade by expanding its coca acreage: consequently Colombia's share of cocaine exports increased in the same period from 23 per cent to 93 per cent. Meanwhile the increased consumer price of marijuana in the US did not go unnoticed by Californian farmers. They started to grow cannabis in a professional way, which reached a turnover at least equalling that of corn (Perkins and Gilbert, 1987). Through Canada, where cultivation of marijuana also began to develop to the sophisticated quality and volumes found today in the West, the improved horticultural technology found its way to the Netherlands, where today the strongest cannabis is raised and exported for the European market and elsewhere. The US consumer market reacted in various ways too, as prices and risks of transport and possession increased. As in the days of alcohol prohibition, consumers looked for stronger stuff: smaller volume with more

12 Tolerance of such health- and eco-destructiveness abroad would not be matched at home: the spraying of pesticides like paraquat would have been unthinkable in the US or in any EU member state.

effect in less time. During the Prohibition era, this led to a preference for rum instead of beer. In the drug market it meant increased demand for cannabis with a higher THC, or other more concentrated substances like cocaine: less bulky, less smell and a lower detection risk for more 'quality' (effect).[13] Less persistent consumers who eschewed all these risks resorted to the socially accepted drug: alcohol (Rasmussen and Benson, 1994). The total market for 'illicit indulgence' may look autonomous, but its segments are inherently interwoven with national and international penal drug policies. Part of drug policy interacts with foreign policy, particularly in the days of the Cold War, revealing the intricate drugs and money connection.

The long-lasting connection between illicit drugs and the Cold War may be read as a sinister chapter in postwar history, which adds a tinge of tension and moral indignation to the narrative of drugs, communists and secret services. However, abstracting from such value judgments, there is little sinister in this connection, which is just about money. As indicated in section 2.2, in the many remote hot spots where the struggles took (and in some cases still take) place between (communist/left-wing) liberation movements and the (neo)colonial powers or national conservative elites, there was and is a scarcity of money and an abundance of valuable drugs, either as a finished product or as a cash crop. Little surprise that the belligerents resorted to the 'local currency' they could lay their hands on. The only problem was that the 'drug currency' was a prohibited one. Use of drug money to support anti-communist or anti-left-wing insurgents implied the violation of the international drug conventions, which had to remain covert because the US was crusading for global prohibition at the same time.[14] This dual policy entailed much deceit and self-deception by mutually competing agencies. As the US was the foremost driven fighter of communists as well as drugs, it bore the full brunt of being blamed for 'hypocrisy'. For ideological reasons or because of simultaneous belief in mutually contradictory ideologies, they never succeeded in publicly selling this duplicity as a simple display of necessary '*Realpolitik*'.[15]

It should be borne in mind that this drug and money connection in foreign affairs applied to only two market segments, albeit very prominent ones: at first heroin and later, in the 1980s, cocaine. This drug and money connection

13 This shift could already be observed when opium smoking and the opium dens were repressed at the turn of the century. Many users shifted to the then available more potent heroin (Courtwright, 1982).

14 See Naylor (1993) for a broader account of the 'insurgent economy'. Resorting to the drugs economy is of course a matter of opportunity. West African insurgents in the 1990s resorted to diamonds.

15 This awkward contradictory position may not have ended with the termination of the Cold War: drug entrepreneurs may again become useful, this time in the war against terrorism.

had its repercussions in Europe, for which reason US foreign policy is an integral part of any description of the developments in Europe.[16] In other drug market segments – cannabis, LSD and other synthetic drugs – this connection was not observed, not because these substances are better or worse, but because they had no economic function in one of the war zones. Therefore we will discuss these drugs in a later section.

The heroin market

Though no drug has escaped the stigma of demonization, heroin (along with crack cocaine) is considered to be at the very top end of this rating. If the bohemian 'artistic' morphine or cocaine user may still have met some understanding – at least outside officialdom – the heroin-addicted skinny junkie is considered an irredeemable loser, exploited by merciless and sinister 'merchants of death'. Like most stereotypes, the 'lost junkie' image did not emerge from fantasy only. As we have pointed out, since its beginning in the US, this substance was mainly used by lower-class male white youngsters in the slums of New York and other east coast industrial cities. After the Second World War, the social class of the users did not change very much, but the colour became darker: heroin became increasingly a 'ghetto drug' (Courtwright, 2002).

During the first two decades after the Second World War the heroin market in the US and Europe was not very significant, compared with the prewar years as well as with the sharp rise after 1965, if measured by the recorded interceptions. The reported worldwide volume of interceptions was in 1969 still far below that of 1936: 465 against 867 kilos (Bruun *et al.*, 1975).[17] After 1970 the seizures started to rise quickly, beginning with 1.466 in 1971 and 2000 kilos the year after. The heroin market had unfolded, first in the US and subsequently in Europe. It would remain a lasting phenomenon.

The development of the organization of this market was not an isolated US affair. If the present popular denotation 'transnational crime' has become a commonly used catchword, the heroin market was characterized as such from its very beginning, in which the European crime scene functioned as an important cornerstone. Much attention is devoted to the Sicilian Mafia and its American counterpart, the nebulous 'La Cosa Nostra'. Even if the participation of the Mafia cannot be ignored, the European involvement

16 Another reason is the more general tendency to the internationalization of US criminal law enforcement in which, as we have seen, drug policy plays a significant role (Nadelmann, 1993).

17 These are seizures reported to the UN Commission on Narcotics and Drugs. It goes without saying that the reliability depends heavily on the reporting discipline and skills of the member states.

began with the earlier mentioned French involvement in the heroin traffic during the first Vietnamese war. In this war the French secret service, Corsican gangsters and the Marseilles underworld played their part in furthering the heroin market (McCoy, 2003; Lewis, 1985). The summarized history is the following:

During the protracted war against the Vietnamese nationalist insurgents, France was financially bleeding white. Hence, the French parliament cut the funds, which affected the secret war operations of the French intelligence services. Desperate for additional funds, the secret service turned to the resources which could be tapped from the local opium industry of the northern hill tribes, the Meo, in northern Vietnam and Laos, as well as the southern river pirates and smugglers, Binh Xuyen. It was all to no avail: the French quarrelled with one of the hill tribes about the price of the opium, after which the tribes colluded with the Viet Minh. This proved to be a vital mistake, as the Viet Minh, supported by the tribes, succeeded in performing what the French High Military Command thought impossible: getting heavy artillery over the hills overlooking the fortress of Dien Bien Phu (McCoy, 2003). The capture of the fortress in 1954 marked the end of the French occupation of Vietnam (Keegan, 1979; Ansprenger, 1966), but not of the Southeast Asian opium industry, heroin traffic and its connection with the ongoing power play.

The multiple connection between on the one hand, the triangle of French politics, drugs and money with, on the other hand, the opium-producing Southeast Asian countries (the 'Golden Triangle') was of importance for the traffic from Europe to the US. French internal politics were particularly important in smoothing the traffic indirectly. The connections between the Corsican-dominated Marseille underworld, the corrupt local political groupings and the French secret service contributed to a relatively benign criminal business climate (McCoy, 2003). The principals in the underworld had less to fear from the police than from competitors. As far as their drug traffic was concerned, their main activity was the export of heroin to the US, commonly described as the 'French Connection'. At first they were dependent on another European crime group: the Sicilian Mafia. Because the handling of cargo in the harbour of New York was 'protected' by the Italian American crime-families ('La Cosa Nostra'), the relationship between the Mafia and 'La Cosa Nostra' contributed to a safer entry into the US. As any trader will usually (if not always)[18] try to bypass a cost-increasing intermediary, the French did likewise, and by the 1960s they succeeded in getting the contraband to the US through Canada and Mexico (Lewis, 1985). At the

18 See Pearson and Hobbs (2001; 2003), who point out that there is far less competition in the UK middle-market for drugs to which they were able to get access than is often assumed. Whether or not this applies transnationally cannot be assumed.

same time they were careful not to attract French police attention by selling heroin in France itself. Apart from that prudent policy, the US prices were more attractive, while a European heroin market hardly existed at that time.

Southeast Asia was not the only source of supply. As indicated earlier, the Sicilian Mafia, or as some sources maintain individual Mafiosi, were important hauliers for the French contraband to the American consumer market.[19] One of the key figures was the notorious American LCN leader 'Lucky' Luciano. Rewarded for his support of the allied invasion in Sicily in 1943, his long prison sentence was commuted in 1946 into a deportation to Italy (Servadio, 1976). Once arrived in Italy, Luciano is alleged to have organized the supply and distribution of morphine (to be refined by the Corsicans) and heroin (Lupsha, 1987). Part of the raw material came from the Middle East via Beirut, but also from a respectable Italian pharmaceutical firm, via bribed employees (Shawcross and Young, 1987). After this supply dried up due to US intervention, Luciano intensified his Lebanese connections, who imported the heroin from Iran, Pakistan and Afghanistan. Being no strangers in this field, it is not surprising that members of Mafia families stepped into this market, after the 'French Connection' was finally suppressed during the 1970s. As we have observed in the previous section, they entered an expanding market.

Meanwhile the Americans inherited the Vietnam problem from the French. Of interest for our story is not the Vietnam drama, but the policy of covert operations in which the local opium industry continued the role it had played during the French occupation. The new strongman of South Vietnam, Diem, realized the importance of the drug and money connection, as well as he valued the success of the river pirates, the Binh Xuyen, in keeping the Vietcong at bay. Against American wishes, he revived the opium trade. At a later stage, the US intelligence service would find itself in the same predicament as Diem and the French secret service. It faced the choice between winning over opium-trading hill tribes against the communist-led national liberation groups or lending support in the fight against heroin traffic, which aggravated the demoralization of the US forces. They chose to

19 It is still a matter of debate whether *the* Mafia, or rather Mafia families were engaged in the drug market or that it was just a matter of individual Mafiosi, acting against the wishes of the nebulous 'Commission' (see Paoli, 2003). The same ambiguity is observed with the Italian American crime-families (Lupsha, 1987). Gambetta (1993) does not consider the drug market to be the core business of the Mafia. Mafiosi drug dealers acted just as common dealers with the outside world of non-Mafiosi fellow dealers. Even if they had some advantages in terms of access, network of relatives and 'muscle', they still did not differ essentially from other wholesale traders. Whatever their social-economic market position, some Mafia families grew fabulously rich, if they were not exterminated by mutual rivalry.

support the hill tribes with army equipment as well as logistical support for their opium trade (McCoy, 2003).

Given the 'domino-theory', according to which the fall of one state (to the communists) would cause all states of the region to fall one after the other, the Americans inherited also the problem of dealing with the restless situation of the adjacent territories.[20] The CIA considered it important to keep the allegiance of the Hmong tribesmen against the Pathet Lao, for which reason it had to tolerate the tribe's main cash crop of poppies. However, it did more than just tolerating, but assisted in the transport with Air America, a CIA airline in Vietnam (Chambliss, 1994).[21] The agency did not benefit directly from the opium trade, but with the tribe's support it could operate cheaply with only a few US field officers working with thousands of anti-Pathet Lao guerrillas (McCoy, 1992). The opium caravans of the tribes operated unmolested, and contributed to the steady flow of heroin to the GIs in Vietnam and the US. When, in 1972, the American GIs left Vietnam, the heroin went along in their wake, whether to other barracks in Europe or simply home (Weijenburg, 1996).

Western Europe did not remain untouched by American attempts to manipulate the pipes and exits of the complicated maze of communicating vessels of the global drug trade. As we have seen in section 2.3, at the end of the 1960s, Nixon was under pressure to outbid his conservative rivals in their extreme law and order appeal. He initiated his 'War on Drugs' and, while the Southeast Asian hill tribe allies of the CIA continued their supply to the US and Europe, he clamped down on other narcotics producers: Turkey and the French laboratories. Historically, Turkey was an important supplier of licit as well as clandestine opium and heroin. At that time, the illicit part was still refined in and around Marseilles. However, closing down this Turkish and French artery actually predictably prodded the market. The first effect was scarcity, which raised the prices and reduced consumption, falsifying the popular inelasticity hypothesis (Rasmussen and Benson, 1994; Grapendaal *et al.*, 1991). Meanwhile after the departure of the US army, the traders in Southeast Asia were left with a substantial stock. Through their networks of co-patriots (seamen and restaurant owners) in the US and Europe, the heroin syndicates tried to sell their product. According to McCoy (1992) the share of Southeast Asian heroin on the American market jumped to about 30 per cent after 1972. The ensuing reaction of the DEA was to

20 Another self-produced heritage indicated in section 2.2 were the lingering remnants of the Guomindan forces, which had settled in Northern Burma after their failed invasions in the South Chinese province of Yunnan between 1950 and 1952. The opium traffic on which they depended was never checked or repudiated by the US (Lintner, 1992).

21 The CIA website asserts that even if aircraft facilities may have been used, it was not a matter of policy. This is plausible, since policy is commonly defined as an official announcement or document by departmental chiefs.

block this flow, but it could not do much about the cultivation areas, where the CIA was still operating. Merely blocking the gates to the US induced the Chinese traffickers to probe other permeable borders: Europe and Australia. Europe witnessed a substantial increase of heroin imports and heroin addicts. In West Germany, the death rate from overdose leaped from 9 in 1969 to 623 ten years later. In the Netherlands, the increase in registered addicts was alarming: from 800 in 1970 to 10.000 five years later (McCoy, 1992). Chinese crime-organizations played a role in the supply and distribution. In the Netherlands, the 14-K Triad from Hong Kong set up its 'headquarters' in Amsterdam from where it supplied the Dutch and neighbouring countries (Weijenburg, 1996).

The functioning of the drugs, money and foreign politics triangle did not end with the demise of the US Southeast Asian policy. During the 1980s it continued in another area of politico-military contest as well as of traditional poppy cultivation: Afghanistan. In December 1979, the country was invaded by Soviet forces. The Muslim population unleashed a disastrous guerrilla warfare, which later was supported by the US. Meanwhile the war disrupted the already fragile economy, leaving opium poppies as virtually the only cash crop. The uprooted population, finding refuge in North Pakistan, added to the misery as well as to the cross-border smuggling opportunities. Within this chaotic situation in the alliance between the insurgents and the US, the role of the opium economy should be interpreted. The CIA, through Pakistan's Inter-Services Intelligence, supported the local tribes in Afghanistan and ignored the quickly developing heroin traffic of which it was fully cognizant. The military transports, which brought the weapons north, returned with heroin to Karachi. As in Vietnam, not only local war groups, like the rough Mujahideen warriors such as those under Hekmatyar, but also persons directly connected to the Pakistan President Zia were implicated. While in 1983 Vice President George Bush lauded President Zia for his anti-narcotics programme, in a Norwegian prison cell a Pakistan smuggler alleged (correctly or not) the involvement of Zia's personal banker and surrogate son, Hamid Hasnain. Whether the smuggling was carried out by Afghan fighters, exiles or the top brass of the Pakistan army, the US turned a blind eye (Lifschultz, 1992, pp. 331–336). Pakistan paid dearly for Zia's policy: while prior to 1979, heroin addiction was practically unknown in Pakistan, it jumped to 650.000 addicts in ten years.

As far as Europe is concerned, much of the Southwest Asian heroin found its way either through the port of Karachi to England and other West European markets or through the Kurdistan valleys, Istanbul and the so-called Balkan route to Germany, the Netherlands and beyond (Weijenburg, 1996). A facilitating circumstance was the weakened position of the Chinese crime-groups in the Netherlands due to mutual lethal rivalry. During the beginning of the 1980s the 14-K organization was replaced by the Ah Kong organization with extensive ramifications in Germany, Belgium and

Denmark. The imported ('Chinese') heroin was no longer solely destined for the Dutch market, which was also increasingly supplied by the Kurdish and Turkish crime-families, who were soon to dominate the European heroin market. This development, which is unconnected to foreign policy or secret services, will be discussed later.

The cocaine market

Cocaine is another (stimulating) drug, which also figured in the triangle of drugs, money and foreign policy (Scott and Marshall, 1998). As with the heroin connection in Asia, the underlying paradox was the conflict between the goals of fighting left-wing insurgent movements (or even legitimate governments) in the American hemisphere at the same time as fighting drugs. The first objective requires local support of whoever has power and is also against communism/socialism; the second implies a relentless persecution of whoever is engaged in drugs. All goes well as long as the persons in power are not also (indirectly) related to drug traffickers, but where the latter happens, a choice has to be made. As we could already observe in the Asian conflict area, where foreign policy and the 'War on Drugs' collide, the CIA largely prevails over the DEA. As long as the aims of the CIA were complied with, corruption, deceit and abuse of the US anti-drug aid programmes by local potentates have rarely been an objection to continuation of such aid. The abuse was simply swept under the carpet. For example, in the late 1970s, the aerial spraying of cannabis plantations in Mexico appeared to be a scam: herbicides were unloaded in the desert or fields were simply sprayed with water. If herbicides were used at all, it was for the purpose of extorting fellow drug cultivators to pay to 'protect' themselves from spraying. To the disgust of honest DEA officers, the reports of this fraud were buried, while the State Department praised the miraculous Mexican success in its anti-drug efforts. However, this 'success' was due to a bad drought and not to the spraying of herbicides. It caused merely a temporary reduction in drug production (Marshall, 1991). Given the 'ethics' of this foreign policy, which according to Chambliss (1994) cannot be considered but shady, it is no surprise that the infamous so-called *Iran–Contra Affair* unfolded.

The complex relationships and connections which surfaced during the revelations about the Contra Affair, may be considered one of the most muddled and murky chapters in the US history of its 'War on Drugs' by using drug-money in the war against 'communism' or a left-wing reform government (Scott, 1992). Basically, the covert and corrupt relationship concerned the clandestine support of the right-wing insurgents, called the Contras, against the Nicaraguan Sandinista government, which had ousted the corrupt and US-friendly regime of Somoza in the late 1970s. The Contras undermined the Sandinista government from the neighbouring Honduras and Costa Rica, but were short of weapons and money. However, after the

Vietnam tragedy, in 1982 Congress forbade the White House to spend tax money on another foreign adventure. Like the insurgents in Afghanistan and Indochina, the Contras resorted to the nearest available resource to fill their war chest: the drug traffic, which in this region implied cocaine export to the US. Part of the Iran–Contra scandal was the alleged sale of weapons to Iran worth about $300 million. It seems certain that Iran received arms, which were (with Pakistan aid) diverted from supplies destined for the Afghanistan rebels and which 'was the first major attempt to create funding for . . . the American intelligence community linked to the Contras' (Lifschultz, 1992, 329).

The illicit management of hidden funds other than via commodities or similar-value transfers often needs a financial institution for laundering and funnelling the moneys, without suspicions, to the right destination. Against the background of warnings about the subversive influence of dirty money, the US administration provided a first-hand experience in the shape of the Australian-based *Nugan–Hand Bank*. This financial institution was established in 1976 by a former CIA agent, Michael Hand, and the Australian Nugan as a successor of a parent company, on which board of directors we find persons who listed their address as c/o *Air America*, the air transport firm which (knowingly or not) hauled the hill tribe's narcotics from northern Laos. The principal directors and higher staff of the Nugan–Hand Bank consisted of nine senior American army officers. After Nugan was found shot dead in his car (the official explanation was suicide), it appeared that apart from financing arms smuggling, the bank also served as a money-laundering institution (Chambliss, 1994).

The US relationship to the Contras was opportunistic, reflecting the divisions within the Contras, which consisted of many factions. This provided a margin for action: complicity with the drug traffic as long as a faction was worthy of support, and busting a Contra trafficking ring as soon as the faction lost support. If one 'window' through which the cocaine passed to the US was closed, another (protected) window was opened. High-level military staff and officials in Honduras, who smuggled weapons to the Contras and protected the drug smuggling rings, were left untouched. This did not change after the Contra activities waned and the case was brought into the open in 1987/88. Altogether some 20–50 per cent of the US cocaine imports passed through these 'windows of opportunity' (Scott, 1992; Scott and Marshall, 1998). Price developments are a clear indicator of the impact of the cocaine flood to the US. During this period the maximum kilo price of cocaine in the US sank from $65.000 in 1982 to $46.000 in 1986. The minimum prices for these years were $55.000 and $24.000 (Lewis, 1989). Nevertheless, by regularly arresting non-supported or unprotected traffickers, the US authorities still could uphold to the public and the international community the image of fighting a genuine drug war. Disgusted DEA field officers, who left the service, portrayed another picture of the drug war (Levine, 1990; 1993).

It is difficult to determine whether the absence of the opportunities created by this policy would have resulted in less trade or a different market. Counterfactual 'ifs' in history are difficult to answer. The most plausible answer would be that the policy of 'windows of opportunity' boosted the traffic, frustrated the working of the DEA and eroded the credibility of the US stand on drug prohibition.

This political connection of drug and money has less direct bearing on the European drug market than the Afghanistan intervention. The Afghan (and Pakistan) heroin soon found its way to Europe. The South American cocaine first swamped the US market. When the US cocaine market became saturated, the Colombian crime-entrepreneurs probed the European market in the second half of the 1980s (Verbeek, 2001). The description of the drug-money connection in this section just provides a few highlights in which American foreign policy (or, since it was unofficial and unannounced, American practice) was involved during the deployment of their clandestine covert operations. It goes without saying that this is not 'typically' American. As indicated at the beginning of this chapter, drugs or drug cash-crops just happen to be present and to represent a high-price commodity. In the service of 'higher aims' the belligerents, who are short of money, feel they cannot ignore its financial potential.[22]

It is also a matter of policy prioritization in which various departments and agencies participate, often far from harmoniously. Preserving short-term national economic and foreign policy interests almost always appears to come out as the priority policy, while the drug-control policies have to wait unofficially until the immediate problems are solved. In this way of 'cognitive dissonance', Americans 'in the know' could hold onto their anti-drug ideology while in practice contradicting it, despite serious negative consequences for other jurisdictions. It might have been too much to expect US policy makers to have the candour to follow the imperialistic nineteenth-century British Prime Minister Palmerston in his saying 'my country, right or wrong', but the *Realpolitik* practice was draped in the ethical policy garments of waging a 'just' 'War on Drugs'. A global drug policy was imposed, though at the same time the US and other markets became swamped with drugs, while other countries were blamed for their liberal attitude and leniency.

22 There is little new in this: in their 'heroic' war of the Dutch Republic against Spain (mainly fought by foreign mercenaries), the States of Zeeland made a good profit by clandestinely selling weapons to the enemy. Today they may have sold XTC or Dutch 'nederwiet'.

2.6 The European drug market

As described in the previous sections, the international illicit drug market is to be considered an underground commercial system of communicating vessels. Closing one outlet vessel is likely to have repercussions in other vessels of the system. However, it is not a system in which direct causal relationships between these vessels can always be discerned. Some relationships are clear. The Vietnam clandestine operations in the 1960/70s were clearly related to the increase in heroin consumption in the US, with a smaller and more indirect fall-out in Europe. The war in Afghanistan with all its disruptions in the region in the 1980s had a more direct impact on the European heroin market. The cocaine saturation in the US during (and affected by) the Contra support policy (eagerly exploited by Colombian 'cartels') induced the Colombian drug entrepreneurs to explore the European market sooner than they would have otherwise done. The US market circumstances of the 1980s made it happen sooner. As far as other market segments – cannabis and synthetic drugs – are concerned, the working of the system of communicating vessels is much more opaque. To make the situation more complex, a 'European Union drug market' is little more than a shorthand or an abstraction, despite the existence of the (expanding) European Union. If the European licit market already reveals many cracks of division, the unregulated opaque underground market of illicit drugs will certainly reveal more regional differences than unity.

The European market developments in terms of money and crime-entrepreneurs are difficult to investigate. This is not only because of the relatively hidden nature of the market and the lack of precise data. There is also a problem in the continuity of political and law enforcement attention and the information which it generates. On balance, European law enforcement agencies and policy makers have succeeded in maintaining political attention for the market in general, but because of its diversity, attention tends to shift between market segments. In addition, some jurisdictions have or claim to have more problems with one particular drug market segment than with others, and also for different reasons.

The drug market segments are interconnected on various levels, which does not add much to clarity. On the consumer level, there is the phenomenon of poly-drug consumption and retailing. On the wholesale level, de-specialization has been observed. For example, some Turkish heroin specialist entrepreneurs entered the cocaine or synthetic drug market, while some Dutch cannabis wholesalers diversified to the XTC or cocaine traffic (Kleemans *et al.*, 1998). After all, many traders are just 'freebooters' or generic entrepreneurs. However, despite that observation, some soft-drug dealers were adamant in avoiding any involvement in hard drugs (Van Duyne, 1995; Korf and Verbraek, 1993). So even on a static level, let alone a more appropriate focus on the dynamics, our knowledge of European drug markets is uneven and fragmented, as borne out by the overview of Ruggiero and South (1995) – see also Browne *et al.* (2003) and Dorn *et al.* (2003). To simplify the representation, we will discuss the market segments in separate sections, bearing in mind their frequent, but unsystematic interconnections.

The cannabis market

Cannabis products (hashish, marijuana, weed, grass) can be considered as the 'beer' of drugs. After the Second World War marijuana was consumed by small groups of the 'avant-garde' and, as in the US, the market grew steadily, but not explosively. However, since the late 1960s, cannabis-product consumption has increased steeply, becoming the drug of choice for the young, especially the 'baby-boomer' generation born after the Second World War (Maalsté, 1997; Harrison, 1997). Despite, or perhaps because of the stern warnings of the authorities and adults, smoking pot became an expression of the anti-authoritarian, counter-cultural and anti-consumerist attitude of many youngsters. Falsifying the 'stepping-stone' theory, according to which cannabis 'abuse' was the first step towards the eventual doom of heroin addiction, the baby-boomers have in general become settled citizens.[23]

If we can speak of a 'consolidated' market in the field of illicit psychoactive substances at all, it may apply with some reason to the cannabis market. Its consumption by adolescents and young adults is widespread and not confined to the marginalized drop-outs. To supply this demand, the areas of production range from small farms in Third World countries to attics, balconies and professional market gardens in the industrialized consumer countries (Malyon, 1985; Whitaker, 1987; Van Oosten and Steinmetz, 1995; Weijenburg, 1996; Bovenkerk and Hogewind, 2003). This implies a tremendous ramification as well as stratification of amateur providers, 'tourist' smugglers and professional wholesale hauliers (Korf and Verbraeck, 1993). The wholesale traffickers, whether hauliers, importers or distributors, have attracted broad attention under the denominator 'transnational organized criminals'. However, the widespread amateur supply of the market should not be considered a marginal phenomenon, as is demonstrated for the Dutch market by Van Oosten and Steinmetz (1995) and for Frankfurt and Milan by Paoli (2000). On the level of wholesale international traffic in Europe, Dutch crime-entrepreneurs seem to have played an important role since the late 1970s. Most of the hash transports were hauled in fishing ships and unloaded on the unguarded North Sea beaches (Weijenburg, 1996). The efforts to organize transports of thousand and more kilos (once, in 1990, even 33.000

23 This observation does not in itself falsify the alternative UK 'gateway drug' model, to be elaborated later, for cannabis remains a common, if not logically necessary, entry point among those who later *do* go on to 'harder' drugs.

kilos) should not be underestimated. However, often times the organizational skills proved inadequate and due more to luck than to judgement, the organizers succeeded in getting the contraband ashore (Van Duyne *et al.*, 1990; 1995). Inadequate nautical maps, exploding motors, unseaworthy ships and appalling conditions marked this trade. The hauling of Afghan and Pakistan hashish continued by boat. But irrespective of the channel of import, cannabis kept flowing into Europe and between the European countries, albeit levelling off after 1994, as illustrated by the seizure data in Figure 1.[24]

The Dutch importers were important suppliers to northwestern Europe. Due to higher retail prices much of the contraband is re-exported to the UK, partly also to Scandinavian countries. The surrounding countries, Belgium and Germany, but also northern France, are provided for, not in bulk quantities, but mainly at mid-level or retail level. Usually, foreigners from these countries visit the Netherlands to buy the drugs (not only hashish) directly from retailers (Boekhout van Solinge, 1996).

Though the wholesale transporters and importers were considered to illustrate the 'threat of organized crime' (and prosecuted according to the

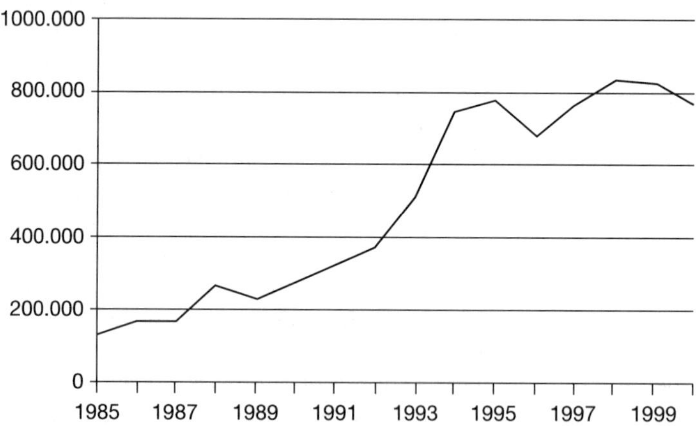

Figure 1 Intercepted amount of kilos of cannabis in Europe, 1985–2000
Source: Adapted from European Monitoring Centre for Drugs and Drug Addiction, 2001

24 The figures in this section concerning the seizures of contraband are amalgamated from the interception figures of the EU member states. They are presented to indicate a rough trend, which is determined by many factors: the success rate of the police, law enforcement intensity, the volume of the supply, accidental huge shipments and sometimes variation in the used statistics. As these factors intermingle in such a way that they are difficult to separate, the figures do not mirror exact market developments but rather approximate trends.

'organized crime' clause in Dutch or German penal law), their organizational 'solidity' or coherence is at best modest. Most 'organizations' are network coalitions of individual crime-entrepreneurs. The inner circle is usually small, consisting of three to five partners. Though such an inner circle reveals differences in 'social weight', this should not be interpreted as evidence of a criminal hierarchy (Klerks, 2000). Sometimes the partners have an additional crime-business of their own, like a distribution network or connections for re-export. As joint ventures they invest mutually their 'shares' in one or more transports and divide the imported cargo or the profits. Almost literally they operate like the early seventeenth-century East Indian merchant adventurers in the days before the monopolistic East Indian Company was established. This organizational pattern is regularly demonstrated in a series of research reports (Van Duyne *et al.*, 1990, 1995; Kleemans *et al.*, 1998; 2002), corresponding to earlier German findings (Rebscher and Vahlenkamp, 1988; Weschke and Heine-Heiß, 1990).

In the Netherlands, most hashish is sold in orderly 'coffee shops'. These are semi-tolerated retail outlets, which are permitted to operate if they comply with a number of strict conditions. The usual conditions are: no hard drugs, no alcohol, no sales to minors, no advertisements, limited stock and no public nuisance.[25] To hard-liner countries like France and Italy, this policy is just as odd as the old Dutch religious policy in the time of the Reformation and the Ancien Régime. The Calvinist regents at that time forbade Roman Catholic worship, but tolerated Catholic churches as long as they could not be seen from the public road.[26] Foreign pressure against this tolerant soft-drug policy, as well as some clamp-downs by a few law-and-order politicians to show the public that the authorities were serious in restoring public order and safety, led to a substantial reduction of the number of coffee shops. The predictable reaction was not long in coming: street selling (which the policy makers wanted to avoid by tolerating the coffee shops) returned again. Only some policy makers and politicians were surprised at this outcome.

25 Within the multifaceted public-safety anxiety the phenomenon of coffee shops became a policy issue. Citizens would feel uneasy in the neighbourhood of coffee shops, seeing all sorts of 'vague, shabby youngsters' entering the shops, while they leave their bicycles against the wall or a tree. Most citizens' complaints were about such 'subjective uneasiness feelings' (Bieleman *et al.*, 1995). As a matter of fact, most coffee shops look 'alternative', but are quiet places to have a cup of coffee: no aggressive alcoholic consumers, just a few quiet, glassily staring figures enjoying their joint.

26 Given this 'odd' policy of tolerance it is worth pointing at its long historical roots and its benign effects: for example, the low number of religious victims in the Dutch Republic: while in Europe the stakes were burning, in the Catholic Amsterdam the *schout* (police officer) warned his heretic fellow citizens to leave town as soon as he heard of the impending arrival of the Inquisition (Mak, 1995). As for France: many of its enlightened philosophers, like Descartes, thought it safer to publish their works in the Dutch Republic.

In the European landscape this form of tolerance is much disputed. The European cannabis market is generally an indoor phenomenon. This applies not only to buying and selling, but also to the production. Home-made cannabis is a widespread industry, very often a balcony-and-attic activity, though professional horticultural enterprises are also regularly discovered. This variation is a function of the nature of the cannabis plant, which is just a herb. Professional cannabis growing developed in the US in the 1980s when the authorities intensified their interdiction and eradication programme, extending later to Canada, especially British Columbia (Perkins and Gilbert, 1987).[27] Subsequently it spread to the Netherlands (Weijenburg, 1996), where it developed almost into a fully grown industry (Van Oosten and Steinmetz, 1995), which will be discussed in Chapter 4. The Dutch traders exported not only their strong 'nederwiet', but also the seeds and techniques. Consequently the home-grown supply in other countries is expanding too, predictably leading to lower prices as has been observed in Paris (Labrousse and Laniel, 2001). It perfectly conforms to the market model set out by Adam Smith, who would smile in his grave, doubtless intoning his own thesis: 'do not beat the iron hand of the market'.

The heroin market

If the cannabis market enjoys a certain degree of openness and some moral ambiguity concerning its 'badness', everything related to heroin is considered *really* evil. The well-known physical and mental dependence it may create is understandably a matter of concern from the perspective of public health policy. Apart from the general moral crusaders' rhetoric against all psychoactive substances and the relentless pressure in international bodies, the skinny 'fix-centred addict' committing depraved and/or criminal acts to fund their habit is usually considered *the* living proof of the wickedness of the 'merchants of death'. Therefore, despite early British experimentation with the 'medical model' and medical prescription of heroin and its substitutes, as soon as heroin consumption became somewhat more widespread in the 1970s, the repressive penal law approach to this market seemed – without much debate – to policy makers and the public to be the most appropriate policy. However, this repressive policy yielded little success: these or new 'merchants of death' have remained in the market. Granted, it is hard to demonstrate the counterfactual: what would have happened if a different policy had been adopted (see Stimson and Metrebian, 2003)?

27 For the home growing of cannabis an extensive series of manuals are published. We mention just a few old guides: 'Marijuana Grower's Insider's Guide' (Frank, 1988); 'Indoor Marijuana Horticulture' (Cervantes, 1983); 'Marijuana Grower's Guide (Frank and Rosenthal, 1978). Of course, the new guides are on the internet.

As we have seen in the previous sections, developments in the European heroin market were directly or indirectly influenced by US Cold War foreign policy. In Britain, France, the Netherlands, Italy and Germany, the late 1960s and certainly the 1970s witnessed the breakthrough of heroin as a market commodity. US and Canadian heroin users, fleeing the repressive climate at home, emerged in Britain, with its benign policy of maintenance through prescription, in the early 1960s. In contrast to the 'middle-aged' British junkies, well-known to their doctors, the new 'drug tourists' were often youthful non-conformists, some with a record of trafficking (Whitaker, 1987; Ruggiero and South, 1995). Despite this influx from abroad and the growth of demand in the 1960s and early 1970s the size of the British heroin market was still limited. Most of the substance was prescribed within the maintenance model or diverted from the pharmaceutical industry. However, restrictions of the maintenance policy in 1969 – itself following a media-fuelled alarm at over-prescribing by a small number of doctors – and changes in the social composition of addicts, who became less reluctant to have themselves registered, changed the market. In addition, heroin, together with other hard drugs, had become an embedded element in the musical youth culture. For some, smoking a joint was not sufficient anymore.

As far as the consumer segment of the market is concerned, it should first be noted that the numbers of problem heroin users is small: around 1 per cent in Dutch and German household and school surveys showed a lifetime prevalence (Korf, 1997; Kraus *et al.*, 1998). In addition there are indications that the big increase in prevalence in the 1980s has levelled off to be replaced by a relative stability: the population of addicts is hardly increasing and new users are less often registered. However, the validity of the methods to estimate the market, either by means of interceptions, drug deaths or self-reporting is debated (Korf, 1997). Valid generalizations are difficult to make: the market remains volatile and changeable, as is also to be seen in Figure 2.

When we look at the supply side of the international heroin market, there are some differences between the countries of Europe. The British Isles were increasingly supplied by Southwest Asia: Pakistan during the 1980s (Wagstaff and Maynard, 1988) and later Afghanistan. Initially a large number of exiled Iranian traffickers were involved. In Britain they were complemented by crime-entrepreneurs with a more traditional criminal history of violent property crime, who diversified into the 'less risky' drug market (Dorn *et al.*, 1992).

In the 1980s, the supply and distribution networks on the European continent changed and widened. The supply through air traffic by the Chinese shrank, while land transport became more important. Most of the supplied heroin found its way via the earlier mentioned Balkan route, which became important after the Afghanistan export increased. The intensive transport between the Balkan countries (including Turkey) and western Europe, comprising in 1990 some two million buses and forty

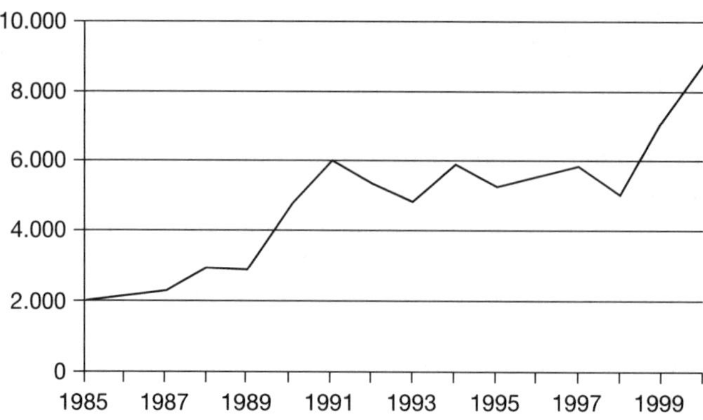

Figure 2 Interceptions of heroin in Europe in kilos, 1985–1999
Source: Adapted from European Monitoring Centre for Drugs and Drug Addiction, 2001

million passenger cars, was ideal for smuggling (ICPO-Interpol, 1992). The heroin is usually not of Turkish origin (though it may have been refined in Turkey), but the Turkish and Kurdish crime-families (which for practical reasons we will denote mostly under the heading 'Turkish') do play an important role in hauling contraband to Europe and distributing it wholesale in virtually all European consumer countries.

A facilitating circumstance is the presence of substantial Turkish minorities in most Western European countries, who still have family ties in Turkey. If the Turkish or Kurdish social-economic nucleus is the 'extended family', it applies to legitimate as well as to illicit enterprises. The extended family, residing partly in Turkey and in one or more European countries provides the organizational blueprint for a fitting criminal enterprise. Given the patriarchal, hierarchical structure of the Turkish family in general, a Turkish family crime-enterprise is likely to mirror this structure, strengthening the old representation of organized crime as composed of hierarchic organizations. Given this organizational family structure, it is not surprising to find a logistic consisting of family points of support for transit in Turkey and distribution in the consumer countries, resulting in an integrated or closed trading line (Van Duyne *et al.*, 1990; Van Duyne, 1995).

This picture applied for a number of years, but changes have been observed by researchers from 1995 onwards. First described by Van Duyne (1995) and confirmed by subsequent research (Kleemans *et al.*, 1998), the family structure loosened. By now a second and third generation of Turkish immigrants entered the traffic. Hardly speaking Turkish and friendly with local Germans and Dutchmen, they formed similar network coalitions as other indigenous crime-entrepreneurs. A practical reason for allying with non-Turkish criminals was the high detection rate of Turks at the customs control points. To lower this risk it was necessary to recruit European drivers and transporters. Meanwhile the route of transport had changed too: the military conflict in the former Yugoslavia shifted the transport lines to Central Europe. According to the reports of the German and Dutch police in 1996, the TIR trucks with the heroin cargo arrived in Poland where it was divided into smaller parcels with different marks for the customers in the Netherlands and Germany. After this repacking, the shipment was re-exported in small vans or passenger cars (IPIT, 1996).

Though the supply by Turkish family crime-enterprises remains clearly discernable, the old trusted pattern has changed and diversified. To what extent the market has consolidated is difficult to determine. It may be safe to conclude that this 'old' drug market is still reasonably thriving and volatile, though there are (for the time being) no signs of the expansion observed during the 1990s.

The cocaine market

Like the heroin market, which may be called an 'old' market, the market for cocaine has long historical roots too. We mentioned in a previous section the widespread abuse of cocaine in Germany after the First World War. However, as far as Europe is concerned, the present professional cocaine traffic is a more recent phenomenon, which as Figure 3 shows, made a 'stormy' entry from almost a zero-level.

It is interesting to note that we are better informed about the wholesale traffic by crime-enterprises than about the retail market and the consumption patterns. The reason is the lack of outward manifestations of cocaine abuse. Cocaine consumers do not 'litter' the streets like the heroin junkies.

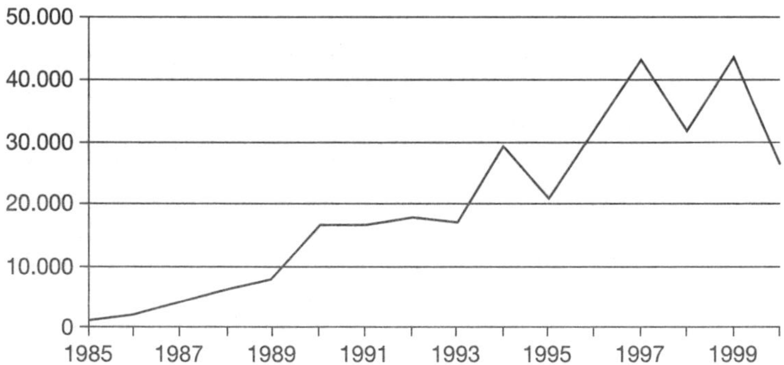

Figure 3 Seizures of cocaine in the EU in kilos, 1985–2000

Source: Adapted from European Monitoring Centre for Drugs and Drug Addiction, 2001

Although many of the latter also use cocaine frequently, it is their heroin habit that brings them to social notice. Though there are heroin 'two-worlders' who use it intermittently, cocaine consumers (other than, perhaps, 'crack' smokers) are more able to combine their habit with the continuation of their professional life and apply less often for detoxification or medical aid. In short, they are less perceived as a public 'nuisance' or a threat against the public order, which leads to less police attention and therefore less information about the daily consumption rate and retail trade. It seems that much of the available information is biased, because it is based on a sub-population who enter the hospital emergency departments applying for treatment, or who have a police record (Boekhout van Solinge, 1996).

The phenomenon of 'organized crime', the professional transport of tons of contraband, attracted most of the attention and was considered related to the notorious so-called Colombian 'cartels'. In the second half of the 1980s, the Colombian cocaine traffickers started to probe the European market (Verbeek, 2001). Since that time a wholesale traffic unfolded. Most of the wholesale import took place by means of sea transport, in which virtually every important port in Europe was involved. Rotterdam is an important entry point because it is the largest European harbour and therefore statistically the main channel for any illegal transport. Apart from Rotterdam, the South American traffickers showed little preference for any particular European country: the cocaine entered Europe from the Baltic ports to the Spanish ones. The preferred ports of entry were a matter of convenience, though Spain still seems to have a slight advantage, because of the linguistic correspondence and the smuggling tradition of the Galician fishermen. In general, the points of entry are determined by the possibility of building up a facilitating support point by fellow Colombians, who reside for some time in the regions of destination. In the literature they are called 'residents', who establish contacts with local crime-entrepreneurs to prepare the facilities for the import and the first layer of distribution (Freiberg and Thamm, 1992; Van Duyne, 1995). In view of the lack of social bridgeheads in the form of communities of emigrated compatriots or relatives in countries like the Netherlands or Germany (as opposed to Spain or the UK), establishing such outposts reflects some strategic thinking. However, the organizational advantages are frequently nullified by the low level of skills on the part of the Colombian 'residents' as well as the local criminals. The fear and awe which the Colombians inspired were no compensation for this lack of competence (Korf and Verbraeck, 1993; Van Duyne, 1995). Indeed, many organized crime groups involved in wholesale smuggling did not reveal the 'mastermind-like' planning, which is often assumed to be characteristic of the Colombian 'cartels' (Zaitch, 2002).[28] After meticulously preparing the

28 The denotation 'cartel', frequently used by the DEA and adopted by other law enforcement agencies, wrongly suggests a hierarchical price and production regulating

means of smuggling (containers, torpedoes under ships, fruit containing cocaine), the picking up of the contraband frequently proved to be a clumsily executed affair. It is difficult whether or not this incompetence is real or rather should be attributed to the tactic of allowing one in five shipments to be intercepted to satisfy law enforcement claims of competence and thus divert law enforcement 'heat'.

The spectacularly large shipments of the wholesale 'cartel' traffickers tends to distract attention from the continuous flow of smaller cargos in the range of a few kilos, which enter Europe by means of the courier, 'mule' traffic (Zaitch, 2002; Bartelink, 2001), often female (Green, 1996). Small parcels are packed on the body, hidden inside the luggage or swallowed (*boleros*) and 'emptied' on arrival.[29] Many of these transports arrive from the Caribbean islands, where the desolate economic circumstances provide the proper receptivity for easily earned extra income. Though the turnover per entrepreneur is smaller, his risks are lower, as the couriers rarely know their principals and their middleman other than by face or first name. To the courier, who swallows large amounts of cocaine packed in condoms (more recently, due to condom breakages, rubber gloves) it is a dangerous job: every year couriers die from severe overdose because of in-flight leakages.

The wholesale distribution networks which are awaiting South American exporters are predictably diverse, reflecting the mobile, multi-cultural criminal Europe: apart from the local traders, Russians, (former) Yugoslavians, Italians or Israelis are involved in the distribution or transit of the contraband to the next retail level. According to Zaitch (2002), the Italians appear to have a relative advantage: the Colombians appreciate their business acumen, many (not all) enjoy organized crime protection in their home bases and they have many social contacts all over Europe.

Reviewing these scattered data, it is fair to conclude that the cocaine market is broadly spread over all the countries in the European Union. Despite that, knowledge about its functioning is less developed than in the field of heroin, cannabis and the next brand of psychoactive substances: the synthetic or designer drugs.

The market for synthetic drugs

Getting 'high' is not only achieved by consuming a distilled 'gift of nature', as is the case with the plant-derived drugs discussed above. Substances

co-operative. Zaitch (2002) and Verbeek (2001) cast strong doubts on this representation of the most important wholesalers from Medellin and Cali. See also Crandall (2002).

29 In the first eight month of 2002 the average seized amount of cocaine carried by air travellers to Schiphol was 3.198 grammes. 'Swallowers' carried on average 692 grammes, while 'body packers' carried six kilos (Maalsté *et al.*, 2002).

with similar effects are also produced synthetically. One of those products, which would for a time conquer the European drug market three quarters of a century after its invention (1898), is MDMA, shorthand for 3–4-methylenedioximethamphetamine. It is a member of the family of amphetamine derivates. Other members are MDA, MDEA. For technical reasons and to further readability we will not give an account of the chemical backgrounds or mention the whole extended family. We will name this group MDMA or by the best known brand name, *ecstasy*.

This particular brand of stimulant was first patented by the German pharmaceutical firm Merck in 1912, but it reappeared as a psychotherapist-commended drug 'to open the mind and feelings' in the 1960s in California (Hammersley *et al.*, 2002; Huskens and Vuijst, 2002). As it was clearly an agreeably (and mild) mind-influencing substance, it attracted the interest of consumers outside the therapeutic context and, as a consequence, predictably the scorn and wrath of the US Drug Enforcement Agency. However, in the 1960s and 1970s the new chemical drug (and its relative MDA) was not yet the arousing substance of the wild rave parties of the 1980s and later. It was a *love drug* of Bagwan Rajneesh adepts and similar Indian 'higher spiritual', free-floating wisdom seekers, who went to Goa with their pockets stuffed with MDMA.

As long as the new drug remained restricted to a small social circle of wisdom seekers and therapists, there was little stimulus towards prohibition. The therapists did not advertise the new drug, because they were afraid that broader knowledge of its effects would attract the attention of the authorities, leading to prohibition. The free-floating wisdom seekers were no reason for concern either, since they were in far-off lands. This silence around the therapeutic use was disturbed when one of the distributors (who remained unknown) sensed the market potential of the medicine. From Boston he established a laboratory in Texas and started to market this still licit *fun drug*. The success was stunning and the *ecstasy* (the new brand name) pill became the drug of choice within the party setting. Given the adage that there should not be such a thing as a drug for *fun*, the powerful Democratic senator Lloyd Bentsen pressurized the DEA for prohibition and qualification in the highest possible classification (schedule 1), though at that time little was known about the physical and psychological effects of the drug. The hearing about this substance turned into a sham, because the DEA declared it could not wait for the final conclusion.[30] After some rearguard actions by psychologists

30 The harmfulness of ecstasy remains controversial and emerging findings about its negative impact on sleep patterns (*Observer*, 19 April 2004) are unlikely to be believed, even if true, by those who take it, since they seldom see any *observable* harm. This sort of issue is a major difficulty for the credibility of harm reduction in preventative as well as law enforcement campaigns.

and therapists, the drug became prohibited in the US in July 1985. After some delay, Europe followed suit.

It goes without saying that the effects of prohibition showed the predicable pattern: first a shift to related but still licit substances and finally the creation of an underground market. The shift was demonstrated by the ingenuity of the pioneers of this stimulating drug. They did not immediately withdraw into illegality, but continued experimenting to design new related substances which were not (yet) prohibited, since the laws were specific (Weijenburg, 1996; Huskens and Vuijst, 2002). The authorities' response consisted invariably in an extension of the list of prohibited substances. Apart from these 'pioneers', the demand side, fanned by the new youth *rave* culture, was such that the market hardly needed exotic experimenters. Though the latter could be useful for production, more important were daring crime-entrepreneurs with extensive networks of suppliers of precursors, chemists (many amateurs, some with professional education), distributors and smugglers. Given the existing drug and other smuggling markets and tradition in Europe, there was sufficient underground infrastructure, means and 'human resources' for this new market development. Synthetic drugs in the form of amphetamine were already produced in many countries of Europe, notably in the Netherlands, from where Sweden was traditionally supplied (Weijenburg, 1996).[31] Changing the production from amphetamine to MDMA was not a revolutionary change. When, after the successful introduction of the substance in Europe in the second half of the 1980s, the market of MDMA proved larger and more profitable than that of amphetamine, many added the new commodity to their production. From the commercial point of view they were right, as is shown by Figure 4.

How the drug fashion entered Europe is of little concern. Various places of introduction are mentioned: Ibiza ('Ecstasy Island'), where house or rave parties were held on the beach, or English ports. Maybe the new fashion entered through both channels of nightlife and partying by adolescents and young adults, spreading both via word of mouth and availability. Given the comparable youth cultures in Europe, the phases in which the new market developed are likely to be very similar. After an initial stage till about 1989 the new substance became increasingly popular, until after 1992 mass consumption set in, as has been described for Spain by Alvarez-Roldán *et al.* (1997). The consumer population of this market proved to be comparable to or overlapping with the hash market: mainly young people, anxiously looking for stimuli, which they find in partying and dancing all night, reinforced by MDMA (or its related stimulants). These are not junkies or drop-outs, but mainly scholars, students and better educated working

31 During the 1990s the Dutch were out-competed by the Poles on the Swedish market because the latter offered purer product (Krajewski, 2001; Hoyst, 1994).

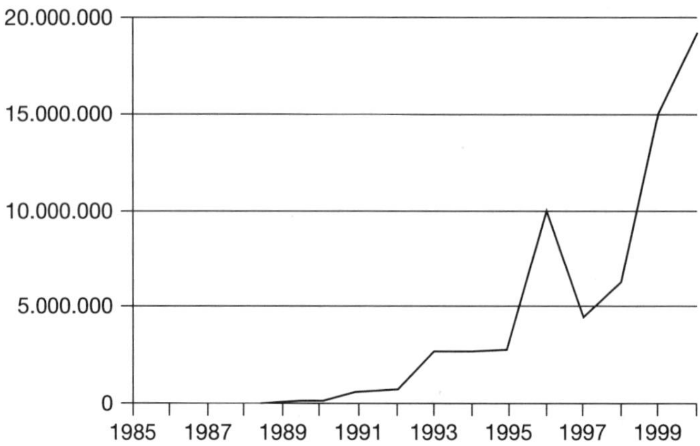

Figure 4 Intercepted number of XTC pills in the EU, 1985–2000
Source: Adapted from European Monitoring Centre for Drugs and Drug Addiction, 2001

singles, who do not need to commit property crimes or resort to prostitution to maintain their consumption (Hammersley *et al.*, 2002).

From the economic point of view, the market for this stimulus brand is very similar to the European domestically grown hash market. It is not determined by Third World low-wage production countries, areas of military conflict, sinister underworld conspiracies or the kind of murky clandestine intelligence machinations discussed in the previous sections. One can consider it a 'spontaneous' industrialized world phenomenon, sharing its mobility and relatively commercial openness. At the consumption level, one finds small-scale dealings on the part of users buying a weekly quota for friends, to cover their own use or just making some extra money. Few such people would consider themselves 'drug dealers', with all the related negative connotations. In the London ecstasy market, these consumer–dealer transactions appear to have become so commonplace and led to so much competition that they pushed prices down (Ward and Pearson, 1997). Given the social setting of the place of consumption, this is not surprising. Of the middle-level segments of the market we are less informed, as the police give little priority to local ecstasy dealers. The research carried out by Korf and Verbraeck (1993) indicates a low organizational pattern of one-person or joint-venture enterprises.

As far as the higher levels of synthetic drugs production and trafficking are concerned, we are slightly better informed due to more intensive police surveillance, albeit that yields the usual collection of anecdotal cases, often under the heading of 'organized crime'. At present, the Netherlands appears to have acquired an international leading market position, particularly exporting to the UK and the US. For this phenomenon, the police provide only the following intuitive explanation. In the southern provinces of the Netherlands (Brabant and Limburg) there was a thriving tradition of smuggling and illegal alcohol distillation. During the 1970s and 1980s, the illicit distillers applied their laboratory skills to amphetamine, exporting mainly to Sweden. After the arrival of the ecstasy market, which in its initial stages was dependent on American imports, they seem to have switched to MDMA production. On the international level they were apparently successful: the transatlantic flow of synthetic drugs was reversed and the US became net importers of Dutch pills. In this reversed flow of contraband there emerged a strong Orthodox Jewish connection, in which young Chassidic Jews from the US (mainly New York) took part in the transportation. The exact relationship and the causes for its development are still unclear. Thus far it seems that they were a component of a kind of triangle between the Netherlands, the US and Israel. The backgrounds of the Dutch–Israeli connection are thus far not clarified either.

As far as the organization of the supply of the Dutch consumer market is concerned numerous small crime-enterprises emerged, as there was little need to set up extensive transport organizations. The wholesale export organizations were more elaborate and were designated by the prosecution and the courts as 'organized crime'. They were characterized by an elaborate division of labour: production, transport, distribution, and criminal management (Van Duyne, 1995; Weijenburg, 1996), preferably separated. They were also characterized by a higher level of violence, resulting in a number of murders (Huskens and Vuijst, 2002; Westphal, 2002).

An important market aspect is the illicit traffic in precursors, the chemical substances that are not the real psychoactive agents, but are required for producing the stimulants. Important precursors are PMK and BMK, used for the production of perfume. Their trade is strictly regulated to prevent their abuse for the production of amphetamine, MDMA and related drugs.[32] Understandably this stimulated the illicit traffic in precursors, which could be acquired in Eastern Europe and China. As the licit outlet for these substances is small, it is difficult to import them wholesale in a regular way with the help of a licensed (front) firm without attracting attention. Therefore the crime-entrepreneurs resort to trusted ways of smuggling, usually by tampering with the descriptions of the contents of the shipment. Do they also enter and function as 'specialist-entrepreneurs'? A University of Tilburg research project analysed the court files of the nine top wholesale precursor and ecstasy dealers prosecuted from 1997 onwards (Westphal,

32 The EU regulation 3677 of September 1990 stipulated the conditions for importation, export and transit. This regulation was amended and extended in January 1993 by the EU regulation 900/92 and 3769/92 and covers 22 substances.

2002). One Chinese exporter proved to be a real specialist and an EU-wide provider, hauling hundreds of litres of PMK to Rotterdam first and (after detection) to Lisbon, from where it arrived in the Netherlands all the same. One entrepreneur acquired PMK by ordering it through a French firm in the Ukraine and Baltic states. There is not only a market for substances, but also for hardware: one firm sold every kind of equipment that was needed for making pills. Other crime-entrepreneurs in this market proved less selective. The remaining sample comprised wholesalers, also for export.

Looking at the European drug markets, their development, diversity and present state, we must grant that only a utopian or a hard-core drug fighter can imagine a drug-free Europe. Otherwise the drug market is part and parcel of a broadly based youth and young adult culture sustained by affluence and a (kind of mild) hedonism, in keeping with the poet Thom Gunn's comment that Elvis (Presley) 'turned revolt into style'. However, drug consumption is no longer an 'act of revolt' by adolescents against an older generation, as in the 1960s. The well-known 'generation gap' of that time hardly exists anymore, though generations naturally still differ: authoritarianism by parents or the 'establishment' is hardly an issue, consumerism is shared by young and old, differences in the musical preferences are less pronounced, leisure dress is generally accepted and the words 'conservative' and 'progressive' have no longer the connotation of 'old' versus 'young'. Within this context most drug consumption is just for sensation and fun. Of course, this may end tragically for the small group of users who get addicted and/or who share needles in insanitary conditions among their fellows, any one of whom may be infected with HIV or other serious hazards. As long as this fun-seeking remains, we have to face the continuation of underground 'hedonist' drug markets. Within this hedonism, the markets will be as little consolidated as any other market that has to respond to 'lifestyle' fashion shifts. In a broader, general sense one may consider it a 'consolidated' and thriving market. However, looking at its market segments, history has shown that these are volatile and whimsical.

Though this observation may be abhorrent to any moralist, this is not a 'moral' conclusion, but the most realistic deduction from the facts and figures since the onset of the anti-drug policy as it started before the First World War in the US. Only one phase in the twentieth century saw an absolute low point in drug traffic and consumption: the Second World War, with its strict military control of all movements of goods and persons. Though that represents an extreme and tragic historical phase, its total control does hint at the high price to be paid for a drug-free world.

3 Commerce, constraints and enterprise features

In the previous chapter we briefly indicated the most common organizational characteristics of crime-enterprises involved in the underground economy of illicit psychoactive substances: criminal trading networks. This common type does not exclude the existence of hierarchic organizations along the lines of patriarchal family enterprises or other types of crime-organizations, like the Sicilian or the Calabrian Mafia. These rough denotations do not provide much insight into the various ways of organizing this trade, the constraints within which the market players have to operate and the ways they cope with them. It is to these we now turn.

The concept of 'market player' requires some elaboration. At first sight it seems to denote the actual traders: importers, exporters, distributors, retailers, user-dealers and finally the consumers. However, one set of key players is often left out of sight: the policy makers, legislators and law enforcement. Though acting as if they are fighting the crime-market and believing themselves to be doing so, they are its inherent cornerstone. Together they constitute the agencies which single out the 'forbidden fruits', determining thereby indirectly their price and profit margins. The nature and intensity of the constraints to law enforcement profoundly influence the structure and operations of the crime-enterprises and the 'natural selection' of its participants or its survivors. If we broaden the concept of the crime-market we should encompass the law enforcement market as well: its budget, mutual legal assistance and power-generation mechanisms including cultural supports and resistance around phenomena such as 'organized crime'. We have seen already a few historic glimpses of this side of the market in the previous chapters. As also understood by Courtwright (2001) in his history of drugs, this broadening goes beyond a description of these substances and their directly related market.[1] At one level, this is a trivial observation: of

1 The European 'market' for drug legislation and policy making has been described by Boekhout van Solinge (2002), describing the 'Brussels ritualism', taking place in a semi-closed civil servant market place of its own right. Irrespective of the level of insight into

course there can be no crimes without socially organized prohibition via a legislature, and no enforcement without enforcers (including the public). However, criminal markets cannot be understood without comprehending how control processes interact with offender motives and opportunities, especially not in fairly consensual activities such as drug trade.

3.1 Organizing criminal commerce

In the previous chapter we have given a short overview of the developments of the drug markets in western Europe. We have reviewed the social and economic processes, which brought a variety of strange bedfellows together. We have also observed that the various market sections did not emerge within a political void, but were stimulated by remarkable foreign policy conditions that ideally would not have been wanted by the Western countries where drugs are consumed. The question we face now is what kind of characteristic features or regular traits can be discerned, or perhaps even what 'mechanisms' are likely to come into existence because of the very underground nature of this commerce.

Product illegality and organizing in a hostile environment

Many obvious and in the literature well-described, characteristics of organizing an illegal business are still overshadowed by 'classical' images of 'organized crime'. We will not rehearse the ongoing debate on the nature of organized crime (see Levi, 2002a for an overview). However, given the longevity of its 'Urbild', the primordial image is still very much alive in the minds of policy makers, legislators and law enforcement officers, and some aspects will have to be referred to here. The image of the conspiratorial, hierarchically structured Mafia organization led by a boss, assisted by a councillor (*consiglieri*) and sub-bosses may be considered the archetype of organized crime. This archetype is not mere fantasy: Paoli (2002b; 2003) elaborates anew its historical and social place and distinguishes this kind of organization from criminal *merchant* organizations. Mafia-type associations (an Italian legal construct), the Japanese Yakuza or the Chinese Triads would have their origins in non-commercial brotherhoods from which they derived bonding rituals and other social and organizational features. Nevertheless, this pre-commercial origin did not prevent them from detecting and from speedily and professionally exploiting the advantages of their closed and violence-prone organizations. An exploitable opportunity was ready at hand in areas of defective state protection: *forced private protection*. For good reasons,

the field, this little cosmos impacts directly and deeply on drug markets, albeit not always as intended.

Gambetta (1993) singled out this entrepreneurial core business for a concise analysis of the Sicilian Mafia as a species of the territory-bound illegal protection industry. A variable in this is the level of masculinity culture, traditional values, brotherhood bonds and expectations on the part of market participants about the consequences of disobedience (Paoli, 2003). Beliefs about control over law enforcement are one component, but 'bad reputation' – enhanced at times by a sensation-hungry media – here may be functional for inducing compliance. Despite the very often ramshackle nature of the Mafia organizations, many characteristics do fit the archetypical image of 'organized crime'. What about 'organized crime' outside the market of forced protection and territorial dominance? Let us make a quick comparison.

The distinction between criminal merchant enterprises and territorially based protection enterprises of the 'brotherhoods' made by Paoli and Gambetta, complemented with the description of 'La Cosa Nostra' by Firestone (1996) as a primitive pre-modern organization, is not an absolute one. In our perspective they share the same underlying psychological principle: entrepreneurs are usually not primarily organization-oriented, but directly action-oriented. Though there are notable exceptions, few ponder about the setting up of an organization as a thought-out blueprint, after which they can venture on a targeted crime-market.[2] They do not think in such terms of established entities, but tend to organize their activities around their core business. Like the usual trader, they organize by doing, being made aware by law enforcement agencies that they qualify as an 'organization'. In crime business the organizational focus is – almost tautologically – the illegal provision of services or products. The concrete way of realizing these commercial activities is to a large extent determined by the nature of the 'commodity' in combination with cultural choices and the way law enforcement actually reacts and is expected to react to this illicit commodity traffic.

Providing protection services or trading prohibited products require different forms of coping with basic uncertainties caused by a fundamentally hostile commercial environment (Van Duyne, 1998). Protection requires full information about the customers in a territory on which one must have a monopolist grip in the first place. In the protection industry there is no room for competing illegal protectors in the territory of operation. Coping with illegality in trading products is dependent on the demand pattern and the conduct of one's customers. Organizing proper access to reliable

2 Some historical exceptions are the 'La Cosa Nostra' figures like Marenzano (who survived his organizational conception by only three months) and 'Lucky' Luciano (who undid Marenzano's organizational blueprint by having him killed in 1931). Other examples are described by the first author (Van Duyne *et al.*, 1990; Van Duyne 1995). In general this observation does not apply to many manifestations of organized *business* crime, in which it is a pre-condition to set out by establishing a real organization, which copies the outward appearances of a legitimate organization, usually in the form of a legal entity.

customers (the outlet requirement), supplying and protecting trade lines against the law and competitors are the basic organizational activities to be undertaken. This does not depend on territorial seclusion but on openness and flexibility within the margins of safety (Reuter and Haaga, 1989). In both illegal industries the crime-entrepreneur 'drapes' his organizational activities over and around the core business product while heeding the same safety requirement of *information management.* As Reuter and Haaga (1989) argue, there are few incentives to develop an organization beyond these baseline requirements.

The basic feature of the criminal entrepreneurial landscape is its pervasive 'Hobbesian' hostility. It is a landscape in which trust is an even scarcer commodity than in normal business life, and in which breaches of trust have far-reaching consequences. Just imagine being an entrepreneur while every person you are dealing with may already be or may become a prosecution witness; your business can be shut down overnight; you may find your lifetime's accumulated assets confiscated and yourself behind bars for a lengthy period. We could add to this the risk of being killed because of the sometimes violent competition or the rough ways of settling debts and other disputes about 'respect'. Within this Hobbesian world of 'War of All against All', information-safety management is an essential requisite for conducting any more than transient business. The crime-entrepreneur has to find a balance between, on the one hand, information restriction and secrecy in order not to be rounded up by the police and, on the other hand, information dissemination in order to do business at all. Let us briefly enumerate the impediments of organizing a crime-enterprise in the prohibited substances market (Van Duyne *et al.*, 2001):

- the crime-entrepreneur cannot act like normal suppliers in a supply and demand market: he cannot advertise and compete openly. This has the consequence that crime-markets of prohibited substances are based on demand;
- he has a *recruitment problem*: how and where can he get reliable staff? He cannot recruit from the yellow pages or the newspapers looking for the most skilled criminal offering his services;[3]
- he has a serious problem in using information carriers necessary to monitor his flow of goods and moneys or dealing with fellow criminals: whether paper or pencil or devices for electronic data-processing for information storage, they are all potential *evidence carriers*.

3 A noteworthy exception was found in a newspaper ad in which a cannabis wholesaler asked for an 'adventurous captain'. As a matter of fact he had run out of his stock of seamen as well as 'clean' boats for hauling the cannabis from Pakistan to the Netherlands (Van Duyne, 1995; Klerks, 2000).

These technical information risks are insignificant compared to the inherent risks of the *human* information carrier. While doing business, he has to cope with continuous risks of leakage to competitors as well as to the police. One does not need to think of outright 'ratting' and betrayal in the first place, but also of unintentional bragging of underlings or conspicuous display of sudden wealth attracting the attention of the police.[4] Given these impediments, one may wonder how crime-enterprises succeed in developing and thriving at all. This applies particularly to trading psychoactive substances, in which the negative penal consequences in the event that this human risk management fails, are the most severe.

We do no need to elaborate the basic motivations for engagement in this trade: 'easy' revenue which enables a luxurious life, popularity (and sex) or at any rate an escape from poverty because of lack of other economic opportunities (Van Nostrand and Tewksbury, 1999). It goes without saying that these general motives are not so unique as to have much explanatory value. More important is (a) being acquainted with a sufficient number of existing traders, (b) to have sufficient confidence and trust to sooth the fear of the threats of the hostile landscape and (c) to have access to a sufficient number of trusted customers. Granted, these conditions overlap considerably. In this milieu one does not get acquaintances without being trusted because of having corresponding social backgrounds, characteristics, skills and attitudes. Socially one must be recognized as really 'being involved' in the market, while one's attitude must radiate sufficient secrecy to be trustworthy. These are basic human traits, but a pre-condition for the building up of a regular and continuous traffic in illegal products.

Being considered trustworthy, because one has the reputation of being secretive (and the other way round), furthers the business, but at the same time it has important constraining effects on the scale of the crime-business one is able to develop and maintain. Trust is basically a dyadic relationship between two people, though not exclusively. One cannot trust too many people, nor being trusted by too many without straining one's capacity in terms of 'social time' to maintain and control relationships. Too many trust-relationships may have a diluting effect, which could be detrimental to the execution of hidden operations, or at least decrease their efficiency. This has been illustrated by Morselli (2001) in his network description of a broker, 'Mr Nice', in the wholesale hashish trade. Mr Nice's most efficient operations

4 Reuter and Haaga (1989) notice that professional wholesalers eschew customers who behave conspicuously. Also the head of the Philadelphia-based Bruno family pressured his members to avoid ostentation (Haller, 1994). Likewise the hash trader Chessplan, described in Van Duyne et al. (1990) and Van Duyne (1995) insisted that his fellow smugglers put their crime-money in a Luxembourg bank account while keeping a low spending profile. He was a cheeseparing character himself, nicknamed by the Canadian importers 'the scrooge', but due to this trait he maintained a high survival capacity.

were conducted by small networks in which he brokered, averaging 2.4 contacts per consignment which involved various groups of sellers and buyers. His most effective shipment load was around 1000 kilos; increasing the load resulted in less efficiency. A similar case of efficiency trade-off was observed by Van Duyne *et al.* (1990) and Van Duyne (1995), following the career of some of the wholesalers. Mr Chessplan (see previous footnote), one of the smartest wholesale traders emerging in his research projects, started with a well-directed, but extensive as well as expensive network, stretching from Eastern Germany over the Netherlands to Norway. After his arrest and prison term in the late 1980s, Mr Chessplan scaled down to the position of middleman or rather broker (though sometimes buying wholesale in his own name). Despite another arrest and moderate prison term, he survived as an affluent crime-entrepreneur, operating with a small 'organization' in the form of a flexible network, which would not even be rated by the prosecution as 'organized crime'.

Comparing the research findings concerning 'organized crime' operations in the drug market with the general notion of organized crime, the outcome tends be a scaling down of the organizational representation. Given the need to survive in a hostile entrepreneurial environment (if corrupt and/or violent control cannot be assured) the entrepreneur's safety management does not provide a pay-off for anything more than short-term operational schemes per consignment. The execution of an operation may each time be performed by a differently composed crew drawn from his available network. This explains the high variability in the shapes of organizing operations, which by law enforcement 'hindsight' are often reconstructed as an 'organization', being essentially shifty pragmatic networks and joint ventures, a recurrent finding since the 1920s.[5] Why should a crime-entrepreneur strive for a settled organization, with all the disadvantages of fixed staff knowing each other and developing some kind of a 'collective memory', eventually to be tapped by the police? This seems to be a rhetorical question, which it is not. Despite the wisdom expressed above, the tendency to 'drape' the organization around the core business may nevertheless be conductive to more continuous and larger organizations. This may depend on a number of factors: on the cultural and social landscape – including corruption potential and longer-term networks of trust-generating friendships that may survive geographical dispersal (Hobbs, 1997) – in which the entrepreneur operates, but also on ambitions and personal choices not all of which are based on perfect knowledge or made with intelligence.

5 One of the first researchers on organized crime in the 1920s, Moley, observed that 'the conception of organized crime as a vast underworld organization, led by a 'master mind', with workers, lieutenants and captains was melodramatic nonsense'. See Woodiwiss (2003), elaborating the tenacity of melodramatic concepts in this field.

Transcending and using the network delta

Despite the fact that the research literature in Europe as well as in the US repeatedly describes the organized crime phenomenon in general and the drug market in particular in terms of network relations, the police and policy makers typically appear to have adopted few of these insights (though there are clusters that do). The police continue to speak of crime-organizations as clear (menacing) entities and policy makers follow suit and enact laws aimed at combating them as discernable 'beings'. There seems to remain a gap between the recurrent findings of the researchers and the official representation by many of the authorities.

The grounds for this gap may be twofold. On the one hand there is the tendency of the police to interpret the operations and relationships within crime-enterprises and between crime-entrepreneurs and their executives from the familiar organizational charts and blueprints they get handed down during training courses. This goes together with the usual 'organized crime' vocabulary, whose importance in constraining rational debate should not be underestimated.[6] On the other hand, it should not be denied that some crime-entrepreneurs do succeed, albeit temporarily, in establishing a real 'classical' top-down led organization. This can be the outcome of chance and haphazard development, but history also records a few cases of identified crime-entrepreneurs deliberately striving to transcend the common level of pragmatic short-term network operations. Though far from being representative, this occasional pyramid structure strengthens again the traditional 'organized crime' representation. In the perspective of police and prosecution, such a representation is conceptually easier, while it also looks more impressive to present a complex organizational chart of the main defendants as leaders of a *real* organization. Except where it would undermine their case, prosecutors are unlikely to present their organized crime case as an example of a pragmatically, loosely functioning network.

When we look at the cases of wholesalers, who achieved such a big turnover and obtained a 'Mr Big' reputation among the organized crime squads (but also in their milieu), we find little unity. What unites them is their success in stretching the constraints of the illegal market, albeit temporarily. Making a very rough division, we have on the one hand the 'indigenous' crime-entrepreneurs and on the other hand, crime-entrepreneurs from ethnic minorities.[7]

6 Researchers, working with the organized crime squads, may share the experience of the first author, who noticed that during their daily work the detectives talk about networks and shifty relationships, but on the more formal level of reporting they resort again to the usual 'organized crime' wording. See Reuter (1983, p. 5) and Levi (2002a) on the persistence of official doctrine and imagery. Though even where relationships are described as networks, it is difficult to avoid hierarchical images, a fact that also applies outside 'organized crime'.

7 Though we will use the term 'ethnic' throughout this book as denoting residents who

Among the 'indigenous' (Dutch) crime-entrepreneurs the first author investigated, one entrepreneur, Mr Bruinsma, actually displayed the expressed ambition to establish 'real' organized crime in the Netherlands. This ambition proved to become his undoing.

Mr Bruinsma: Mr Bruinsma was the son of a wealthy soft-drink manufacturer, who deliberately opted for a criminal career. During the late 1970s and early 1980s Bruinsma gradually developed a wholesale hash importation and distribution 'firm' with a friend and a girlfriend. The firm became one of the biggest, if not the biggest supplier for the Netherlands and beyond. Bruinsma succeeded in obtaining sufficient credit in Pakistan for multi-thousand-kilo hash shipments, which were unloaded in the darkness of night on the beaches of the North Sea. Apart from being just a wholesale importer, as his girlfriend associate saw it, he also glorified himself as a real underworld boss. This did not remain unchallenged, resulting in multiple killings (Middelburg, 1992; 2000). While his ambitions (and his cocaine consumption) increased, the organization of his core business became cluttered. Being no longer satisfied with the successful large shipments, in 1989 he wanted to make a last 'real' big stroke: a haul of 35.000 kilos, called the 'mountain'. This consignment failed, leading to bitter rebukes against his fellow investors. Meanwhile, Mr Bruinsma had become a major target of the police. Whether Bruinsma's whimsical behaviour, the loss of the 'mountain' or the intensified police attention scared his fellow crime-entrepreneurs is difficult to say, but it is a very plausible assumption that his entourage wanted him to leave the business. He intended to do so and sold his real estate corporation. Two weeks later, in June 1991, he was shot (Middelburg, 1992). Only a fraction of his considerable 'heritage' was found. The two boxes containing the unsorted paperwork of his heritage revealed more chaos than structure.[8]

Whether or not he was the real organized crime boss of Amsterdam, it is interesting to observe that the carrying out of his core business followed along the usual lines of the network of co-investors and available aides for the dangerous 'wet jobs' (landing of the cargoes on the shore, Van Duyne

themselves or whose parents originate from countries outside the EU, it is a strange discriminating concept. It is usually reserved for people from the Middle East and beyond and coloured people. No one speaks of 'ethnic' English residing in Spain, or 'ethnic' Dutchmen in Rotterdam, though within a decade they will be a real 'ethnic minority' in that city.

8 A nickname of Bruinsma was the 'tall guy' (de lange), whose shadow proved to be long indeed: in 2003, the second son of the Dutch queen announced his engagement to a 35-year-old woman, who as a 21-year-old student had been befriended by Bruinsma when she took part in his sailing events. When the shadows of the past came to light again, the ensuing media hype was such that the prince was obliged to renounce his rights as potential heir to the throne.

et al., 1990). Was it just a network with an over-ambitious leader, or a real organization in which he himself believed? The police made many complicated 'organograms' to approximate the 'Bruinsma organization', parts of which could actually be qualified as such, at least his real estate corporation and his distribution 'shop' as long as being managed by his girlfriend (Middelburg, 2000). But apart from these segments, his criminal firm was essentially a very small inner circle of yes-men, while for his core business, the organization of import operations, he addressed the existing network of veteran smugglers. Many of them came from the fishing communities along the North Sea and the Ijselmeer. In changing compositions, they could be recruited to carry out similar jobs for their fellow hash-import entrepreneurs or, as the police assumed, the 'heirs' of Bruinsma. From their traditional organized crime conception the police vehemently continued to look for the 'successor' organization, called the 'Delta-organization' in the meaning of a hierarchical triangle of command. But there was none (Middelburg and Van Es, 1996). There was just the flat network 'river' delta as of old, before Bruinsma attempted in vain to impose his Mafia-like fantasies.

The observations of Adler (1985), followed by Reuter and Haaga (1989), Morselli (2001) or Kleemans *et al.* (2002) with their emphasis on the dynamics of shifting network relations do not seem to leave much room for projecting such continuous crime-organizations. The various ways drug-entrepreneurs conduct their businesses indicates that the network approach is a good approximation of the illegal market, but not always of the structure of the single crime-enterprises themselves. In this regard, it is of interest to compare the Bruinsma enterprise with what became known of the enterprises of his colleague wholesalers, most of them also specialising in hash trafficking, but one also in the emerging XTC market. They differed in one respect: ambition. They stuck to the craft they were good at: smuggling or the organization thereof. Some of them succeeded in remaining long enough in business to qualify as a continuous enterprise or structured organization. The cases are interesting, because they reveal the tension between, on the one hand, the requirements of commanding a fully fledged large smuggling enterprise within the constraints related to its illegality and, on the other hand, personal choice and a stable leadership style. One enterprise showed characteristics which corresponded closely to the police clichés; another enterprise was led like a normal firm with a boss and a fixed staff, characterized by normal non-violent stable social relationships, as described below.

Jan Orange and Mr Stadholder: Jan Orange, a stocky peaceful man, who acquired the taste for smuggling as the truck driver of big Dutch–Belgian VAT-scams, invested his money in a hauling firm, which transported large shipments of hashish on behalf of many wholesalers, a few of them connected to the network of Bruinsma. His cover cargo consisted of oranges and other fruits from Morocco. He had a fixed crew of drivers, who got normal wages plus a good bonus for smuggling. Those who did not dare to smuggle were not pressed to do so: without reproach they could transport only oranges instead. In cases where drivers were arrested he took care of their families, for social as well as for the tactical reason of ensuring their loyalty (free lawyer for husband available, also abroad). Indeed, the firm stuck together when Jan Orange was arrested, suspected of being involved in the 35.000 kilo hashish consignment. Nobody made any statement and the prosecution dropped the case. Jan (and his son) are still in business.

Normal and steady social relations existed also within the hash-enterprise of Mr Stadholder, who also acted as wholesaler with a fixed middle management (the executives were more often recruited ad hoc). His peaceful operation made his firm an uneventful undertaking. Being a risk-eschewing entrepreneur, he prudently delegated his transport business to his middle management, carving up the main area of operation in Spain into two or three sections, in which they were to operate like 'stadholders'. The enterprise operated safely and silently without attracting police attention until the mishap of one of the truckers getting a heart attack in the middle of Spain while hauling a large cargo of hash. The detection of the hash load and the truck led to Stadholder himself.

Stadholder embodies the transition of *central-player* to *peripheral-player*, creating a distance between himself and the basic operations, though he cannot be characterized as a broker (Morselli, 2001). He was the general manager of a stable transport/import firm with a reliable delegation pattern (Van Duyne, 1995).

There is no contradiction between the illegal network, with its short-term relationships and shifting coalitions, and the existence of continuous enterprises as organizational entities. If the latter provide safety for the core operations, the organizer as well as the executives grow into a more coherent organization. Depending on backgrounds and experience some, like Stadholder and Jan Orange, who had an 'upperworld' business background, may be more naturally inclined to follow a more stable upperworld model. Most drug-entrepreneurs originate from the informal shadow economy and will feel more at ease within the network of informal relations. However, this informality does not exclude the development of a command structure to monitor extensive and complex trading lines for which more than shifting relationships are required. The cases which have come to light underline the vulnerability of such large undertakings, aggravated by a gangster leadership-style as demonstrated by *Boris Batterbrain* (Van Duyne, 1996a; Klerks, 2000).

Batterbrain: The multi-ton hash-importer Batterbrain was a sophisticated organizer of sea smuggling lines, one of the few drug entrepreneurs who managed to monitor several consignments at the same time, instead of operating on a one-by-one project basis. This implied much logistics and 'human factor control' with a more than usual visibility and interception risk. Contrary to Mr Stadholder and Jan Orange, Batterbrain held his captains personally responsible for interceptions, or suspected them of having stolen the intercepted cargo. He made clear that a personal responsibility implies the risk of getting the barrel of a gun against one's head or being taken 'for a ride'. Because of this management style his network of human sources was eventually exhausted, which induced him to more violence to get a new crew or to acquire a new untainted ship. This proved his undoing, as was also the case with Mr *Horseshoe*, a fellow wholesale hash importer and exporter to Britain. Cheating his customers, beating up his crew in front of others as an exemplary warning proved to be a poor power substitute for smoothing human relations in the way Mr Nice, Orange or Stadholder did.

Apart from these personality deficits, monitoring such extensive operations proved generally to be counterproductive from the point of view of information management. For example, the more control Horseshoe exercised, the more evidence he created for the police overhearing his conversations.

Rising above the network delta by stretching the inherent constraints in the underground economy actually proves to be a risky undertaking. Those who tried went down because of their ever-extending trading lines, which dominated a segment of the trading delta. This had the unintended and unexpected effect of increasing their vulnerability, because while acquiring the reputation of a real wholesaler, more became known of them to the investigators. Subsequently they moved to a higher position on the list of police priorities, if only to prevent them from becoming considered 'untouchables'. As far as we can determine, most of those ambitious wholesale organizations were rounded up in the 1990s. Only a few of the main players, like Chessplan, are still at large, though it is uncertain whether they are still active traders or what their market position looks like. Therefore we do not wish to rule out the possibility of 'Big Fish' being unknown to the police. However, it is important to distinguish between those who are outside the intelligence loop altogether and those who are known but have the skills, discipline and resources (human and technical) that inhibit collecting sufficient legally admissible evidence for conviction.

Family enterprises and networks

It should be noted that the crime-enterprises described in the previous section were composed of Western European criminals, many of them being long-term acquaintances, but usually not relatives. We can observe another organizational picture when crime-entrepreneurs can resort to closer relationships like an 'extended' family, usually of foreign origin, which may entail closer and safer bonds. From the point of view of risk management, operating through family ties is a natural choice for escaping the human factor constraints of the illegal market. In addition, without explicit planning the family provides the blueprint for the organizational structure to be adopted. If, in many cultures, the family is the usual unit of legitimate economic activities, it is no surprise that crime-entrepreneurs adopt the same cultural formula.

This observation is a very general one. It does not do justice to the huge variety of (criminal) family businesses in western Europe, due to the cultural differences of settled minorities still having strong ties to their home countries. For example, in the Turkish families the head of the family is a man, a real *pater familias*, a man of authority determining the activities of the other relatives. This results in a natural hierarchic organization as is often found in the complicated police organograms presented as evidence of the hierarchical nature of organized crime. However, these police organograms are little more than 'family pictures'. Compared to this, describing a Caribbean crime organization is much more difficult. Families from this region, particularly if they are of a Creole descent, are much more matriarchal, in which the mother plays a major role in holding the family together, while the male partners frequently come and go. If a such a crime organization has a family structure, one finds brothers, half-brothers, distant uncles and half-nephews, etc. operating almost without a clear 'command structure'. For example, criminal files of Jamaican and Surinamese smuggling crime groups look quite chaotic and one may be tempted to call this 'unorganized' crime. However, this may be a wrong characterization. Like a hierarchical Turkish crime-family, the Jamaican or Surinam crime-family just partly mirrors the way its society is culturally and economically structured of which the (illegal) entrepreneurial community is a part. Even if operating within a family structure is adopted to cope with the constraints of illegality, it does not yield a homogeneous picture.

When we look at the Turkish wholesale heroin traffickers who according to the police, provide about 85–90 per cent of the European heroin consumption, we find an interesting phenomenon, which reflects within a rather short time span a cultural and organizational development. In the 1980s we found 'integrated family trading lines', by which is meant that the export from Turkey, the transport and the first points of import in Germany or the Netherlands was organized by one extended family, often dominated by the *baba*, the *pater familias* in Turkey (Van Duyne *et al.*, 1990). This did not exclude cooperation between families, though one finds more reports of bloody feuds than shared commercial interests (Bovenkerk and Yezilgöz, 1998).

After an increasing number of police successes, the traffic did not abate but the police noticed a change towards a 'cell structure': small groups of criminals (frequently relatives) operating with little knowledge of other 'cells'. Was this a new strategic way of coping with the hostile trading environment or merely a common police construction. Or did independent families, living already for a long time in western Europe and having only thin connections to their previous homeland, enter the drug market? A number of case studies showed that the 'cells' were not the firmly closed-off disciplined entities that the police claimed. 'Cells with little plasma and a permeable skin' was Van Duyne's (1995) concluding remark. It is more plausible that the 'cell-presentation' of organized crime is another organized crime projection of the police, this time derived from the anti-terrorist security model. Actually, Turkish families are strewn all over Europe having still many connections in Turkey, where influential men of respect are able to recruit relations in Europe as support points for logistic purposes (Flormann and Krevert, 2001). However, it is doubtful whether the support points are the professional, disciplined and secluded 'cells', to which tasks can be delegated at will. Often, delegating to 'cells' within a sixty-person family proved to be disastrous, owing to the bungled execution of the tasks. Resorting to untalented members of one's family appeared to be as big a security risk as using distrustful outsiders or as the prying eyes of the crime squad. Leading family heads sometimes had to travel from Turkey to the 'front-line' to supervise basic 'front line operation'.

Alongside such extended families, which still exist, many local families were observed in the Netherlands and Germany, which formed networks or temporary alliances. Some acted as logistical links in the operational transport and distribution chains, which for safety reasons appeared to be longer than the rather short transaction chains observed by Reuter and Haaga (1989). Granted, the length of the transaction chain may in these cases be determined by the risks inherent in the transportation. Extra links are required by an intermediary towards specialists and providers of facilities (e.g. preparing cars, providing safe houses) in the transport business (IPIT, 1996). These were often times independent crime-entrepreneurs, servicing various import-export connections, strengthening the metaphor of the trading network. Later Kleemans *et al.* (1998) would more strongly emphasize the 'shifty network' phenomenon, which was not so much a 'new' style as the belated observation of an ongoing development.

As time and social integration of the Turkish minority went by, coping with the constraints in the cross-border wholesaling also changed. Increasingly criminal files and police reports mentioned stronger relations with non-Turkish traffickers' networks as well as the recruitment of non-Turkish drivers after continuous arrests by the Austrian, German and Dutch customs. One of the first examples of 'criminal integration' with Dutch fellow traffickers was observed in an Amsterdam criminal file of a major heroin importer in 1994, described by Van Duyne (1995) as a 'first swallow' of what the police called a 'modern Turkish criminal entrepreneur'. Subsequent research by Kleemans *et al.* (1998) confirmed the progress of inter-ethnic co-operative criminal trading networks. Another development was the search for new routes and methods to neutralise police controls. The

Balkan route, having become troublesome because of the Yugoslavian wars and increased controls at the Austrian border, shifted to the east and to Poland and the Czech Republic. In addition many consignments did not cross the EU borders in their original wholesale form. As described in Chapter 2, the shipments were re-packed in Poland and sent in smaller parcels, each market by shape or colour, to the importers/distributors in passenger cars or small vans to Germany or the Netherlands. In some cases, the packages destined for individual customers were prepared in Turkey. This suggests a rather direct connection between the importer/distributor and Turkish exporter (see page 38).

Organizing criminal commerce in a hostile entrepreneurial landscape is by its very nature a matter of continuous improvised adaptation to new threats as well as opportunities. A full and detailed account of the various forms of coping with the constraints would merit a specialist volume in its own right. Suffice it to conclude that this network-like delta landscape is hardly conducive to continuous 'organized crime' enterprises. Nevertheless, amidst this shifting functional patchwork, extensive organising crime-families did (and still do) – for some time – reach a form of stability.

Using networks and 'organized crime'

Given the profitability of the drug market, it would have been a miracle if forms of organized crime, like the 'traditional' Italian organized crime groups, the Mafia, the Camorra, the N'Drangheta or the Nuova Sacra Corona would not have taken part in it. The role of the Mafia in the emergence of the European heroin market has been described in Chapter 2. Furthermore, Italian–American organized crime did not shy away from the drug market, though not all leading members of the crime-families agreed to this.

Given the participation of the Mafia, does its way of operating in this market differ from what is considered their territorial core business of forced protection? The answer is partly affirmative, as the Mafia did (and does) not necessarily *directly* take part in the traffic. In the first place, Italy was and still is an important transit country for those transporters who want to avoid the Balkan route. Protecting the passage of contraband consignments safely through an organized crime territory in southern Italy can still be considered to be the core business of the Mafia or Camorra, according to which they levy their Mafiosi protection 'tithe'. The same applied to the laboratories in the 1970s, established in Sicily and protected (and exploited like any other enterprise) by Mafia families (Gambetta, 1993, ch. 9). This was not their only form of drug involvement. They were also attractive intermediaries between the exporters in countries in the Middle East (Turkey, Lebanon) and the importing main consumer country, the US. This advantage was due to their historic connections with the Italian-American organized crime-families controlling the waterfront in New York (and control over corrupt criminal justice bodies, which was an element in the 'purchase plan'). In addition they invested directly in smuggling enterprises, remaining separate from the executives, like the fishermen operating in their spare time, as has also been the case with cigarette smuggling.

On the basis of the available evidence, one can conclude that the drug smuggling of Mafiosi is not fundamentally different from that of other illegal enterprises. However, instead of only relying on external networks, the problems of the illegal environment need not be met by external network relations only. Gambetta (1993) refers to Mafia families who mentioned the 'internalization' of smugglers as mafiosi in order to enhance security and reliability of supply. Perhaps this represents an exceptional situation. The reverse side of this hasty adoption of outsiders was a shallow incorporation of Mafia norms and values (Paoli, 2003). In most available cases, the cross-border transport operations are network relations carried out by independent entrepreneurs with only a few contact points to the Mafiosi principals, preferably by means of an intermediary.

The tendency towards small network organizations does not exclude the use of large criminal external networks, which can be maintained for wholesale transport operations by keeping the component parts of the network separate. A detailed and interesting analysis of such a wholesale cocaine smuggling organization has been carried out by Natarajan (2000). His mapping of the surveillance information per suspect reveals a large and ramified network, with a characteristic contact density per member and level. Both top (Colombian bosses) and low end (executives) of the trading network had a low contact density, though for very different security reasons. The leader of the operations had, as chief executive, predictably a high density and range of communication.

There is not a single model of coping with the entrepreneurial constraints due to market illegality. There is a tendency towards small crime-organizations or single entrepreneurs having around their core business pragmatic and changing network relations with fellow-entrepreneurs. Despite this frequent observation, more extensive lightly led organizations regularly develop.

3.2 Market functions/diversity and players

Given the challenges arising from the illegality of the drug market, the next question concerns the market players themselves: who are they? The elaboration of the previous sections makes clear that there is hardly a common denominator or type of market player. There are various obstacles to finding a clear answer to this seemingly simple but actually too broad question. As usual, reality defies any attempt to design an all-embracing typology or classification. Attempts to create hypothetical categories in this freebooter economy may yield rather temporary and arbitrary results due to changes in the market environment and its population. In addition, any outcome will partly mirror the *couleur locale* or temporary local market developments, like the rise of the Albanian hash traffickers in Italy (Ruggiero, 2000). Despite all the 'transnational crime' rhetoric, which applies mainly to the wholesale supply and export enterprises, most drug traffickers appear to be rather 'parochial'. They prefer to remain within the networks they can oversee, either territorially or through their personal cross-border network relationships.

A potential approach would be to address the 'market player' issue by means of the categorization of the level at which the players operate in the market. Curtis and Wendel (2000) differentiate between freelance distributors (street level), socially bonded businesses (distribution) and corporate-style distributors. This is a functional classification, which is not the only conceivable one. Pearson and Hobbs (2001), in their study of UK middle market drug distribution, differentiate between middle and upper level markets. These partly overlap with socially bonded business and corporate-style distribution. Together they allow a few glimpses of our elusive market players.

One may also concentrate on the bigger market players, as have been targeted in the Dutch research projects on organized crime: the wholesale importers/exporters or the upper levels of the regional drug market. However, due perhaps to the lack of behavioural expert reports in the criminal files, the information about the persons involved is meagre. The most detailed information from these investigations concerns 'the criminal finances', as these market players generally realize annual turnovers of more than one million euros. The financial investigation (for the recovery of crime-money) sheds some light on the (*financial*) behaviour of these market players, which may reveal interesting differences, for example along the line of ethnicity. Some ethnic minority market players still have their 'social-economic home' abroad, in their native country, leading to a different pattern of financial management (laundering as well as spending) than that of their socially and domestically 'integrated' fellow entrepreneurs or indigenous criminals.

In short, we have a potentially very broad range of market players, which contrasts with an extremely limited amount of validated information. We will sift that information looking for elements of social, psychological or economic profiles.

Diversity of major market players

For the researcher as well as the public, the first question concerns the personality of the actors under study. What sort of people willingly take risks that can lead to loss of freedom, assets and sometimes even life, aiming for wealth which can be confiscated overnight? Who are these 'calculating' risk takers? As remarked before, this leading personality question is the most difficult to answer because of lack of data. Even if we had a valid general personality psychology – which remains contested – few major drug entrepreneurs have been investigated by behavioural scientists. Such an investigation is usually carried out to determine to what extent a defendant may be held responsible for his aggressive behaviour, for example manslaughter, murder or a sexual offence. Most drug entrepreneurs are not charged with such offences – with very rare exceptions such as elderly American crime bosses – and they will certainly not deny culpability because of mental deficiency or insanity. Similarly, judges and prosecutors will not be inclined to order a behavioural investigation for sentencing purposes when the charge concerns only smuggling drugs. The punishments demanded and meted out are usually determined by the estimated or determined volume of contraband trade and the assessed position in the 'organization'. Surveying the literature on organized crime bosses, Bovenkerk (2000) observed that while the social aspects of organized crime have been amply studied, clinical psychological investigations appear to be absent. This leaves us virtually with no other data than journalistic biographies, our own impressions from the criminal files and interviews of detectives handling these cases. What image do we obtain, when we put all these little scattered fragments of the profile mosaic together?

What transpires from interview-based studies, like the one carried out by Reuter and Haaga (1989) is the relative normality of the entrepreneurs in the first place. To the interviewers they may have posed as such, presenting their favourite image as 'plain businessmen', albeit trading the wrong commodity.[9] Even if we assume that they were keen to present their 'good side', like any other human being, the business image does not deviate substantially from other observations or from the image we derived from the study of about 150 files which the first author analysed for various research projects. As a matter of fact, the better the suspects operated as *real* businessmen, the more boring the criminal files were to read and the better their businesses.

Given the business image, one would expect a rationally calculating risk taker. We doubt whether this does justice to many of the higher level drug-entrepreneurs, who continue their operations in a hostile entrepreneurial environment after having amassed sufficient wealth to retire from business. Van Duyne (2000) refers to the off-the-record statements during interviews in which drug-entrepreneurs conveyed to the detectives that they 'do not care for the big money anymore, [but] the excitement of outsmarting you guys' or boasting to be the only one who the law never could get.[10] It is reasonable

9 For safety reasons the authors did not interview potentially violent inmates in high security prisons, which may have yielded less 'plain' crime-entrepreneurs.

10 These were Mr *Horseshoe*, who was actually outsmarted by the police (Van Duyne, 1995) and the earlier mentioned Mr Chessplan, proving right, up till now.

that for some of the crime-entrepreneurs there is more at stake than big, easy money only. Excitement and ego enhancement, sometimes reaching the level of pompous self-inflation, should also be taken into account as behavioural stimuli. If we compare the phenomenon of 'edge working' in dangerous sports, as described by Lyng (1990), with the 'criminal entrepreneurial edge working', we recognize many similarities. For example, the criminal files of the international drug entrepreneurs, running the highest risks and longest sentences, do not reveal a reckless gambler's behaviour, but a challenge of testing one's skills by handling ever bigger and more dangerous consignments, like Mr Bruinsma and Mr Nice. Granted, they proved to be self-overestimating edge workers, challenging the system with a stubborn perseverance. They should have heeded the examples of Al Capone, Escobar, Gotti and other conspicuous challengers of the authorities. In one way or another they all came to grief. In contrast to them the quiet, reserved Gambino died peacefully in his own bed. The pompous Gotti, who killed his successor Castellano, provoked the authorities into a 'get Gotti' rage (Blum, 1993). In the end they got him and he died in prison, in 2002. (His son was also jailed when he took up the 'Family' mantle.) Compared with similar ego displays of many 'captains of (licit) industry' and big-time corporate fraudsters, such character traits related to (criminal) edge working should not be considered a reflection of a specifically pathological *criminal* mind. Bovenkerk's (2000) comparison of licit and illicit entrepreneurship and Levi's (1994) discussion of the role played by the culture of masculinity in major frauds may be more than mere speculation, though the lack of systematic data fall well short of proof.[11]

Being hampered in carrying out proper methodological research we have to proceed like an archaeologist describing a Neanderthal community on the basis of a few bones, a tooth and an arrow point. But if a Neanderthal may be as silent as a top criminal, at least he does not lie. What do our criminal 'Neanderthal' remnants convey to us? Looking through the material, ranging from criminal files to sensational 'true crime' journalistic books, many differences and just a few generalities emerge.

The general picture of the perpetrator is male, usually older than 30 and lower class. That is hardly informative, because behind this shallow sketch much diversity and many exceptions can be observed.

11 Regretfully most literature on organised crime focuses on the organized *underground* economy (particular drugs), which is due to the way organized crime is defined (Van Duyne, 1996b). The picture would be more balanced if organized *business* crime were addressed from the same entrepreneurial angle as the 'traditional' underground crime-entrepreneurs and not defined away (Woodiwiss, 2003). This is clearly the case in the work of Fijnaut *et al.* (1998) classifying 'corporate' law breaking as 'organizational crime'. Analytically as well as empirically these 'definitions' fail to denote or delineate any proper phenomenon at all.

First the exceptions. Indeed, at the top levels of the drug trade women are rare birds, but they do exist and not merely as the woman or girlfriend 'of' some man. The girlfriend of the earlier described Bruinsma is a good example (Middelburg, 2000) of a strong-willed woman, making her own decisions within the enterprise. The same applies to a Turkish mother, head of a Turkish-German drug family enterprise, under the name of Kaba Arslan (the 'hard-handed lioness'), who was feared for her rough ways of handling non-complying fellow criminals or debtors (Van Duyne, 1995; Flormann and Krevert, 2001). Kleemans *et al.* (1998) provide additional examples of the active role of women in crime-enterprises. Nevertheless, the share of women in the number of arrested suspects for organized crime is about the same as the general percentage of arrested female suspects: 11 per cent. Is this rare participation of women due to the high prevalence of violence in the higher levels of the drug market?

The answer to this question is likely to be 'no'. While the occurrence of violence cannot be denied, it is not an all-pervasive 'natural phenomenon' of the drug market, but a human factor of choice. In the first place not all the wholesalers have a background of violence before they entered the drug market, though understandably the violent ones attracted the most attention of law enforcement and 'true crime' authors alike. Books about criminals like Curtis Warren, Gilligan, Bruinsma or Horseshoe would be utterly boring to read if these were solely devoted to their smuggling enterprises.[12] These criminals can be classified as 'diversifiers' from their original craft: violent property crimes (Dorn *et al.*, 1992). It is difficult to estimate their importance in terms of turnover or the continuity of the market. Their personal yearly turnover in monetary terms exceeds €1 million, but their arrests appeared to have no influence on the price level of the commodities they are trading. Is this because they are never arrested all at the same time, which would have an impact on the supply, or because they are only a small, but 'colourful' group of the major drug suppliers? Or because within the total supply from small and middle-level suppliers their share is insignificant? Lack of data leaves this question unanswered, but it casts doubts on the supposed dominant role of these wholesalers on the drug markets.

Apart from these criminals, for whom violent problem solving is not unusual, there are many other major dealers, who deliberately avoid violence.

12 See: Huskens (2001), Mooney (2001) or Barnes *et al.* (2000). A simple frequency distribution of the number of pages devoted to the psychological profile of the criminal personalities compared to other topics shows that the former topic does not go beyond a few meagre pages. The rest is filled with a shallow description of the criminal (violent) landscape and the spelling out of the exploits of the crime-squad. The exceptions may be the biographies of Al Capone (Schoenberg, 1992), Meyer Lansky (Lacey,1991) and the Kray brothers (Pearson, 1973). One may wonder why crime is considered so exciting, while most criminals are so boring.

This does not mean that they do not pretend to resort to violence in cases of bad debts, although they know they cannot fulfil the threat (Desroches, 2003). As a matter of fact they 'hitch-hike' on the general reputation of violence in which they have no part. They differ from the 'diversifiers' as far as their backgrounds and lifestyle are concerned: more bourgeois middle-class and more settled. It would be wrong to consider them amateur market participants because of their more middle-class backgrounds. They range from experienced insiders starting as user-dealers to professional transporters, who use their know-how of the transport sector for smuggling. In the Dutch research projects on organized crime they were particular active in the cannabis market, which may be due to the traditional social acceptance of that substance in the Netherlands. Desroches (2003) makes the same observation concerning high-level cannabis traders in Canada. Unfortunately the latest Dutch 'organized crime monitor' (Kleemans *et al.*, 2002) has remained too shallow in its analysis of the social backgrounds as to be informative. In the Dutch research project on criminal finances (Van Duyne *et al.*, 2003, Meloen *et al.*, 2003), similar middle-class wholesale hashish traders could be identified, and measured according to their style of spending their crime-money; we would describe them as petit bourgeois. It is not clear whether and to what extent they interact with the 'real', i.e. violence-prone, criminal dealers from the 'traditional' underworld. The market for cannabis products is large enough for them not to be thrown into each other's criminal company.

The importance of ethnic backgrounds is discernable in the heroin wholesale market, as far as the Turks and Kurds are concerned. In section 2.5 we have observed that the pattern of the Turkish family enterprises has changed. However this does not imply that the wholesale importers from Turkey have been replaced by Dutch or German traders. This applies also to the UK: the import from the Netherlands and Belgium is acquired from Turkish or Kurdish major dealers. Though the ethnic cohesion in north-western Europe has weakened, no cases are known of independent German or Dutch traders importing directly from Turkey. One may add: 'for the time being', as active involvement of Kosovo-Albanians, Bulgarians, Romanians and Macedonians is reported. Though they buy from Turkish and sometimes Iranian wholesalers in Istanbul, they operate as independent entrepreneurs (Flormann and Krevert, 2001).

The backgrounds of major players in the cocaine market are much more diverse: cocaine is not a Colombian monopoly. Of the major exporters from South America to western Europe the kingpins in Cali or Medellin have been arrested or killed in the 1990s, without stemming the flow of cocaine. Apparently, beating 'cartels' does not reduce drug availability much. This is certainly the case if we follow Zaitch's (2002) argument that this term is rather the product of law enforcement projections. Indeed, new 'cartels' arise as quickly as the DEA (and the local, national auxiliaries) root them out. The

DEA even speaks of the 'Surinam cartel', supposedly headed by the previous putschist Desi Bouterse, army commander, and (ex) strong man of Surinam (Haenen, 1999). When prosecuted for multiple cases of export to the Netherlands, Bouterse was acquitted on most counts, though procedural aspects played an important role. At the European side of the traffic a motley crowd of professional indigenous and South American local smugglers look after the handling of the import of the contraband (Zaitch, 2002).

The backgrounds of the major ecstasy (and amphetamine) traders range from traditional underground thugs from the trailer camps to academically educated figures, who rightly or wrongly claim to be driven by some sort of idealism (Korf and Verbraeck, 1993). According to their philosophy, people should share in their psychological experience. This is not just a hypocritical statement to justify a lucrative trade, since the ecstasy trade grew out of spiritual free-floating esoteric deeper wisdom-seekers, though it is a convenient technique of neutralization. Amphetamine has more often been related to the world of sport and boosting sporting performance. The market for ecstasy is relatively young and less dependent on the craft of wholesale transport logistics as the consumption market can be provided by local producers. If importation from cheaper regions like the Netherlands is preferred, smuggling the pills in a few bags does not require much organization either (Gruppo Abele, 2003). Nevertheless, in the first half of the 1990s, some hashish smugglers and amphetamine producers stepped into this market. Some developed large enterprises, exploiting the price differential with the British Isles, as the following example demonstrates.

The United Pill Peddlers: A combination of two major crime-entrepreneurs ('The United Pill Peddlers'), from the traditional trailer-camp milieu (Van Duyne, 1996a; Weijenburg, 1996), operated from the Netherlands and Belgium. The group imported the precursors, produced the pills, and exported them in shipments of 100.000 and more to the expanding British market, making a turnover of €150 million. It was a large, tightly led, disciplined organization, integrating all production and transport processes. A partly independently operating Belgian doctor provided the precursors, and was shot by unknown killers when released from prison.

This section of the market of synthetic drugs is characterized by mainly indigenous Dutch entrepreneurs. Do these criminals dominate the synthetic drug market? There are no indications for such a domination. Rather they are flanked by many smaller entrepreneurs of various nationalities (Gruppo Abele, 2003), whose social and educational backgrounds seem to be higher than the above-described traditional crime-entrepreneurs (Korf and Verbraeck, 1993). Such a higher educational level is not only observed among the dealers, but also among the chemical technicians, as the production of ecstasy is not without dangers, requiring specialized skills. In addition to this social complexity there are traders in equipment and precursors, who operate on a cross-border basis. Due to better monitoring it has become more difficult to obtain laboratory equipment, machines for making tablets, and PMK or BMK. To procure such items, licit front firms and international networks are required, particularly for access to Eastern European and Chinese providers (Westphal, 2002).

We may conclude that diversity in the population of market players prevails. We do not exclude that a potential common denominator for one 'profile' or (more likely) various profiles may exist. However, that remains pure speculation as long as we have to work with raw (police) data, which are too poor to provide a lead for more advanced trait analysis. Nevertheless, one (tentative) conclusion may be made: a considerable part of these illegal markets is not based on the dreaded folk image of 'transnational organized crime', but rather on normal, flexible adventurer-entrepreneurs. Since time immemorial they have operated internationally, but for no other reason than the availability of products or the lure of price differences. Given the expansion of the market worldwide, though, their number has increased.

Middle market and wholesale levels

Dividing the drug market in 'layers' like retail, distribution, wholesale and 'middle level' has a deceptively commonsensical appearance of clarity. Pearson and Hobbs (2001), studying the 'middle market' in Britain, illustrate the ambiguous nature of this concept. There are many middle markets or rather 'layers' distinguished by the volume of merchandise being handled. As a rule, importers are not classified as 'middle marketeers', but as wholesalers. The latter sell their commodity to a small number of wholesale distributors. As every link in the chain of transactions connects a higher and a lower part of the market, the term has little descriptive value. It loosely denotes the very diverse intermediate trading layers: those between shipping from production countries and the proper consumer market.

Within Europe this broad denotation knows many exceptions. For example, distributors in the local or regional middle market may operate as importers as well. Cross-border trafficking between the Netherlands, Belgium, Germany and France is partly carried out by local distributors, who spend a weekend in Amsterdam, Rotterdam or Antwerp returning with modest amount of dope for their friends or customers (Van der Torre, 1996; Paoli *et al.*, 2000). In addition, part of the demand for psychoactive substances can be met by local or regional production: synthetic drugs and hashish are produced all over Europe. Cannabis production ranges from amateur attic sites (for producers' own use or as a putting-out system (Bovenkerk and Hogewind, 2003)) to professionally functioning green houses. Similarly, the production of artificial stimulants like ecstasy can take place in modern mobile laboratories as well as in a ramshackle shed.

This fragmentation of the drug market allows the opportunistic and pragmatic drug traders to shift between the many overlapping layers of transaction. Nevertheless, other market players, being known for years as wholesale importers or distributors, are more stable than the above observations suggest. This may be brought about by bonds formed as a consequence of ethnic and/or childhood friendship or prison affinities. Such stable bonds can sit alongside more fluid relationships. With these reservations, we give a brief account of what has been presented as middle and wholesale markets.

The middle market

As can be deduced from the previous observations, the middle market as observed by Pearson and Hobbs (2001) is broad and diverse. What kind of market players does it encompass? The general picture the police convey about the middle-level traders is that of criminals who have a finger in every criminal pie as long as it yields money. This police portrayal is not wholly consistent with research findings. It does apply to a certain section of market operators, having a general criminal background of (violent) property crimes: the criminal diversifiers whom we have metaphorically met before (Dorn *et al.*, 1992). Indeed, there is a broad lower class of mobile criminal 'jacks of all trades', usually locally based, who have a share in the drug market. Pearson and Hobbs (2001) refer to traditional urban localities in Britain. The Netherlands is aware of similar traditional criminal 'pockets', often kinship- and partly neighbourhood-based networks, partly from poor urban quarters or from trailer camps. Apart from a high degree of violence, they are traditionally known as mobile entrepreneurs, car mechanics and dealers (changing the identity of stolen cars) and hash dealers. However, representing the rough and conspicuous side of the drug market, they are more likely to attract police attention, thereby contributing to the dominant picture of a violent market in which the 'traditional' criminals prevail.

Contrasting with this representation are the findings concerning networks of crime-entrepreneurs, whose businesses are centred on one favoured commodity. This does not exclude step-overs to adjacent fields, but this happens often as a sideline business (Kleemans *et al.*, 2002, Dorn *et al.*, 1992). Even if there is a tendency to branch out to other commodities, many appear to opt for strict dividing lines as we have pointed out before. For example Korf and Verbraeck (1993) and Van Duyne (1995) mention hash entrepreneurs, who did not want to do any business with cocaine dealers, eschewing the Colombians because of their reputation for violence. Similarly, Pearson and Hobbs (2001) quote dealers in hash as well as ecstasy, who thought the heroin and crack market immoral and just 'junk'. Likewise, the study of the Gruppo Abele (2003), comparing the synthetic drugs markets in Amsterdam, Barcelona and Turin, confirmed the image of a mainly specialist market, though with national exceptions. In the Netherlands there are cross-overs from hash trafficking to ecstasy production, while at the distribution and retail level a mixed trading of all sorts of stimulants has been observed: this includes, in addition to ecstasy, hallucinatory mushrooms, LSD and cocaine. In this regard they respond to the demand of the dance scene, in which the demand for heroin is low, though in interviews such economic choice may be dressed in ethical garments.[13]

Brokering – in all its variations – is a recurring phenomenon in the various segments of the middle market. It typically consists in buying multiple kilos of heroin and cocaine, 20–25.000 tablets of ecstasy and 10–20 kilos of cannabis, though the variation may be larger than this. This may depend on market access and distance to the consumers, though the number of transaction links are estimated to be four or even fewer (Reuter and Haaga, 1989). Lower-level drug brokers seem to be more engaged in multi-commodity transactions. More important is the frequently observed structure of the brokers or middle men (or at times women, Dunlap *et al.*, 1994). Most act alone, aided by a few runners connecting them to their customers, of whom they know little and vice versa. The same applies to the runners, delivering the packages, but not always being charged with picking up the money, which may be carried out by another person. To complicate the picture, some of the runners also had their independent side-businesses, some are to be characterized as junior partners, while others get paid per delivery. Sometimes, at least in the UK, taxi drivers (or motorcycle business delivery employees, especially for City service sector workers) deliver the packages and return the payments.

It is interesting to observe the low level of actual *violence*, at least in the Netherlands and UK, though it may always loom in the background. Occasionally a violent dispute breaks out in 'turf wars' over the control of lucrative business areas as well as more casually, over the perceived display of insufficient 'respect'. Independent brokers rarely appear to compete violently. Rather, there is little real competition or a fight for turf, perhaps due to the steady demand and a sound tendency not to attract police attention by overt violence.

Concerning the *type of mediation* Pearson and Hobbs (2001) discern three modalities. In the classical form of brokerage they 'oil the wheels' of trade by connecting the seller and the buyer, for which they ask a commission. This assumes a rather open flow of information and a great degree of trust in mutual silence about the nature of the contacts. There are not many examples of this classical form of brokerage. In the second form of brokerage, the strategic middle position, the middle man sees to it that the buyer and seller do not know each other, actually exploiting their lack of knowledge. This seems to be the most common form of brokerage, which also fits to the safety

13 In the UK, as in Italy, in 2003–4, changes in the nature of the dance scene appear to be reducing the popularity of ecstasy.

requirements of the illegal market. Buyer and seller usually do not wish to know each other at all and, for security reasons, are happy to have a link in the person of the intermediary between them. This results in a compartmentalization, which is the third type of brokerage, though it seems to fuse with the second type. The intermediary deliberately keeps buyer and seller apart so as to create the need for his/her role and financial 'cut'. This may stimulate both parties, especially the seller, to try to manoeuvre the discovery of the other, to gain the intermediary's profit margin. The brokerage can be cross-border as is observed in the ecstasy and cannabis traffic from the Netherlands, in which case the manufacturer remains behind the broker, passing the orders from foreign importers.

Cross-border wholesalers

The 'players' of the wholesale cross-border import and export traffic have been less intensively researched than the middle-market-level players they are supplying. This is perhaps due to the fact that they are at the top of the market pyramid, in which there are fewer major players around or willing to talk with researchers. Where they are unconvicted for such offences, there are also problems attached to researchers explaining how they came to learn of their existence, as well as physical and legal security issues for both parties. Therefore, much of the evidence is bound to be anecdotal, depending on the 'narratives' deduced from police files. These may be broadened by a few journalistic biographies, which may be popularized versions of the same files or heavily constrained by defamation risks. We are better informed about the operational characteristics of their enterprises and the conditions they are working in.

To what extent do the wholesalers' enterprises have different characteristics from the middle-level drug brokers? For example, are they more likely to be commodity specialists, more (or less) violent and do they lead big, hydra-like organizations?

The question of whether wholesale drug traffickers are generalist or specialist criminals reappears regularly. As mentioned before, the image conveyed in police (and ensuing media) reports is that of the 'criminal finger in every pie', but there is insufficient empirical support for this proposition. In general the observations tend to uphold the picture of specialization, but not universally. The level of specialization is the outcome of a variety of opportunities as well as criminal entrepreneurial social position, skills and also a matter of personal choice. Referring to the basic skill of the crime-entrepreneur as an information and risk manager, one may wonder why he should opt for being a generalist. As we have elaborated in the first section of this chapter, engagement in many kinds of criminal undertakings implies a spreading of managerial skills as well as risks, because one becomes dependent on a variety of fellow criminals, who possess those skills (unless one is a rare multi-skilled criminal genius). This is possible as long as the entrepreneur is able to maintain control. However, this is difficult when it comes to long-distance, cross-border traffic. Therefore it is likely that a generalist crime-entrepreneur is more inclined towards local enterprises, which enables day-to-day direct control. The 'local hero', as described by Morselli (2000) or the career of the Kray brothers (Pearson, 1973) fit into this pattern of territorially bound general criminal undertaking.[14] This does not imply that cross-border traffickers necessarily fit into the picture of 'global, transnational' crime-entrepreneurs. For much of their business they are based on local relationships from which they form network ties with other localities: the 'glocalization' of crime-entrepreneurs, as Hobbs calls them (Hobbs, 1997; Hobbs and Dunnighan, 1998).

If we compare this kind of local general crime-entrepreneur with the wholesale contraband trader, we find other entrepreneurial conditions, which give a comparative advantage to the trend towards specialization. It goes without saying that the basic conditions of such a trade are supply and transport access. Given the secretiveness of the illicit market, there is no free shopping around to broaden access to alternative sources of supply or demand, as would be required for 'perfect competition to obtain'. As a matter of fact, bulk suppliers are cherished as valuable 'possessions', though the supplier may deliver to other wholesale buyers as well. The international hash entrepreneur Horseshoe punished his junior partner severely when he operated in what Horseshoe considered '*his* line' without his permission (Huskens, 2001; Van Duyne, 1995). Single and separate supply lines appear to be the rule instead of organizations having their 'tentacles' everywhere. Personal choice and risk management also play a role. We have already referred to crime-entrepreneurs who deliberately do not want to become engaged in what they consider 'tricky stuff' or partners of other markets who have acquired a reputation for violence. Others may simply not be sufficiently ambitious to expand substantially or do not come across such opportunities. This state of affair is not simply a product of the inability to trust other market participants, but of inherent information management problems in illicit markets in which the State takes a hostile interest.

Despite these findings, there are also many examples of side-businesses of wholesalers in adjacent market segments or a change-over. For example, the police have indicated that many previous Dutch hashish-entrepreneurs have changed over to ecstasy (Gruppo Abele, 2003). Similarly, Kleemans *et al.* (2002) and Pearson and Hobbs (2001) mention shifts to other market

14 The structure of *La Cosa Nostra* (Firestone, 1996) and the Sicilian Mafia (Gambetta, 1993) fit partly into this pattern, though the Mafia protection core business did not stop them from participating in the drug business, either as 'protectors' of dealers or refiners in their territory or as direct individual participants.

segments, sometimes (predictably) facilitated by the broadening of criminal networks while serving a prison sentence. Whether or not aided by prison contacts, spreading of the network to fellow crime-entrepreneurs, who are already well versed in that market segment, has advantages of shortening the 'learning time' and providing safety. The new expert may fend off some of the new dangers, though it may be a poor substitute for one's own specialist know-how. Actually, many crime-entrepreneurs were caught while dabbling without experience in their new market segment, either because of clumsily executed operations (e.g. wrong techniques for dodging custom controls) or insufficient support network points (Kleemans *et al.*, 2002).

Within the supply lines, brokers, keeping buyer and seller apart, are also frequently observed, depending on the nature of the access. Access through family relationships, as is frequently the case with Turkish heroin family enterprises, is naturally a very direct one. Rather, the whole chain of purchase in Turkey and subsequent export can remain in one entrepreneurial hand, even if the closed family structure has been partly opened up. We do not know whether in Turkey the purchase of products is conducted via brokers. This cross-border family access is not observed with the wholesaling of cocaine, cannabis and ecstasy or amphetamine, where brokerage seems to be more important. Unfortunately not many brokers are recognized and described as such, being prosecuted under the over-inclusive charge of drug trafficking and organized crime. This is not an omission but a technical consequence of investigating and prosecution under the legal label of drug trafficking and organized crime. In addition, most brokers do not perform the 'pure' brokerage role of merely connecting two parties. Frequently they have more to gain from keeping the parties apart, in which case they have to arrange the transport and the delivery as well. For example, in the course of transporting the contraband, the 'broker' Chessplan was technically the owner of the shipment, which obscured his primary brokerage role. Connecting the buyer A and seller B he also became a prominent member of an 'organized crime group' comprising also A and B, who did not know each other.[15] This extended role contrasted with the real brokerage of the Pakistani, Fouad Abbas, mediating between wholesale deliverers in Pakistan and the Dutch purchaser, who also organized the transport (De Stoop, 1998).

Mr Abbas: Fouad Abbas was one of the busiest brokers between the bulk producers of hashish in the north of Pakistan and major Dutch importers, who supplied the north-western European market as well as Canada. The Dutch consortium provided the shipping for more than 200.000 kilos of hashish, of which 115.000 was lost because of interception and

15 Though one boat with a few thousand kilos of hashish was intercepted around Honolulu in 1993, he got away with it due to lack of investigative capacity and mistakes by the detective involved.

embezzlement by the 'Hakkelaar' himself, the most prominent man of the consortium. The Dutch consortium did not know the hashish-exporting Pakistani, who only traded via Abbas. Abbas also took care of the management of the proceeds, which were handled through his diamond business in Antwerp and London. The Dutch, mainly from the traditional trailer-camp milieu, were not easy customers, bullying and implicitly threatening their broker, while not paying their debts. When the consortium was prosecuted, the broker saved his skin by becoming a 'crown witness' after settling for a payment of €810.000 to the prosecution, which dropped the charges against him.[16] It was a good deal for one of the biggest hash brokers, which, as a side effect, hampered his prosecution in Belgium.

The availability of a broker is not a necessary condition for a successful drug enterprise. Westphal's (2002) account of the precursor market concerns among others a Chinese-Dutch wholesale supply line for BMK.

Zeming and Koggel: The Hong Kong-based Chinese businessman, Zeming, exported in the late 1990s 12.000 litres BMK under the cover of peanut-oil directly to a Dutch partner, Mr Koggel, who sold the product to a few regular customers, but also directly to British ecstasy producers. Koggel was an authoritative figure, who demanded to be obeyed, if necessary by extreme violence. One day, to 'relieve his frustrations', he shot a member of his group, suspected of disobedience, in cold blood through the head. (Much to his undoing, since it yielded a life sentence.) As Zeming now felt the heat of the Dutch police, he changed his routing from Rotterdam to Lisbon, from where the contraband was transported by truck to the Netherlands. It seems that in this second phase, he may have used one or more intermediary brokers, though the police report was unclear on this point.

Summarizing our own observations and the findings from other research, we consider that there is no firmly delineated brokerage phenomenon. Rather, this fluctuates at both wholesale and retail level, due to the general fluid and shifting nature of the drug market. A broader brokerage function is important, but the pure selling of information between two parties is less frequent than acting as short-term principal in between a relatively short chain of transactions.

The access to *transport* facilities appears to be less secluded than access to bulk supply. The wide range of inventive methods of getting contraband to the destination goes beyond the scope of this book: everything which has a hollow area, from human beings to coconuts, is fit for smuggling. More

16 The Dutch Procedural Code does not recognise the figure of 'crown witness', but the witnesses in this trial were labelled as such. They obtained attractive out of court settlements, which were widely contested. One of these settlements invoked a rebuke from the Appeal Court and the dismissal of the case.

important is the question whether the transport function is a vertically integrated component of the crime-enterprise or a separate enterprise itself, providing transport services. Again the picture is highly fragmented. This is partly due to the constantly mutating nature of the market itself, partly to the safety requirements leading to compartmentalization of who-knows-what ('I had to deliver to John, whom I did not know' or 'I met the guy in the pub') and the opportunities for the police to unveil a whole transport line.

During the beginning of the 1990s, the Dutch hashish and the Turkish heroin wholesalers arranged their own transport, which was to a large extent incorporated within their enterprises. This resulted in large enterprises, which were well-controlled and protected against robbery by fellow crime-entrepreneurs. However, we observed earlier that these were also more vulnerable to police investigations. Around the middle of the 1990s, in the cannabis market the picture shifted to an externalization of the risky transport: there were sufficient daring seamen and hauliers with a broad experience in smuggling. This was not a sudden innovation after the police had rounded up a few big 'self-transporters'. Finding new opportunities for transporting large shipments did not take long. Freelance seamen had already engaged in smuggling since the 1970s/80s. Many came from fishing communities in the province of North-Holland, reappearing frequently in the police reports (Weijenburg, 1996). Facilities for professional road transport were also provided by professional hauliers: as an illustration we recounted already Jan Orange, who started as a transporter for VAT smuggling rings between Belgium and the Netherlands (Van Duyne *et al.*, 1990; Van Duyne, 1995). Also, for risk-control reasons, the Turkish heroin trading families began to rely on non-Turkish transporters. The impact of the law in this bustling market never lasts long.

The transport picture of the ecstasy and the cocaine markets does not reveal any evidence of an 'incorporated' transport section in the enterprises. The ecstasy (and amphetamine) is usually transported in bags and suitcases by hired freelancers, as was the case in the Israel–Netherlands–US smuggling route (Huskens and Vuijst, 2002; Gruppo Abele, 2003). The fragmented descriptions of the length of the supply lines indicate that these used to be short as well as shifting, depending on instantaneous network relations. For cocaine smuggling more professional organizers are hired, particularly for bulk transport using legitimate firms for clearance at the customs. Besides this wholesale flow, there is the ongoing mule train of 'swallowers and stuffers' between the Caribbean islands and western Europe (Bartelink, 2001). This accounts for only a small part of the imports, while unduly increasing the caseload with the police, courts and prisons.[17]

17 Especially female prisons in the UK are heavily populated with African and Caribbean 'mules'. The British authorities have tried various programmes to try to stop the traffic

As far as the size of the wholesale enterprises is concerned, a recurring finding is their relatively small size. The exceptions are the Turkish family firms and the previously mentioned 'self-transporting' hashish enterprises, which did not show up again after their dismantling. A general observation is a partnership of two of three fellow criminals, who do not necessarily need to be equals, forming the inner ring of the organization. For separate operations, particularly concerning transport and warehousing, specialized executives could be recruited through the network relations, which are within the 'social orbit' of the crime-entrepreneurs. In this regard there is little difference between the wholesalers and the middle-market entrepreneurs.[18]

The last potential characteristic is the *violence*, which is considered to be an *a priori* feature of the crime market in general and the drug market in particular. According to the police and referred to in the popular literature, violence looms large on the horizon of all drug transactions. Shootings in large British and Dutch cities (e.g. Amsterdam, Birmingham, Bristol, London, and Manchester) seldom escape without mention of the connection to local rivalries over 'turf' and images of groups of (often foreign) organized criminals 'moving in' on cities or smaller towns. Compared to this general picture, the research-based literature stresses the low level of violence, referring to the relationships of trust as a condition for success. How can we properly reconcile these opposing representations? In the first place, many recorded occurrences of 'underworld violence' have little to do with the drug trade or other business conflicts. Because the victim is allegedly connected with crime figures or is a criminal himself, the violence is considered to be an 'internal conflict settlement'. When it appears in the subsequent investigation that the reason for the violence is revenge for an insult, defiling of honour or simply a family tragedy, the report is hardly ever rectified (Van der Port, 2001). In the second place, the potential for violence is not homogeneously spread over the criminal business population. The criminal 'diversifiers' (Dorn *et al.*, 1992) with violent property-crime backgrounds have a lower threshold for violence than the more settled bourgeois hashish or ecstasy salesman, who nurses his network. Members of some ethnic minorities, particular in which the defence of 'honour' is valued highly, resort more often to violence, for personal as well as for business reasons. For

at the source, including stimulating more active interest in Jamaica in interception prior to departure. This sometimes yielded fruit, though with what net impact on drug availability is more questionable. In the Netherlands various emergency measures have been tried too, but in the end they all proved ineffective. At the time of writing the 'swallowers' are simply sent back to Curaçao if there are no other aggravating circumstances.

18 At this point a difference in interpretation between the law enforcement agencies and empirical researchers may emerge, the police describing a larger part of a network as an organization than researchers.

example, the collection of bad debts is often accompanied by threats, violence and kidnapping. Debt collection is not necessarily always related to drug trafficking, but may have other origins, like gambling. However, violent debt collection may backfire. The acquisition of a reputation for violent dealing may instil 'shock and awe', but may also produce avoidance by fellow traders, apart from creating potential (resentful) informants and attracting police attention. Inter-ethnic rivalry may also contribute to violence, like the take-over of the heroin market in Munich by the Kosovo-Albanians in the 1990s, resulting in three killings (Flormann and Krevert, 2001). Such striking examples are often put forward as characteristic features. However, when we finally compare the violence rate with the financial interests at stake and the volume of the daily international and local trade, we cannot explain its ongoing success (against all odds) from the threat of an allegedly all-pervasive violence. We do not want to suggest that the European drug market resembles a cosy 'bazaar': (deadly) violence does occur, but it is not a 'pillar' of these markets. Trade is generally not furthered by 'lead and dead', but by silver and silence. This observation is expressed by many researchers (Reuter and Haaga, 1989; Van Duyne *et al.*, 1990; Van Duyne, 1995; Desroches, 2003). The successful traders appear to be those whose files are boring to read.

3.3 Just another market?

Should we consider the drug market as 'just another market', albeit with the wrong commodities? There is no unambiguous answer to this question. The point is in the last part of the sentence: the contraband nature of the commodity, which shapes the market. However, this is not something unique to the drug market. If we compare the drug market with the clandestine cigarette market as described by Van Duyne (2002) and Von Lampe (2002; 2003), we find comparable features. The difference is the even lower rate of violence in the clandestine cigarette market, for the time being.[19] Otherwise we find an equally thriving market with a motley collection of participants, ranging from amateur-smugglers to highly skilled professionals, transport service providers and shifting pragmatic network relations.

In one respect, the drug market as an entrepreneurial and basically capitalist phenomenon remains baffling: the strange absence of competition as well as monopoly. As Reuter and Haaga (1989) observed, in the opinion of their interviewees, entering and progressing in the market involve a low risk rate compared to the huge revenues, and (in our words) involves social

19 The violence between Vietnamese in Berlin in the 1990s did not concern violent competition between cigarette traders, but the extortion by fellow Vietnamese (Von Lampe, 2002).

capital rather than financial capital. The fixed inventory is modest and the business capital consists almost entirely of 'good will' by knowing reliable suppliers and customers, nursing their confidence (instead of bullying them).[20] So, 'If the cocaine and marijuana trades were truly functioning as ordinary markets, the competitive pressure from eager new entrants should have driven down these extraordinary returns eventually, unless there were significant barriers to entry'. But Reuter and Haaga, along with the other researchers, do not observe such significant barriers. To demonstrate such barriers, they should have interviewed people who had an opportunity to enter this market, considered doing so, but in the end decided against. Presumably, such respondents are difficult to find.

We can only speculate about the causes for this deviation from the basic capitalist principle in a market populated by capitalist adventurers. When we abstract from the majority of entrepreneurial people who do not want to pass the 'blue line', there are still sufficient potential entrants, who may be lured by the big returns but still do not enter this market. Given the relative opacity of the market, some simply do not come across opportunities, because they are operating in another social-economic niche. For example, in the Netherlands and Germany Van Duyne and Von Lampe, mentioned above, found little overlap between tobacco and drug markets. However, there was a frequent overlap with the brand piracy market. Selling untaxed articles as well as brand piracy products was for some of the smugglers just a normal parallel market activity. Others may be deterred by the severe law enforcement regime regarding drug trafficking, though this may be only one of the thresholds. Given the overcrowded prisons partly due to the influx of convicted drug dealers (as well as from those who commit offences to purchase their artificially highly priced products), the effectiveness of the intended deterrence may rather be a matter of perception.

In the beginning of this chapter we referred to the fact of illegality as a critical market shaper, which results in an opaque demand market. Opacity serves security, but sets limits to the ease of entry and the extent of the network of customers one can serve. It takes time to handle and penetrate this opacity. Entry as dealer takes time and goes along a gradual developmental path, often depending on existing legal job opportunities (adjacent entry) and acquaintance with a few trusted people already involved in the market. Rationally developing relationships of trust is more important than flashing an exhibition of recently acquired wealth (Curcione, 1997; Reuter and Haaga, 1989). Entry through the circles of addicts is not a popular option: junkies are considered a nuisance and unreliable (Tewksbury, 1999).

20 This falsifies one of the generally stated tenets of the crime-money recovery policy: taking the means from criminals to reinvest their crime-money into their enterprise, thereby preventing the development of an economy of scale.

Entrance through financing one's recreational habit by selling to friends and acquaintances is often quoted as a 'quiet' beginning. Murphy *et al.* (1990) distinguish other developmental routes of becoming a (cocaine) seller: becoming a connoisseur, getting high-quality product by buying larger amounts and reselling a part of it; apprenticeship, going around with a veteran and learning the required skills. Still, most user-dealers do not advance much further, either because they are satisfied with financing their habit by marginal dealing or because they do not have the right network links. At the higher levels of the market with increasing risks, the networks narrow: there is little incentive to 'conquer' the market if one has sufficient trusted customer-traders whose demand can be met by selling the commodities from a few trusted wholesalers, importers or producers. This may (partly) explain the finding that the 'lure of the big profits' has less effect than it would have in a really open capitalist market. At the same time, it raises question marks about the repetitive statements about rationally calculating criminals aiming at 'profit maximization'. It may be more realistic not to attribute more rationality to our illegal entrepreneurs than to our licit ones, who also operate (or blunder) within a bounded rationality, as Simon (1972) observed. If few corner-shop salespeople want to become multinational corporate executives, why should we assume that drugs dealers have a uniform set of ambitions? Of course, some forms of drug *taking* distort people's rational judgement about their capacities, and *desistance* from drugs dealing and other serious criminal careers such as fraud may be made more difficult not just by 'addiction' to lifestyles (Levi, 1994). It may also be more difficult to desist because of the fear of becoming a target for criminal predators, who know that criminally obtained assets are there to be seized. Unprotected retired offenders are in a poor position to seek legitimate law enforcement protection.

4 Drug markets in action

An orderly description of a basically fragmented socio-economic phenomenon like 'the' drug market seems a *contradiction in terms* or an impossible endeavour. It must cover the well-known skinny and shabbily dressed young drug runners whispering to tourists 'stuff, sir?' on a bridge in Amsterdam, as well as the head of a hierarchically operating crime-family carefully planning a large shipment. In addition, each country or region and each commodity may have its own social market characteristics. Further, as we have noted in the previous chapter, drug markets can mutate quickly, due to the constant pressure from the law and changes in consumer preferences.

Despite all this, we have also encountered in the previous chapters some recurrent features, deviating from traditional images: the market is not a monopolistic one, not led by extended hierarchical organizations, but by small enterprises within changing network relationships, in which many traffickers actually perform the role of broker. Underlying these entrepreneurs are the consumers. Quite dissimilar to the position of consumers in the licit, regulated markets, many consumers are not just passive purchasers, but acquire part of their consumption by 'servicing' the market. This may range from being on the look-out for cops, doing errands for dealers, carrying packages, guiding tourists to the outlet places for drugs, to selling to friends for a small profit. Not all of them are street junkies covering the expenses of their addiction by dealing, stealing and prostitution. These smaller market players are entrepreneurs in their own right and may be quite bourgeois in their outlook (Kemmenies, 2000). This differs from the 'retreatist' label given to drug takers in Merton's typology of adaptations to *anomie*. It indicates many-faceted economic interactions between consumers and traders in many-sided markets.

To describe such a broad spectrum would need a full volume instead of a chapter. In order to make a selection within the framework of this book, we will sift the available empirical material in order to shed light on the operations of the markets and the broad outlines of the related finances. These concern not only the wealthy drug barons, some of whose finances will be investigated in the following chapter. Of equal importance is the picture of the daily market, which is to be found in the big cities, where we meet the less conspicuous local, smaller-scale dealer, often a user-dealer. It is partly for this reason that the convenient legislative binary split between possession and trafficking is so misleading a guide to drug market operations.

4.1 Drug markets in some European cities

The retail parts of drug markets are mainly an urban phenomena, at least in the West. The places where customers meet suppliers are usually the inner cities, or rather 'hot spots' in poor districts near the city centre, sometimes a park, as in Zurich, or some streets around a railway station, but the market can also develop in lower-class suburbs. In Germany and Italy the functioning of the drug markets of Frankfurt and Milan have been investigated, the result of which will be compared with the findings of other studies.

The European Monitoring Centre for Drugs and Drug Addiction commissioned the Max Planck Institute to carry out research projects in Frankfurt and Milan. Apart from analysing documentary sources, the researchers interviewed numerous law enforcement officers, and dealers and their users, either in the street or in prison. In the previous chapters we have met some diversity and changeability. Our question is now whether the outcomes of these research projects reveal some commonalities of these markets in terms of their commercial features, structure and developments.

Frankfurt

The history of the Frankfurt drug market shares many features with other major western European cities. Starting with the youths of the counterculture flower-power movement, experimenting with all kinds of psychoactive new substances, the consumption of drugs and the related market has remained. Many of the rebellious youths have become decent citizens, though a tiny percentage remained hooked on 'smack'.

The present-day drug market of Frankfurt has various layers: outdoor selling at different places for different substances as well as selling indoors or in semi-closed places (Paoli, 2000). The market players range from newly arrived immigrants from Kosovo, North Africa and eastern Europe to second-generation migrants, the children of 'guest labourers' (*Gastarbeiter*). For any illegal market, part of the transaction costs consist of the time and efforts of customer and seller to come together. These costs are primarily determined by the intensity of police control policy, which has varied over time here, as elsewhere. This is particularly important in the rise and fall of drugs 'hot spots'.

The open drug scene, particularly concerning heroin, was a phenomenon of the early 1990s. As was the case with the Platzspitz in Zürich (and 'Platform Zero' next to the Central Station of Rotterdam) the open market in the Frankfurt Taunusanlage became a place of misery and dirtiness. The scene of dealing and openly injecting the portions of heroin was repugnant to the citizens and nearby businesses alike, evoking sufficient political pressure for subduing this open market place at the end of 1992. After rounding up this market a peregrination, or rather the scattering and fragmentation of the open scene began. A part of it moved to the Central Station quarter, but also to the safe injection rooms which had been established for heavy drug users in the second half of the 1990s. There, the number of users was, at about 150–200, less than a third of what it once was: 600–800. In addition, many moved to quieter quarters, where they were less harassed by the police, while outdoor dealing went indoors.

From a commercial point of view, the actions of the police were successful as the transaction costs increased: customers had to spend more time and energy to get their product, waiting in uncertainty as the suppliers became more careful. From the perspective of public order, the police actions may be called moderately successful. Economically they just diverted the dirty water of a central pond to a multitude of little creeks and brooks.

The research project reports a preference of dealers to migrate from street trading to indoor trading among regular customers. We have met this conduct before: no heat from the police and dealing only with trusted customers. This represents a higher level of doing business. It requires social capital, reliability towards customers and trusting the supplier to deliver the promised quality and quantity. If one does not want to deal in one's own house it also means having fixed meeting points in pubs, in or near discos or other semi-closed localities such as hard-to-police municipal housing schemes.

This description of daily business applies mainly to the substances heroin and (crack) cocaine, usually combined, the so-called poly-use. Looking at the market for the two other main drug commodities, cannabis and ecstasy/amphetamine, we find other commercial characteristics.

Cannabis, as a kind of beer of drugs, is the least problematic product, for consumers and small/middle level traders alike. The German police meanwhile have come to view hashish users as no more 'essentially' criminal than beer drinkers, and to think that few hashish smokers develop a bad habit for other, stronger substances, just as few beer drinkers end up as schnapps-drinking drunks. Hashish smokers are far more socially variegated than misfits or drop-outs and do not generally need to commit property crimes to sustain their use. Whatever the views of the policy makers and politicians about the criminal status of cannabis consumption, at the level of daily law enforcement in Frankfurt, consumption has *de facto* become tolerated. This has made transactions of consumers and local traders, being no longer constantly chased, more comfortable. Trading inconspicuously indoors, they create no public nuisance and thus provoke no complaints to the police. At this level we observe a smooth market summarized by the tautology: a little criminal because it is illegal.

The other contemporary drug of choice, ecstasy, shares many of the social characteristics of the cannabis market. Being a drug for partying, dance festivals, techno music, raves and parades, there is hardly an open scene of unsavoury users as the ecstasy is sold in and around these events. The consumers interviewed go to school, university or have a job.[1] Of course, apart from potential longer-term effects, ecstasy is not an unproblematic product, creating its own habitual users. These may finance their habit by trading with friends and acquaintances, thereby forming the consumer-dealer layer which is generally observed in these illegal markets.

Given the ubiquitous presence of these illegal markets, how are the supply businesses organized? As far as the heroin and cocaine supplies from the local or regional wholesaler are concerned, the pilot report provides little additional case information. The general picture is that of small crews, operating within family or friendship relations. Few small and middle-level suppliers are dependent on the presence of wholesalers, as they obtain their commodities from the Netherlands and, less often, Belgium, which can be reached within a few hours. This applies particularly to cannabis products (about which in a later section) and ecstasy, though also to amphetamine and LSD. Even to those users who are not dealers, it is profitable to spend a weekend in Amsterdam or Heerlen, near the German border, to replenish their stock and to buy in addition some for their friends. Among the many 'ants' (*Ameisen*), there are also wholesalers, however more in terms of quantity then in terms of organization, which is not needed for just picking up a few kilos of hashish from one of the many 'coffee shops' in the Netherlands. The precautions are moderate: 'look like a decent businessman and in the absence of border control you can be in Amsterdam within four hours, back in the same day, deliver or store the goods and be at work in the next morning'. This pattern results in a short, three-level chain of transactions: importer, middle man and customer. The practice of buying drugs in the Netherlands has the important structural consequence that no big dealer or ethnic group of dealers succeeds in becoming dominant. Even if some individual or group would want to control the market, it is not obvious how they would manage.

Milan

The drug market of Milan shows many of the characteristics we have already recounted concerning the Frankfurt market. This applies particularly to the drug-using population, beginning experimentation in the 1970s, which does not mean that before that time, there were no drugs. The drugs of choice were heroin and cannabis products. The heroin-using population gradually became older, as in the Netherlands, Germany and the UK. Apart from this steady group, the consumption of hashish became prevalent in all layers of

1 Rakete and Flüsmeier (1997) report similar findings: about 80 per cent of their interviewees are higher secondary or grammar school students.

society. Cocaine, always available, was since the mid-1970s mainly used in two remote sections of society. It was used in the underworld and the *beau monde*, the top and low social circles, probably sharing the same *ennui* and craving for excitement. In the last decade of the twentieth century, the consumption pattern was complemented by the designer drugs, while the consumption of cocaine spread to other users. As a matter of fact, drug consumption 'normalized', according to Paoli, in the sense that drug use is found in all layers of (Milanese) society. This might be expressed as: 'illegal but normal'. The consumer population was extended by foreigners from various corners around Italy: the Balkans, particularly Kosovo-Albanians, and North Africa. For a demographic historian these features are interesting, just because they are so common to the western European metropolises: globalization from the bottom up.

More interesting than these recurrent features of the user population (allowing for local variation in Europe) is the development of the composition of the drug entrepreneurs, who tried to find an economic *niche* in this market. Like elsewhere in Europe, at first the drug traffic was carried out by like-minded circles of idealists bringing in small shipments in their battered Volkswagen vans. According to legend, it did not take long before the Mafia stepped into the market. It would first have boosted cannabis and subsequently have the commodity withdrawn from the market to replace it by cheap heroin. That would have been an evil though commercially clever scheme. 'Typically Mafiosi', one would think. However there is no evidence substantiating this clever policy. Actually, the underworld of professional property criminals as well as the Milanese settlements of south Italian crime-families reacted with a considerable delay to the new commercial opportunities. Being already engaged in cigarette and car smuggling, they had the right antecedents. According to the report, the 'Ndrangheta group of Sergi became dominant in the Milanese market, but due to his contact with a figure from the local underworld.

The course of this history is of interest, not because of the sudden acquisition of fabulous wealth by organized crime families, but because of its social consequences. Social cohesion within families has always remained solid, to which their social rites and a moderate division of wealth contributed. The bosses were rich, but not so staggeringly richer than the underlings as to create dissent. This changed because of the huge drug profits. However, the newly accrued wealth of the bosses did not contribute to the strength of the families, but rather evoked envy among the lower-level executives, who became 'fed up of eating only crumbs, while the chiefs were pocketing billions'. The complainants were often *not* ritually affiliated, which had its effect when the law clamped down on the drug wholesalers operating under the bosses: many became *pentiti* (Paoli, 2003).

Before that happened, the 1980s brought booming business for the crime-families, and the Milanese underworld partly carved up the city into quarters in which families exercised a monopoly. For example there was the long-lasting alliance of the Coco-Flachi group, with Franco Coco Trovato being a high-ranking member of the 'Ndrangheta. This group covered not only part of Milan but also the Lecco area near Lake Como. By incorporating some independent drug enterprises, the organizations grew in size with an accompanying division of labour. Nevertheless it is telling for the flexibility of the market that partial domination of the Mafia families did not lead to a rigid stratification. According to one of the leading members of the Coco Trovato group, his fellow dealers from the Sergi group imported hundred-kilogram cocaine shipments to sell directly in lots of one or two kilos to many lower-level dealers. The territorial domination did not lead to exclusion of other drug entrepreneurs or monopoly price-setting. Also the Mafia organizations remained mainly 'price takers', accepting a market price, while engaging other groups or outsiders to form a temporary 'crew' for a particular deal or job. Though the data are not yet fully investigated, the pattern which has come to light thus far does not fit into the generally observed pattern of small ephemeral organizations.

Did these crime-groups and families succeed in defying the constraints inherent in the illegality of the drug markets? Partly, but the market itself changed. The influx of illegal migrants, desperate to eke out a living, meant that a number of them entered the underground economy of drugs. Their presence was not only felt on the retail level, but also the wholesale and importation levels. For example Moroccans import the hashish produced in their homeland, like the Albanians smuggling their marijuana from Albania (together with cigarettes and migrants).[2] Though direct causal relations are difficult to establish, it is likely that the emergence of ethnic-minority dealers was furthered by the decline of the south Italian organized crime groups.[3]

Is the Milanese drug market 'back to normal', characterized by loose structures and short distribution chains? To a certain extent that is correct, though the drug market is different from where it started in the 1970s. Despite the 'zero-tolerance' rhetoric of the mayor, drug use is 'normal' in the sense that it is no longer a distinctive social feature or considered a personality disorder. Compared to the first 'drug wave', with the exception of cannabis, the prices of drugs have gradually gone down in Milan. Given the general increase in

2 It is interesting to observe that in north-western Europe hashish from Morocco is mainly imported by *Dutch* transporters (Fijnaut *et al.*, 1996, Van Duyne, 1995). The suggested explanation of the Dutch transportation experience is somewhat thin, as any country can develop such skills.

3 Becchi (1996) observed a kind of 'overcrowding' of the Italian drug market. According to a police estimate there are some 10.000 higher-level traders (importers, distributors, wholesalers) and 65.000 market participants in total. This contradicts the picture of an organized crime market monopoly, given the relative managerial inefficiency of the Italian criminal secret societies.

buying power, this implies a greater availability. This is provided for by small enterprises within market conditions which are again relatively open. The contribution of foreigners to the importation and distribution of cannabis and heroin reflects the increasing ethnic heterogeneity of Milan. Though in this regard comparable to Frankfurt, the nature of the foreigners can make a difference, like the Kosovo-Albanians, who are active heroin importers as well as distributors. However, they are not bulk importers and operate apparently from deposits in Eastern Europe, as the Turks/Kurds are also doing presently in their supply operations to Germany and the Netherlands.

These characteristics apply to a large extent to the Frankfurt drug market described earlier. An important difference is the shorter distance from Frankfurt to the Netherlands, which contributes to lower prices, while lowering the need for organizing the supply.

The main findings of this research project agree with the description of Ruggiero and South (1995) of the London and Turin drug markets, though the methods of research themselves do not allow a precise comparison. For example, the description of the Turin drug scene appears to focus on heroin alone. Nevertheless, in this city too a development from amateur dealer in the beginning to territorially controlled markets in the 1980s by professional criminals could be observed. Likewise, the latter did not encourage the drug commerce in their quarters, fearing that increased police attention would jeopardize their craft. However, the changing criminal climate and the lure of big profits caused a change of mind. When the power of a central group crumbled in 1984, the market fragmented again.

What is interesting is its relation to organized crime. In section 3.1 we discussed the criminal figures who purposefully strived to transcend the commercial delta. Though initially partly successful, all their attempts came to grief. Looking more closely at the markets for the three main psychoactive products we observe the same attempts, sometimes initially succeeding, but soon the market resumes its flat delta shape of creeks and brooks.

4.2 Ecstasy and raves in three cities

The closing remarks of the previous section apply to the synthetic drug market for amphetamine, ecstasy and all other amphetamine-like derivates. Though some bigger organizations of enterprising underworld figures have been observed and described before (Van Duyne, 1996a), these just occupied temporarily a segment in an ever-increasing market. As a matter of fact, there appear to be few incentives for rising above the disorderly commercial 'delta'.

From the late 1980s onward, ecstasy, the 'love drug', has become well established in the orbit of all-weekend rave parties and techno music, being an integral part of the international youth culture. Given this state of affairs we may assume (a) a fair degree of comparability between Western cities and (b) local 'industries' for manufacturing or cross-border trafficking to provide young people with the coveted substances to endure the relentless nocturnal stimulus onslaught.

The Italian non-governmental organization Gruppo Abele, together with the Spanish IECAH and the Dutch Transnational Institute, carried out a research project comparing the ecstasy markets of Amsterdam, Barcelona and Turin. The researchers collected data from informants of the police as well as from informants of the market. The research groups did not approach informants from the top-level manufacturers and suppliers of precursors, which section has been investigated independently by the University of Tilburg.

Amsterdam and beyond

Without proclaiming Amsterdam as the organized-crime city in the Netherlands, there are good analytical reasons for studying the Amsterdam drug market area (apart from more pragmatic reasons). The city is situated near Schiphol, an important gateway to North America, one of the most important consumption areas. Even if not based in Amsterdam, smugglers heading for the American markets may foster (safety) connections in that city. Conversely, importers from America may find it convenient to do business in Amsterdam. Whatever the business reasons, the Synthetic Drugs Unit (SDU) confirms that 70 per cent of their ecstasy investigations are connected to the Amsterdam area. This does not imply that Amsterdam is also the production area. Most of the production facilities are still situated in the southern provinces of the Netherlands, although a spreading to the regions adjacent to Amsterdam has been observed (SDU report, 2002). In fact, commercial and organizational relations between Amsterdam, the Dutch hinterland and, as we shall see, regions far beyond are continuously fanning out. The role of Amsterdam is better understood as the crossroad of many commercial transactions in the ecstasy market.

The pattern of the synthetic drugs market consists of upperworld external relations for obtaining laboratory equipment and precursors, and the mainly domestic criminal relations of production. The transport side is rather unsophisticated and is mainly courier-based.

For any major synthetic drug producer, whether amphetamine or ecstasy, it is essential to obtain the BMK or PMK precursor and the right equipment.

Zeming's BMK supply: In section 3.2 on the function of the brokerage in the middle- and upper-level markets, we described the operation of the Dutchman Koggel and the Chinese Zeming. The latter played a vital role in supplying BMK. Though he was very important, he was not a monopolist. A few years earlier a fellow precursor trafficker, Sunset, scoured eastern Europe in search of PMK, at first aided by a Slovak national, who ordered the PMK from legitimate firms in France and Moldavia. Subsequently he had the MDA powder processed into pills by a Latvian firm. Originally, the firm processing the powder produced remantadine pills against influenza, which was now used as a cover for re-exporting to Belgium. As far as could be determined, the Slovak was actually a co-organizer, arranging the production process in Riga, for which Sunset delivered three chemical analysts. Later, the precursor trade was restricted because of new legislation, and subsequently Sunset set out to try his luck in the Ukraine. Here he also failed and in the end he sank down to the level of a small retail seller of BMK in the Amsterdam market (Westphal, 2002, p. 106).

Obtaining precursors requires some cross-border scouting or networking in the legitimate industry. The same applies to the supply of all kinds of laboratory equipment, like flasks, retorts and for the end process, machines for making pills. One criminal firm, operating behind a licit cover, was actually specialized in the supply of such essential equipment, which could be obtained on a no-questions-asked and no-invoice cash payment basis.

Next come the production and wholesale distribution levels. According to the Dutch police, there are a limited number of figures operating on this level: about eighty to ninety. We have studied nine of these professionally led crime-enterprises (some already described above and in 3.2). In four of these, the leading entrepreneurs had a violent criminal background and tended to operate more top-down, if not hierarchically. Others operated on a peaceful, collegial basis. They all operated in an extremely secretive way, even if their chain of transactions was a short one.

Top-down firms: Two of the hierarchically led enterprises were famous or notorious in their own milieu. One, run by *Headers and Master*, cheated their fellow entrepreneurs and got away with this. The executives were held accountable to Mr Master, who was himself accountable to Headers. Both remained in the background, leaving the operation to a salesman and a chemical analyst. The warehouse was at a separate location from the laboratory, headed by the analyst, who was carefully shielded. The enterprise not only produced and exported synthetic drugs, but also imported hashish from Morocco.

The other wholesaler's firm, called '*Alpha and Omega*', was headed by a charismatic leader, who tightly pulled the strings of the separated sections, which were also hierarchically organized. The laboratories were lodged in separate locations. The transport and export to the UK was put out to an outsider. The risks were further reduced by using automobiles rented by the firm: the underlings were not to use their own cars during operations and were told only shortly beforehand where to find a car of the firm. Telecommunication was strictly coded; careless talk was punished.

The other drug enterprises were less tightly structured. All were small and had their own commercial *niche* as far as the sales were concerned. One of them, the small '*Postal Organization*', was in essence a small Dutch-Jewish delivery service, either sending by post or by hired messengers. The latter were recruited from the Jewish community in Brooklyn. Being devout orthodox students without a criminal record, this case, and other cases in which Israelis were involved, received much media attention. However, the estimated value of the ecstasy pills exported to the US (often via Paris and Spain, see below) of €800.000, is large, but not exceptional. The picture of the Dutch–Israeli–US network is not yet clear (Huskens and Vuijst, 2002) and it is reasonable to assume various parallel flows to the US. Indeed, there is ample room for parallel 'postal export services'. The market is apparently big enough, and the traffickers do not reveal much competitive behaviour (see also Pearson and Hobbs, 2001; 2003 for UK parallels). The Gruppo Abele mentions co-operation between the network focal points, for example concerning the supply of hardware or precursors.

At the wholesale level and at mid-levels, the organizational structure soon becomes looser. However the market is constantly changing. On the one hand, the report mentions a 'small world' phenomenon mainly dominated by white males between 25 and 35, some of whom know each other well. On the other hand, other ethnic groups with sufficient drug market experience in for example cocaine, also stepped into this market. Apart from the Israelis mentioned above, there are also Turks, Moroccans and West Indians. The Dutch Antillean groups, encompassing also Dominicans with contacts in Colombia and the US, operated a kind of triangular traffic system: importing cocaine to the Netherlands and exporting ecstasy to the US. A Surinamese group not only was involved in wholesale distribution, but also sold retail, a phenomenon often recounted. Mid-level and even wholesale distributors who buy tens of thousands of pills at a time sell them to a lower level, but also directly to friends and acquaintances. Some operate on the open market, in or around discos (the primary information for the police) and other locations of the 'night-time economy' (Hobbs *et al*, 2003), but others work in the closed settings of private homes. This 'hidden' market is mainly a matter of better educated and well integrated native Dutch white males.

Barcelona

In Spain, ecstasy consumption became a fashion in the second half of the 1980s, in cosmopolitan settings and in holiday resorts like Ibiza. Subsequently it spread to countercultural groups and then to the raves and house-music happenings. Its popularity increased around 1990 to become a mainstream drug a few years later (Alvarez-Roldán, *et al.*, 1997), sharing the wider European trend, inclusive similar symbols on the pill, together with adulteration (Gamella *et al.*, 1997).

The old city of Barcelona, 12 per cent of whose population is between 15 and 24 years old, did not remain outside this trend. It has a lively youth culture with an extensive proliferation of bars, discotheques, raves and musical events. One third of its population comes from other Spanish regions, while about 8 per cent is of foreign origin. Sharing such characteristics with most European metropolises, it has similar youth culture and drug problems. The perceived ease of drug acquisition is high (80 per cent), even higher than in any other country of Europe. Correlated with this high degree of availability, the drug market is spread across the city: a diversity of street markets, private places and dance and nightlife scenes. The participation in the drug market, either as user/dealer or mid- or higher-level trader runs through all social-economic classes of society. However, the police observed an increasing participation of youngsters with a higher educational and social background. As in other European metropolises, the dance scene is the usual outlet for stimulant drugs: synthetic as well as cocaine, the consumption of which expands in summer, weekends and holidays and shrinks in winter, reflecting the tourist and partying season.

The Madrid Barajas airport is the first import gateway for air transport, Catalonia is the transit zone for imports by vehicle. From Barcelona and surroundings, much of the ecstasy and other synthetic drugs is transited to other parts of Spain. Not all ecstasy is imported, as production also takes place in the coastal area in and near Barcelona. Imported ecstasy is frequently obtained in the Netherlands, which produces the paradox of the differential availability perception in the Netherlands and Spain. The 'ease of drug acquisition' is on average 80 per cent in Spain, as mentioned above, against 60 per cent in the Netherlands from where the drugs are being imported (Gruppo Abele, 2003, p. 109). This may be considered surprising, given the image of the Netherlands as the 'Mecca of drugs'. Are the Spanish importers better informed about the Netherlands than the Dutch themselves?

The wide availability hardly requires much organization by all kinds of unsavoury figures from the underworld. The following very simple and most frequent distribution chain for synthetic drugs is described by a police source:

> A Dutch courier, or the importer directly, brings the pills from Holland by car or bus and delivers them to the buyer, who is at the same time the person responsible for distributing them in the area. At this level there is merely a client/supplier relationship with the producer. It is neither a network nor an organization. The Dutch do not want to maintain structures. They are only interested in moving large quantities of pills. This is why the price of pills at this level is very low (for example €0,30 each). The 'first buyer', who distributes large quantities of pills also sells them cheap (for example €1,30). Local laboratories are beginning to appear at this stage; established by people who want to expand their profit margin. In this case, not only does the profit margin increase since they sell at higher prices (for example up to €9 each), but they also assume more risks. At this level we find young people connected with the leisure environment who have risen from lower to the upper sales level.

The local market reveals the loose and fragmented network structure, or rather the lack thereof, as observed earlier. The mid-level dealers, who are employed in the night-time leisure industry, buy their product either from local producers or in the Netherlands. With an average educational background and economically integrated in licit employment, they like to show off their acquired wealth. Next to these indigenous traders, the police also observe networks of foreigners working in the expanded tourist industry of the Catalonian coast and further south, importing drugs to distribute alongside their regular job performance. A Dutch settlement of citizens along the Catalonian coast, the Levant and Costa del Sol, is said to form an incipient well-organized network of drug importers. They are joined by settlers from the Maghreb with connections in the Netherlands, which facilitates their supply.

The retail market, consisting of young user-dealers, has few distinctive characteristics, revealing the usual pattern of dealing to pay for expensive drugs and parties. Those who work their way up in the market may save enough to enhance their prestige by flaunting their new flashy 'play-things'. However, the difficulty in demonstrating a licit origin for money spent on a luxurious lifestyle made some change their fancy car for a more modest type.

At the wholesale distribution level, the police have recorded some non-violent competition, as the distributors try to keep 'their' section of the city for themselves. The simplest method of removing an interloper is an anonymous phone call to the police. However, even without such peaceful removals, it remains difficult to intrude in settings in which the dealing is based on trusted buyer–seller relationships.

If the local market requires little or moderate organizational acumen, internationally operating crime-enterprises do not leave Spain or Barcelona untouched. The internationally operating Israeli–Dutch–US smuggling ring emerged also in the Barcelona area, where the kingpin, Mr Tuito, was arrested in 2001. Mr Tuito is said to have bought up whole stocks from laboratories in the Netherlands, to be smuggled by couriers to the US. After his arrest, another Israeli took over till he was also busted a few months later in Barcelona. Apart from this perhaps unique international connection, an interesting phenomenon is the 'barter' trade by networks which usually deal in other substances. When demand for ecstasy increases, they barter their products for synthetic drugs. For example, Moroccans export hashish to the Netherlands, accept ecstasy or other synthetic drugs as payment, and sell these in Spain. Is this an exception to the previously stated specialization in the drug market, or is this barter trade just a side business? The report provides no information to answer that question, but it demonstrates the economic use of existing trafficking routes, contributing to further diversification even if it concerns only side businesses.

Turin

The street market in Turin has changed significantly since the government clamped down on the open market places in squares and parks, and repressed the Mafia-type organizations and networks. The market, the interaction of demand and supply, has not been eliminated, but the social pattern of the market players has changed. Usually supply and demand try to meet, but with the traditional supply being repressed, the users began organizing their own supply, forming small distribution networks. However, the street market did not remain empty for long, as immigrants from abroad moved in. Either they are less easily deterred because they are used to harsher police repression at home, or they simply consider that they have no other means of livelihood or no place to operate from. Their place in the synthetic drugs market is hard to determine. Given the finding that many user-dealers see to their own supply, preferring dealings in closed settings and between friends and acquaintances, it is likely that the role of foreigners is marginal.

Obtaining synthetic drugs from the Netherlands seems to be a preferred supply route, although the rapporteurs point at a possible overvaluation of the Dutch supply market. According to the US Drug Enforcement Administration 85 per cent of the ecstasy in Italy originates from the Netherlands, but the Italian law enforcement agencies suggest a figure of 42 per cent. Other countries like Belgium and Slovenia have recently become important suppliers, to which other central European countries like Poland, the Czech Republic and Slovakia can be added. All of these joined the EU in 2004.

The phenomenon of self-supply leads to an interesting observation: a thriving illegal drug market without 'organized crime' in the sense of well-structured drug-enterprises and Mafia participation. Small networks of 'freelance' importers travel by car or train to the Netherlands, where they buy from a known supplier a few thousand pills, which can easily be hidden. There are many advantages in this way of doing business. The Dutch entrepreneur does not need to take the risks of organizing a major export operation and the Italian importer, while keeping his haul small (a few thousand pills), reduces his risks on his cross-border return trip too. Larger shipments (21.000 pills from Rotterdam to Turin, 2002) have been observed, but the general picture is that of *ad hoc* operating freelancers, working alone or incidentally accompanied by a few people for specific tasks, like driving or storing the contraband. Together they are socially bonded suppliers, operating in small circles of friends, neighbourhoods, mutual cultural contexts, etc.

The people described above come from all social layers of the Turin and Piemonte. The most frequent type of dealer has no other criminal record or background than his present market participation, next to his regular job and his participation in the music scene. The group with a criminal background are familiar with the traditional urban underworld as well as with the musical scene, which provides them an outlet. Another discernable group is more involved in other illegal businesses networks, for example former Mafia associates. Given the suppression of Mafia activities in the area, they try to find an income for themselves, for which the open synthetic drug market provides moderate opportunities.

A drug market without 'organized crime' is not a contradiction in terms. We have observed a similar situation concerning the supply of hashish in Frankfurt: individuals or small groups of like-minded entrepreneurs scouting Europe to replenish their stock. 'Organized crime' is not an inevitable concomitant of the drug markets. Local circumstances, like easy availability, moderate law enforcement pressure and low risks may increase the number of market players while lowering the need for organization.

4.3 Weed in the attic and organizing crime

In the chapter on the development of the drug market, we have already referred to the domestic industry of home-grown cannabis. In many ways, cannabis is a rewarding plant and with relatively little effort, anyone willing to do so can grow a few plants yielding enough marijuana for their own consumption and a surplus for selling to friends or to a local dealer. As referred to in section 2.5, since the beginning of the popularization of cannabis consumption in the 1970s/80s, (self-defined) idealists, professionals and amateurs have been engaged in improving the cultivation of the cannabis plant (Van Oosten and Steinmetz, 1995). In the late 1990s, the ongoing horticultural professionalization of indoor growing of cannabis plants also resulted in a professional 'putting-out' system in the Netherlands, as was common in pre-industrial production processes, such as the textiles industry in Britain.

The method of putting-out is basically simple, but exploiting it commercially requires extensive social organization. Large-scale growth of cannabis indoors in a commercial setting requires much space, for example a large shed, and equipment, which is widely available in so-called *grow-shops*. It also requires staff to look after the plants and much electricity. However, there are many risks connected to maintaining a large plantation of thousands of plants. The production can be detected because of its smell and the high electricity consumption (especially when many other people in the area are doing the same thing), while the plantation is difficult to defend against fellow criminals. Thefts of expensive equipment and complete harvests are frequently reported, though not to the police. One technique of risk reduction is to invite people who have nothing to do with the hashish-enterprise itself to allow the growing of cannabis plants in their dwellings. In underprivileged quarters and trailer camps, many people are easily persuaded to arrange their attic, spare bedroom or any other place on behalf of some 'unknown person'. Frequently all they have to do is to water the plants until the harvest, which is carried out by another stranger. Raising and taking care of cannabis plants is barely if at all considered to be really criminal. The expected 'penal costs' are low, while it yields a handsome marginal income to supplement meagre social security payments or a low-paid (illegal) job.

The 20 cases of 'putting out', described by Bovenkerk and Hogewind (2003), provide a lively but incomplete picture of the variety and organization of this criminal putting-out system. The incompleteness is due to the way the police handle these cases. The police operate according to a quick sweep approach: rounding up a plantation, destroying the plants and making a few arrests. As the occupants of the dwellings either only admit to have been growing these plants once, are scared to say more or really do not know more than that 'a man called John' brought them the small plants and some 'other man called Pete' gathered the leaves, there is little information about the organizational backgrounds of the trade or traders. Deeper investigation to trace the responsible lead personnel does not appear to be a police priority in the Netherlands or, very largely, elsewhere. This means that organizational backgrounds of offenders have to be deduced from the ways the plantations are equipped, operated and the yield is collected.

Various features of indoor cannabis growing allow the plausible deduction of an entrepreneurial approach, which transcends the individual grower. For example, a standardized installation for lighting and watering the plants in a number of nearby premises or in the trailer camp, while the growers clearly do not know where it comes from. Another rather unambiguous indication is the gathering of the leaves by a special crew instead of by the grower himself. As in 'black labour' picking primary foodstuffs (from fruit to seafood), the crew can consist of illegal immigrants, housewives, divorcees and/or of social security claimants 'doing the double' (i.e. working and claiming). The police have recorded cases in which the gatherers were transported in small buses with shuttered windows. A technical problem is the electricity. During the night, the plants have to be lit by so-called assimilation-lamps (freely available from Dutch grow-shops), which consume much electricity. To lower the costs or not to alert the electricity company, the electricity meter is bypassed, which is a dangerous job beyond the skills of many illegal growers. Sometimes the inspector of the electricity company is bribed or pressured to bypass the meter.[4] The growers themselves are

4 If the illicit electricity usage is sufficiently great, this may show up in a central information unit of the electricity company, whereupon the police are informed. Apart from victimizing the electricity company because of theft of electricity, the overuse of the available supply in a neighbourhood by too many illicit growers may lead to a power failure at other households.

instructed to learn by heart a cover story in case the police carry out a house search. Intimidation to tell 'the right story' has also been observed. It is assumed that on behalf of background figures, other aides try to recruit would-be growers to allow their spare rooms, shed or attic for cannabis growing. Finally, physical violence has been recorded, but not invariably: in certain regions the organized indoor growing took place peacefully.

It would be jumping to a false conclusion to deduce that behind all this is 'organized crime'. Apart from the lack of clarity of that theoretical concept (Van Duyne, 2003; Levi, 2002a), too little information about these organizing background entrepreneurs is available. However, it is safe to assume some long-term planning, financing and division of labour, and a capacity to control a neighbourhood sufficiently to prevent undesired behaviour, like 'informing'.

The consumer market is not supplied solely by this organized indoor growing of cannabis. Apart from smaller amateur and larger professional independent indoor growers, there are also professional wholesale growers, planting in the open field between maize or in large sheds of farms or factories with a potential of thousands of plants. The production of these wholesalers is probably too large for domestic consumption in the Netherlands, though it is unknown how much is exported.

At the time of writing, it seems that indoor growing is more widespread in the Netherlands than in the surrounding countries. In Belgium, some sixteen plantations were closed down in 2002. In England and Germany, the home growing of weed is still comparatively rare, though some hydroponics efforts have been made, following the example of the Dutch and often using Dutch lighting equipment. For the Germans, it may be more attractive to buy the marijuana in the Netherlands than to risk severe punishment if caught with a plantation. Only in France does the phenomenon of home growing seem to be so widespread that it competes with the import of hashish from Morocco (Labrousse and Laniel, 2001). The steep increase of the investigations and confiscation (in 1990 1.591 and in 2001 a total of 41.000 plants) reveals the growing appetite of the French to produce their own joints. The Dutch may become out-competed by the Gauloise-weed, though, for the time being, not by the Albion- or Teutonic-weed!

The features of the restless, changeable, partly organized illegal drug markets are not unique. The illegal cigarette market reveals very similar characteristics while (for the time being) overlapping very little with the drug markets (Van Duyne, 2002; Von Lampe, 2003). The difference is the licit nature of the nicotine product. The similarity is the massive illegal supply of untaxed cigarettes bound for the jurisdiction with the highest excise, the UK, carried out by small networks of brokers and transporters. Around the professionals, there are numerous market players, usually from the lower income groups, who are willing to supplement their income. In between there are some 'heavies', but not as the driving force of the market.

5 The volume of drug money and money management

In the previous chapters, we described the various drug markets and their motley crowd of participating adventurer crime-entrepreneurs. Unpacking the constituents of fear of crime is a complex task, since it is not always possible to strip out the demonology of social stereotypes from other aspects of the harm done by the acts themselves. Imposing an abstract rationality necessarily does violence to the emotional 'logic' that reinforces opinions and real experiences. Nevertheless, it is important to try to disentangle whether the fear and concern that drug dealing inspires comes from the commodities themselves or from how dealers are believed to organize themselves and what other activities they may engage in. One of the aspects of crime that has been presented in the last decade as a real threat is the financial potential that profits from illegal drugs may have brought about. This concerns not only the negative role models to society at large offered by the more or less spectacular unjust enrichment from crime. More menacing still are the alleged hundreds of billions of narco-dollars, narco-euros and narco-pounds which are considered to provide a harmful leverage over the economic and political 'control chambers' of free democratic societies. Though the argument neglects that clandestine political finance and bribes can be given in unlaundered cash, it is assumed that to exert that influence, some or all of those moneys may have to be laundered to give them a façade of ill-deserved respectability. This makes money-laundering a connected evil.

In the present state of our knowledge, it is not possible to determine how influential money-laundering is in fanning the 'fear of drugs'. It seems to us that it is more a consequence and a 'folk image' than a cause of these fears. Whatever its importance in the political realm, as something politicians and police chiefs can include in their end-of-conference *communiqués*, money-laundering has not been examined specifically in crime seriousness surveys and indeed, social tolerance for it and for other activities such as buying illicit software from criminals has been highlighted as a problem of deficient public awareness (NCIS, 2003). However, looking at the ways in which this menace is presented, one may discern various assumptions. The first assumption concerns the amount of drug money available. There is a curious disconnect between the total sums said to be laundered world-wide and the evidence about narco-influence. The global sums evoke an image of almost unlimited riches available to drug syndicates for penetration of the licit economies and society. Yet it is only episodically that vast sums are associated with any particular country or crime group. The second assumption is that the drug money is laundered. This assumption begs the question as to the precise meaning of the concept of laundering. What counts as money-laundering? The third assumption is that drug dealers, or at any rate the major ones, aspire to use their (laundered) moneys to obtain some corruptive power bridgehead into the upperworld. What empirical support do we find which may validate these assumptions?

5.1 The volume of the drug money

The question of the amount of the drug money, and for that matter of all the crime-moneys, has been approached with some ambiguity. On the one hand, attempts have been made to produce serious estimates, which have been criticized from a methodological point of view as mere 'guesstimates'. On the other hand, that criticism was neither refuted nor responded to, which smothered any debate on the issue of the magnitude of the drug- or crime-money threat. However, that was not a silent recognition of the invalidity of the proposed estimates, for without even referring to the methodological comments, new estimates have been put forward which doubled or tripled the initial estimates. Subsequently these figures obtained a political life of their own, being repeated regularly in official reports and by the media trawling their own electronic press cuttings.

The FATF approach

The first comprehensive attempt to estimate the global volume of the drug money was carried out by the Financial Action Task Force on money-laundering in 1990. Van Duyne (1994) analysed the far-from-transparent report of the FATF Working Group Statistics and Methods, and concluded that from a methodological and analytical point of view, the figures presented had to be considered at best contestable. The assumptions were unfounded and untenable, the statistics were unreliable and the application of arithmetical techniques to reach high total figures incoherent (Van Duyne, 1994; 2002).

Its basic assumptions were:

- the '*golden ten per cent rule*': only 10 per cent of the contraband is intercepted, for which any substantiation is lacking.[1] This is a dogma

1 Higher interception rates, as is the case with cannabis, are much more likely, as was well known at the time of the FATF reporting. For example, Rasmussen and Benson (1994)

going back to the 1930s when it was mentioned for the first time (Korf and De Kort, 1990, p. 22);

- the *street-level price calculation*: at this level of the drug trade, there is virtually no laundering (in the strict meaning of the word), given the fact that most street dealers are also users and their net disposable profit is very small;
- the *price level of expensive places*, like London, despite the fact that in most other reports Amsterdam is considered the 'Mecca' of the drug trade because of its much *lower* prices;
- the '*high-end multiplication*': this means that of any range of figures, the multiplications are carried out using the *highest* ends of the scale resulting incompetently or deliberately in systematic over-estimations.[2]

These assumptions were applied to three approaches to assess the volume of the production of drugs:

- the UN estimations of world drug production, qualified in the report as 'very uncertain';
- the consumption needs of drug abusers, qualified as of 'doubtful reliability';
- seizures of illicit drugs, of which the rapporteurs remarked that it 'raises significant methodological problems'.[3]

Undeterred by their own qualifications of the applied premises as invalid (defying the Aristotelian basic rule that no conclusions can be drawn from invalid premises), the report continues without additional argumentation in the next section: 'Using these methods, the group estimated that sales [of drugs] amount to approximately $122 billion per year in the US and Europe, of which 50–70 per cent or as much as $85 billion per year could be available for laundering and investment'.[4] The underlying elaboration of this remarkable specimen of arithmetic and methodology could be found in an obscure unpublished addendum.

estimate that a third of the cannabis shipped to the US is intercepted (in the 1980s), an estimate also put forward by the Dutch representatives in the working group on statistics. After duly mentioning this dissenting opinion, the working group continued its estimates on the 10 per cent basis without any further reasoning or arguments.

2 The Working Group justified these methods by stating that all measurements in this field are anyhow under-estimations.

3 Chapter 1: Extent and nature of the money-laundering process.

4 Dutifully the report mentions that 'One Task Force member estimated global profits at the main dealer level, which might be most subject to international laundering, to be about $30 billion per year'. In the subsequent consensus about the bigger numbers, this lower number was forgotten.

With this 'methodology' the FATF succeeded in convincing high-level policy makers that the global figure of the gross-proceeds amounted to a sum of $300 billion (the UN's 'very uncertain' estimation). The reader may also notice that in the above estimation not the 50 per cent but the 70 per cent has been taken as the multiplier. One may also pay attention to the subjunctive phrase 'could be available'. This contains a double contingency, which implies simply the *possibility* that there is a certain amount of money which *might* be laundered sometime. This formulation sounds cautious and restrained, but intentionally or not, has a strong public relations effect. It is predictable that such vague and cautious formulations tend to be transformed into *affirmative* phrases: so much money *is being* laundered. In this sort of way has the public image of the money-laundering threat been created. In public policy terms, such 'awareness-raising' may be a necessary impetus for action, but this does not make the data any more accurate or less speculative. Later on, the initial subjunctive in this formulation has indeed been turned into a simple affirmative 'is', after which these figures have become canonized. Many academic commentators have in practice used these figures without demur or comment.[5] The current official estimate provided by the United Nations Drug Control Program (UNDCP) is even higher, ranging from $300–500 billion. In an unconscious global echo of the statement wrongly attributed to gangster Meyer Lansky that organized crime in America was 'bigger than US Steel' (Lacey, 1991), the UNDCP report of 1997 states that 'in 1994 this figure would have been larger than the international trade in iron and steel, and motor vehicles'.

In view of this evaluation, the estimates presented in the FATF report cannot qualify as valid or as a guide for further refinement. The effect of the FATF statement was comparable to the fraudulently concocted figure of addicts by Hamilton Wright's report for the US Senate in 1910 (Courtwright, 1982). According to Thoumi (forthcoming), in 1999 the FATF did make an attempt to obtain a more reliable estimate and hired a well-known drug economist to that effect. Using all the available data, this economist came to an estimated range between $180 and $250 billion, probably based on retail sales. Though we consider that this figure is large enough for social concern, this led to a debate within the FATF, as some member countries expected or wanted a larger figure. In the end, though there was some debate about the extent of fraud and tax evasion and whether these should be included in the estimates, none of the studies were published, leaving the existing FATF and IMF claims as the only official 'data' in the public domain.

5 The academic literature does not contain many authors independently and critically scrutinizing the quantitative or policy making claims of the FATF. See in this regard Naylor (1999), Reuter (2000) and Reuter and Greenfield (2001), to be discussed later.

This leads to the question whether there are other sources of information. And if that is the case, is this information validated?

As far as the global estimates are concerned, the answer to this question must be an ambiguous 'hardly'. The reason for this state of affairs is not only the hidden state of the financial management of this market. Hiding financial aspects of trade and industry is inherent to any market, if only to avoid or evade the tax authorities or delude investors. More important is the cluttered layering of the chain of transactions between production and consumption. Each transaction generates added value: profit plus business costs for the entrepreneur. The latter means income for the providers of services like transporting, guarding, stashing the commodities or managing (or 'laundering') the money from the distribution points back to the wholesaler. In addition, income from (and on behalf of) all these illegal transactions is created where it is also spent, in sectors of the upperworld, not the least for legal advice and bribery. In short, much drug money seeps through the fingers of the drug entrepreneur into many greedy as well as innocent hands. This is as difficult to estimate as to assess the proportion of the grey or black labour in the building industry or hidden domestic services in the Gross Domestic Product. At best, economists claim to be able to estimate the proportion of the unofficial economy relative to the GDP (Hughes Hallet, 1997). If measuring the hidden economy is already traditionally hotly debated (Frey and Pommerehne, 1982), the singling out of separate branches of the crime-industry is well-nigh impossible.

Given these considerations, we are still left with the open question of how to approach the difficult issue of approximating the volume of drug money. 'The' drug money is of course an amalgamated concept, the components of which consist of the money generated by the markets for the separate commodities. The four well-known main varieties are: heroin, cocaine, cannabis products and synthetic drugs, which contain an ever increasing number of sub-types. One form of estimation is relatively simple: if we know how much is produced, we can fairly estimate the volume of the sales at the retail markets. Some estimation parameters concerning proportionate loss to interception may have to be inserted (the 10 per cent dogma or some other estimate that is not a universal constant). Business costs can also be inserted, as the FATF did (but such costs are income for the service provider). This makes just as much sense as calculating all the 'tobacco money' in an economy by estimating the acreage under cultivation, subtracting unknown losses and pilfering, and declaring the legal and illegal sales as the world's 'tobacco money'. Unlike the tobacco industry, in the drug industry every link in the chain of transactions from raw product to street-level turnover is much more fraught with uncertainty (Labrousse and Laniel, 2001). All industries experience 'shrinkage', and no RFID (Radio Frequency Identification) tags are yet available to track illegal drugs in the way that happens increasingly to industrial products from production to consumer. The area under cultivation is often difficult to assess, crops can get lost, a small part of the product may be consumed by the producer, while large consignments may become confiscated, simply lost or traded against other commodities of uncertain value.

The assumptions made in estimating the drug money as formulated above are basic to the approach of the UNDCP, equating the volume of drug money to the retail expenditures or the street-level turnover. The defects of the approach are aggravated because it does so, often without sampling sufficient points to obtain a correct total estimate. Reuter and Greenfield (2001) carried out a re-estimation taking the added value within trade flow as their point of view, arriving at a more modest $20–25 billion annually. They looked at the plausible value (not the same as profit margin) added in the chain of commerce and determined the largest mark-up in the cross-border import-export link for heroin and cocaine. For heroin, the mark-up for export from Pakistan to the US was 2.700 per cent; for the export of cocaine to the US, it was 2.100 per cent. But the increase of added value measured in absolute dollars or euros is to be observed in the industrialized consumption countries. However, these moneys accrue to a motley crowd of local distributors of various sizes, dealers, user-dealers, spending daily as they go. To these two markets, in which a limited number of production countries and wholesalers in the upper levels of the trade chain do play a role (though not a monopolistic one), one should add the much more fragmented markets for cannabis and synthetic drugs. In these markets, indoor production can take place anywhere. Granted, the limited number of very rich wholesalers, affluent intermediaries, reasonable well-to-do distributors and common user-dealers, all spend 'drug money'. However, in terms of socio-economic weight, it is highly questionable to add them in the way done in the official UN and US estimates.

Confiscation and seizure surveys

It is a commonplace that no official statistics generated by enforcement are reliable, reflecting as they do the efficiency and resources of law enforcement agencies as well as the underlying phenomena. This is particularly true in crimes without specific victims or where reporting rates are low, as the resources devoted to crime control 'create' the public awareness of the levels and forms of criminality. Thus, the burst of police and prosecutorial training in the UK to implement the Proceeds of Crime Act 2002 (and perhaps the creation after 2006 of the Serious and Organized Crime Agency in the UK) can be expected to generate a shift in resources and increased competence levels, which will result in more information about the financial activities of major criminals.[6] Despite this ambiguity and unreliability, official data

6 The addition of some eighty-six financial investigation officers as well as increasing pressure on judges to impose and see through confiscation orders, compared with earlier periods will yield more case information (Levi and Osofsky, 1995; PIU, 2000).

on drugs-related confiscation and money-laundering cannot be neglected. What do the official figures teach us?

The assumption underlying this question, that there are sufficient official statistics in the first place, was recently falsified by the valiant attempt of the Max Planck Institute at Freiburg to make a survey of this topic (Kilchling, 2002).[7] In a broad survey of the state of affairs concerning the recovery of the proceeds of crime in Europe, the institute succeeded in obtaining data from eight countries: Germany, the Netherlands, Austria, Hungary, France, Switzerland, Italy and the UK. It will evoke little surprise that the national statistics do not allow any international comparison. Actually, they are not maintained for this purpose, let alone for study and analysis of particular subjects, like the amount of drug money. However, even in purely national interest terms, they proved to be in a pretty bad shape, with important omissions on key variables such as assets confiscated related to the kind of crime. Sometimes only the crime category is mentioned, but not the amount of confiscated or forfeited money. Other statistics mention aggregate confiscation figures without any relation to predicate offences.[8] In short, the European judicial 'book-keeping' proves to be in a very poor state.

Of the national contributions presented, only the German and British ones contained some information about confiscations in relation to drugs (Kilchling, 2002; Levi, 2002b). The statistical analysis of the confiscation results in Italy – though problematical in comprehensiveness and validity (Vettori, 2003) – were most detailed. However, they did not provide the details that would enable us to separate out the contribution of the drug industry from proceeds of other crimes. The statistical system – as presented – of the other countries do not appear to reflect any serious attempt to connect the volume of crime-money, let alone drug money, to confiscation law enforcement results.[9]

The German situation is made more complicated due to the federalization of the judicial system and accompanying statistics: the non-comparability of the national statistics in Europe is amplified by that of the fifteen German Länder. Despite this drawback, Kilchling analysed the statistics concerning seizures (*vorläufig gesicherte Vermögenswerte*), differentiated according to various

7 See also Transcrime, 2001, for a study conducted for the European Commission.

8 If crime categories are indicated they can nevertheless be very misleading. For example, the police insert the offences in the order of the maximum penalty, and often mention a next higher category. Thus, a reported assault with only slight injury is booked as an attempt to murder if the assault weapon could have been lethal. When the outcome of the prosecution and trial is not included in the form, and the offender is only convicted for causing a minor injury, the case still counts statistically as 'attempt to murder'.

9 The contribution of Daams (2002) about the situation in the Netherlands is misleading because the author did not address available data bases permitting cross-comparison, but confined the analysis to data from the recovery support unit of the Public Prosecution.

Table 2 Drug-related seizures (in Deutschemarks) in eight German Länder, 1999

Land (region)	*Number of drug cases*	*Mean DM*	*Total DM drug money*	*Drug money as % of the value of all seizures*
Nordrhein-Westfalen	1152	14.501	16.705.900	12
Berlin	22	32.243	709.349	2
Bayern	50	38.321	1.916.049	3
Niedersachsen	194	44.524	8.637.732	18
Sachsen-Anhalt	–	–	444.956	4
Rheinland-Pfalz	20	82.618	5.935.329	16
Brandenburg	5	25.506	127.530	3
Sachsen	25	10.835	270.887	13
Total	**1.468**	**23.670**	**34.747.732**	11

Source: Compilation of Tables A 4.1–4.8 in the addendum of Kilchling (2002).

crime categories, including drug offences, for 1999. The results of eight Länder are presented in Table 2.

The statistics of Table 2 seem to be more revealing of the differences of law enforcement activities in the represented Länder than of the relation between drugs and crime-money. Despite this reservation, the volume of drug money (in terms of seized assets) exceeds that of the profits of most other forms of crime, even if the range is large: from a mere 2 per cent to 18 per cent. However, the value of the seized assets in fraud cases appears to exceed all other crime categories.[10]

Levi (2002b) provides some data, but they are not readily comparable. In 1999/2000 there were 131 confiscation orders made in England and Wales, with a value of £2.759.000, and 61 forfeiture orders valued at £4.411.000. There were 77 orders outstanding worth a total of £5.361.000. These cases concerned imported or exported money seized by the customs or police, because they had reasons to suspect that it was connected to drug trafficking. Subsequently, official data show that in 2001/2, 1300 confiscation orders in relation to drugs and non-drugs were made. The Exchequer received £25.200.000 in respect of recovered assets in 2001/2, including £4.630.000 cash forfeitures relating to drug trafficking controls. In 2002/3, the value of receipts recovered from confiscation orders relating to drugs and non-drugs was about £40m, and over £6m was recovered from cash forfeitures relating to drug trafficking controls. Using the £25.200.000 figure exposes the dip

10 The values could not be added as the component tables of the eight Länder mentioned different names for this category of property crime, like deceit, ill-faith. This illustrates the inconsistency between the statistics of the German Länder.

from £30 million in 1999/2000. It should also be noted that recent and current investigations of alleged customs & excise misconduct in failing to disclose information about contact with participating informants throws many of these successes in *non-drugs* confiscations into doubt, since some substantial funds may have to be repaid.

Nonetheless, a Home Office press release (24 February 2004) is upbeat in noting that '£55 million in suspect cash has been seized by police and customs officers since December 2002; £37.6 million has been confiscated over the past year . . . . Police will receive a third of all recovered assets above £40 million next year, increasing to 50 per cent in 2005/06.' As for what these asset cases tell us about money-laundering techniques, with the exception of property involved in one restraint order of £1.040.000 (Central Criminal Court, 9 February 2004), many of the cases reveal cash storage and/or transfer overseas. Thus, Greater Manchester police arrested one man with £11.000 of cash but no drugs in August 2003 and re-arrested the same individual on 3 February 2004, sitting on a pile of cash totalling over £10.000 next to 5 kilos of amphetamine. In London, the search of a South American's house found £161.245 in cash which was seized and ordered to be forfeited in November 2003. In other customs & excise and police drugs cases, sums of up to £1 million in cash per case have been forfeited following deliveries by security firms to premises under observation, or in properties and businesses run by persons convicted of drug trafficking offences. The Proceeds of Crime Act 2002 allows for cash to be forfeited in such circumstances unless the person can demonstrate to the court on a civil standard of proof that it has been acquired legitimately.

The modesty of scale of successful confiscation elsewhere in the UK – at least prior to changes from the implementation of the Proceeds of Crime Act 2002 – is illustrated by the fact that in 1999/2000, seventeen orders valued at £822.700 were made in Scotland compared to twenty orders with a total value of £630.504 in the previous financial year. In Northern Ireland, only four orders were made in 1999 with a value of £149.359 compared to two orders in 1998 for £94.800. The data from the criminal statistics are set out in Table 3 (Home Office, 2002), to which one should add that in 2001, almost 25.000 drug offenders (well over half sentenced) were additionally required by the courts to forfeit cash and other instrumentalities of crime.

The Dutch statistics will be elaborated in the next section, using more complete data than were provided in the Max Planck review.

Surveying the strategic information management of the law enforcement agencies, we have to conclude that they do not give any indication of or support for claims about the huge volume of drug money. We do not imply that this shows that there is far less drug money than claimed, but it shows that the financial magnitude of the problem does not force itself upon the official statistics. It is difficult to attribute this to the poor state of the 'policy information and data management' alone. Whatever the potential

Table 3 Offenders ordered to pay confiscation orders for drug-trafficking offences by amount, England and Wales, 1996–2001

	Offenders sentenced at the Crown Court for drug trafficking					
	1996	1997	1998	1999	2000	2001
Total sentences for drug offences	7.373	8.370	6.998	6.577	6.458	6.653
Confiscation order not made	5.816	6.904	5.755	5.568	5.622	5.876
Confiscation < £1.000	1.117	1.032	855	682	525	454
£1.000–£3.000	217	224	185	147	159	155
£3.000–£10.000	118	127	111	99	69	77
£10.000–£30.000	64	56	56	45	51	47
£30.000–£100.000	32	19	26	23	20	30
£100.000–£300.000	6	6	7	9	11	10
£300.000–£1 million	1	1	1	2	1	3
£1 million and over	2	1	2	2	-	1
Total with order made	1.557	1.466	1.243	1.009	836	777
Orders made as a % of eligible offenders	21	18	18	15	13	12
Total amount confiscated	10.471.336	5.620.003	6.970.535	16.107.414	5.002.493	7.979.793
Average amount of confiscation order	6.725	3.834	5.608	15.964	5.984	10.27

explanation, we observe a remarkable gap between the fear of drugs and drug money, on the one hand, and the poverty of reliable figures, on the other hand. Why do the assumed staggering amounts of drug money not force themselves on statistical parameters, despite attempts at concealment? One possibility is that the figures discussed relate to law enforcement cases leading to *conviction*, and European police and customs are not finding sufficient of their assets to convince the courts that they should be confiscated. (One remedy for this is considered to be toughening up civil forfeiture or tax regimes, or changing substantive or procedural law to make convictions/funds-stripping easier.) Unless the possibility of generating reliable data is discarded on *a priori* grounds – in which case figures should no longer be used by officials – it appears that the official concerns about the drug money have not stimulated any observable interest in basic fact-finding among the law enforcement agencies or responsible policy makers involved. Unless there are plausible bureaucratic causes which prevent obtaining a proper insight into this phenomenon, one may seriously consider other hypotheses: either the demonstration of the fear is mainly politically motivated and/or there is less drug money than is officially assumed, or the drug money appears to be less menacing to the economics of the upperworld than is usually alleged. A more detailed description of what upper-level drug traders do with their ill-gotten profits may shed some light on these questions.

5.2 The analysis of the 'big earners'

It may be a more useful strategy to gain some insights into crime-money by building more slowly from what we patchily know about 'big earners' in the drugs market, instead of focusing on macro-level 'data'. The reason for this is that the economic conduct of small-time drug traders with no or moderate surplus savings will differ little from that of the average property offenders (fraud included), spending their loot as they go. Big earners, who have acquired so much net profits as to generate (forced) savings and who possess the potential for a significant social economic leverage, may be considered to be more plausible social threats.

An investigation of the socio-economic role of the drug money of the big earners would amount to a survey of all those wholesalers of whom we have a sufficiently accurate description for this purpose. This approach has been adopted by the University of Tilburg (Van Eekelen, 2000), which has been extended by the Research Department of the Dutch National Detective Institute.

In the first phase, the University of Tilburg carried out a pilot study based on the criminal files of convicted offenders with a confiscation recovery order of at least €45.000 (Van Eekelen, 2000). Of the twenty-one cases, thirteen concerned drug trafficking. Two of the drug wholesalers (a Dutch hash dealer and a Turkish XTC trafficker) had criminal assets of more than €500.000.

The pattern of money-management and the precipitation of the crime-money in the upperworld of only these two really affluent crime-entrepreneurs reflected some degree of business acumen. As far as laundering was concerned, the Dutch hash dealer made a real attempt to clean his money by means of the well-tried and tested loan back method. The cleaned money was invested in real estate, catering and a loss-making advertisement firm. The Turkish crime-entrepreneur did not launder in the sense of 'cleaning' his crime-money, but simply carried it physically out of the Netherlands and invested it in real estate in Turkey and in a 'gold and currency' firm, which was put in the name of his three brothers. The pattern of the financial behaviour of the other offenders was less impressive: their crime-money was primarily spent on their 'daily needs', which of course exceeded those of average workers dependent on their regular salary.

The outcome of this pilot study did not answer our questions conclusively, but it provided the first, more systematic view on the financial behaviour of the higher echelons of the drug market. The follow-up research project by the Research Department of the Dutch National Detective Service expanded this approach, while there was also access to the national data base on confiscations from 1993 onwards. Though the methodology remained the same, the base line for case selection was increased to €450.000 (one million Dutch guilders at the time). As the research question was 'the precipitation of the crime-money in the upperworld economy', the case selection concerned all kinds of offenders: drug traffickers, fraudsters, embezzlers and other 'classical' property criminals. For our analysis, we will highlight the findings concerning the selected drug traffickers only.

The database on confiscations contains 159 offenders estimated by the *police* to have obtained a minimum of €450.000 illicit profits per case (not per offender). From this population, 52 cases were selected, which contained 25 drug offences. Of the 27 remaining cases, 21 concerned fraud and 8 varied between money-laundering, organized property crimes and women trafficking. In 23 cases the offenders were foreigners or ethnic minorities from Morocco or Turkey. The Turks were mainly involved in heroin trafficking, while the Moroccans were less specialist, trafficking in hashish, cocaine and XTC. The criminal cases had all been tried in the lower courts, in which also the drug-trafficking benefits had been determined. During the research, a number of confiscation cases were still pending trial in the appeal courts.[11]

11 In the Dutch system of criminal law, the forfeiture procedure can be separated from the main trial: first the predicate crimes may be tried and in a subsequent procedure, the prosecutor can open a financial investigation and demand recovery of the estimated illegal profits.

Levels of determining crime-money

Determining at the micro-level of investigated and sentenced individual cases the amount of crime-money per convict suggests more solid grounds to work from than is actually the case. This procedure proves to be as arduous and ambiguous as the assessment approach on a macro-level, though it allows more insight into aspects like gross proceeds, costs, net profits and the subsequent management of the crime-money. The point is that there are various procedural levels at which, for each individual defendant, the amount of his income from the drug offences with which he has been charged, has to be determined as precisely and transparently as possible. In the end, even if there is disagreement, it is the independent court that determines the amount of the illicitly obtained advantage. Even if every party in the trial may disagree with that verdict, this is the only indisputable *de jure* fact. That is what we have judges for. However, this *de jure* fact does not mean that it is a mistake to include data from the police and prosecution in our analysis.

The following procedural levels of determining the amount of crime-money can be discerned in the Netherlands:

The police and the prosecution

At this level, the first assessment of the illegal profits is carried out. At this procedural level the investigation squad – frequently a specialized financial unit – performs a special financial investigation, which is reported separately. Apart from observable facts like recorded income, purchases and expenses, the investigators may have to make assumptions about the nature and the 'trade rhythm' and the period of business. A frequently applied method is a simple extrapolation of the observed profit margins to the whole assumed time span. Thus when it is the opinion of the police that the offender has been dealing for two years and his average weekly turnover is known (or estimated), the police (prosecutor) simply multiplies his profit margin times the number of weeks, allowing some reduction for business costs. Taking the sum of the police/prosecutor calculations as the best approximation may lead to an overestimation: dealers are also sometimes ill, go on holiday or have problems with their suppliers or delivery staff, or may have been cheated.

The first instance trial level

The court (usually consisting of three judges in the Netherlands) has of course a different role and has to respond to the pleas of the defendant. For example the defendant may wish to challenge the claim of the prosecutor that he has been selling dope for fifty-two weeks per year, because he has been ill for a month and has gone on holiday for another six weeks, while during Christmas time he had run out of stock. If the court thinks this a plausible defence, the amount of illegal profits and thereby the amount of 'drug money' will be deducted. Business costs such as transport of goods may also be deductible.[12] However, such costs are income for the accomplices or aides and are therefore still crime-money, and for our investigation drug money.[13]

If the convict and/or the prosecutor do not agree with the sentence of the lower court they will appeal.

The appeal court

Three higher judges will look into the case afresh. Pleas from the defendant and prosecutor, rejected in the lower court, may be accepted, leading to new, frequently lower assessments of the illegal profits.

Hence, there are three judicial assessment levels of the 'financial reality' of the drug moneys. However, this assessment of illegal profits in the verdict does not equal the sum of money finally stipulated in the recovery orders: given the financial situation of the convicted offender, the court may moderate the amount of money he/she will have to pay to the state. This implies that the total of the *recovery orders* cannot represent the total of the drug moneys (or other types of crime-money): it is always an under-estimate.

Given these ambiguities, the best we can do is to consider the *de jure*-determined volume of the crime-money being the bottom line of the phenomenon. It goes without saying that there is much more drug money around (including moneys under the control of persons never charged or, if charged, never convicted), but in the absence of serious analysis, the extent of that will remain a matter of speculation. The 'plausible' estimates of the police and the evaluations of the public prosecutor in individual cases are usually arrived at conscientiously, though they may nevertheless contain inflating distortions.[14] More inflating distortions are to be expected if we move further away from the investigative and judicial basis. Even if from an empirical point of view the judicial estimates are far from satisfactory, they provide the most cautious basis for our study.

12 This is the so-called 'net earning' approach. In the UK and Germany, the gross earning approach is used, which implies that the money to be recovered encompasses business expenses plus earnings (Alldridge, 2003; Kilchling, 2002).

13 This means that the total of the *de jure* determined illicit profits of the convicted offenders are not equal to the amount of crime-money. But where ends the taint of crime-money? If an accomplice is paid, it remains crime-money; if the fees of the defence lawyer are paid some still think that crime-money, but if the trader pays VAT and income tax (some semi-tolerated hash dealers are very conscientious about that), the crime-money is gentrified.

14 Neither the police nor the prosecution office will agree with this position. They will argue that *their* assessments are invariably conservative and that they can detect only a slice of the reality. This is a plausible proposition, albeit an agnostic one.

The confiscation database of the Dutch criminal justice system can illustrate these difficulties, though only for the total numbers of forfeiture and recovery procedures, not differentiated for drug offences. The reason for this is not the omission of the nature of the charges in the data entries, but because – as elsewhere in Europe – drug charges are frequently subsumed under the organized crime charges. However, the entry 'organized crime' also covers other predicate crimes, like human smuggling, organized fraud and other crimes. Also the connection between the appeal court statistics and the lower courts proves to be a difficult one, as the registration numbers in the appeal cases are changed without connection to the first instance numbers.

Table 4 provides an overview of all the recovery cases started between 1993 and 1999. As indicated, there is a gap between the courts of first instance and the transfer of the finalized cases to the Central Recovery Office: that gap is due to the appeal courts. However, there is some approximation as the Central Recovery Office also receives the recovery verdicts from the appeal courts for further execution. We have divided the cases in three categories: 'small' recovery cases up to €45.000; the middle range of €45.000 to €450.000 and the cases against the 'big' criminal earners of more than €450.000.[15]

This table makes clear that the amount of crime-money at the police level is very much different from the assessed amount after the full course of judicial procedures. The gap is huge: of the €460 million initially estimated, just under 3 per cent was transferred to the Recovery Office, of which at the time of writing 0,75 per cent was finally recovered! The recovery rate from the 'big earners' is even well under 1 per cent, which seems to make a mockery of the system. Actually, though the table provides an idea of the evasive reality of the crime-money, it does not present a proper picture, because much of the shrinking amounts of recorded crime-moneys may be due to many procedural causes: cases are still pending appeal; there are out-of-court settlements of frozen or recovered funds with the prosecutor; an acquittal of (part of) the charge, or a legally allowed moderation of the court to recover less (or even nothing) of the illicit profits determined, because of the personal circumstances of the defendant; or that the Inland Revenue Service had already taken so much from the defendant that there was nothing left,[16] etc. This implies that the amount of crime-money may have been

15 Before the introduction of the euro these figures were about *f*100.000 and *f*1000.000.

16 The Dutch Tax Authorities were a mystery: when the researchers tried to find out how much the fiscal recovery office actually collected from convicted fraudsters, it appeared that they could not provide figures. At the time of writing, this mystery has been partly solved: the local fiscal recovery offices appeared to have the policy of leaving violent taxpayers, as are often found in trailer camps, alone. However, this policy was not reported to the Ministry of Finance, which claimed resounding successes in its criminal recovery policy, instead of losses.

Table 4 Assessed illicit profits at the various judicial levels, divided into three 'income classes', 1993–1999

Phase process	< €45.000		€45.000–€450.000		> €450.000		*Total*	
	total	N	total	N	total	N	total	N
Police	53.868.631	6.236	139.790.339	1107	266.441.759	159	460.100.729	7.502
Prosecutor	44.589.722	5.001	111.791.718	907	216.917.853	117	373.299.293	6.025
Trial court	21.226.220	3.008	27.227.659	468	46.385.987	73	94.839.866	3.549
Appeal court							No direct database matching	
Recovery office	7.261.876	2.079	4.214.207	150	1.821.149	11	13.297.232	2.240
Sums recovered	2.211.624	1.266	1.138.385	88	107.574	3	3.457.583	1.357

reduced for many different legitimate reasons. Whatever the many causes of reduction, it underlines the need to handle the police figures most carefully.

In order to overcome these flaws, a comparison was made between the judicial stages of only those offenders who passed through the *whole* judicial process. This results in a reduction of the number of convicted persons and therefore also in the amount of assessed crime-money.

Table 5 confirms the previous observation that one cannot sensibly discuss the amount of crime-money without taking the level of assessment into account. The figures of the police and the public prosecutor are the highest and hardly differ, which is understandable as the prosecutor depends on the former for formulating the sentence demanded. He may lower the figure if he considers dropping parts of the charges due to insufficient evidence. He may also settle cases out of court or drop the prosecution all together. The ensuing reduction does not look very significant. The largest reduction is observed between the sentence demand of the prosecutor and the recovery verdict of the court. Taking all the cases together, the reduction between the prosecution and the court of first instance is 70 per cent. Differentiated for the three criminal 'income classes' the reduction in the small cases (< €45.000) is 52 per cent; for the middle range (€45.000–€450.000) the reduction is 70 per cent. The approximately 50 per cent reduction from the courts to the recovery office is also substantial, though conclusions are somewhat obfuscated because of the appeal phase, which was difficult to match with the other databases.

The three cases of the 'big earners' do not allow many valid statistics, while many other cases of this category are still under appeal. There are actually many more such 'big earners', namely 159, but only three of them had passed all the stages of the judicial process at the time of the analysis. Obviously, the inclusion of all these pending cases would have made a big difference to the analysis, but it would be inconsistent to include them.

We hope that this statistical elaboration conveys convincingly the underlying difficulties of any valid claim about the volume of crime-money in general and drug-money in particular, based on either police or court statistics. This small statistical exercise also demonstrates that the huge amount of the alleged crime-money obtained by the 'big earners', of whom there are not very many, dwindles towards smaller quantities sooner than is usually assumed.[17]

17 In the study carried out by Levi and Osofsky (1995), the authors found that one of the reasons for the attrition between police and judicial sentences was the judicial resistance to the legislation and the reversal of the burden of proof post-conviction when it came to determining sums to be confiscated. There were no indications that such factors influenced the Dutch courts and the attrition rates there. This may reflect the cultural differences between Dutch and other continental European professional career judges/prosecutors and the situation in England and Wales where people become judges usually after a career representing both sides in court.

Table 5 Assessed illicit profits of defendants, *all* having gone through the three procedural levels, divided into three 'income classes', 1993–1999

Phase process	*< €45.000*		*€45.000–€450.000*		*> €450.000*		*Total*	
	total	N	total	N	total	N	total	N
Police	8.156.647	1.082	7.663.870	76	6.052.632	3	21.873.149	1.161
Prosecutor	8.033.638	1.082	7.450.921	76	6.052.632	3	21.537.192	1.161
Trial court	3.837.327	1.082	2.213.216	76	271.369	3	6.321.912	1.161
Appeal court							No direct database matching	
Recovery office	3.681.356	1.082	1.929.215	76	271.369	3	5.881.940	1.161
Recovered	1.820.309	1.082	963.333	76	107.574	3	2.891.216	1.161

As can be deduced from section 5.1, the expectation to compare the Dutch statistics with those from other countries proved to be unrealistic even if access had been granted. The format of the foreign statistics prevents statistical analysis with SPSS or a compatible statistical analytical programme. In the age of information and intelligence management, many law enforcement agencies and judicial systems still function on the level of the 1970s.

Drug money and the upperworld

Though the attempt to approximate the volume of the drug money proved to be fraught with many measurement problems, an approach based on a case-by-case analysis still may provide us with more insight into the interactions between the 'big earners' in the drug trade and the upperworld. Such an analysis is not necessarily entirely a qualitative, 'anecdotal' study. Taking a big enough sample and projecting the outcomes onto a broader quantitative background (even if shrouded in so much ambiguity) may lend weight to the findings.

What kind of interactions are to be considered relevant for an understanding of the role of the drug money in Europe? These interactions may range from the 'most feared' infiltration of the higher levels of the upperworld, like the financial system, the public administration or trade and industry, to the virtual zero level of hiding the drug money, while apparently living from some registered income, like a social security benefit. As we will see, this is not a hypothetical situation.

Given various kinds of financial interactions it is difficult to order them along some objective yardstick. At face value a kind of 'degree of threat' scale looks like a useful way of judging harm, if it were not so heavily value-imbued and shallowly covered by circular arguments. What is the threat posed by drug money, placed in a bank account, compared to savings derived from income-tax fraud, which are equally deposited in the accounts of the same banks? The banks will handle the money in the same way as all the other deposits: they will loan or invest it at a higher interest rate than they will pay to the (criminal) depositors. To deduce the threat of the drug money from the morally reprehensible deeds confuses values pertaining to the ways of earning money with its potential economic roles for such an offender. For all his crime-money, the latter may not reveal any deviating threatening behaviour, but simply support his family while keeping a part of his assets as a kind of retirement fund. It is only if the ability to retain the funds induces him or others to enter or remain in the criminal market that one may sensibly speak of the harm posed by money-laundering. But then one is rating the harm posed by the profits from the drugs rather than by the laundering. On the other hand, respectable citizens and corporations may funnel legitimately earned money to secret funds for illicit donations to equally respectable public persons, like the erstwhile Chancellor Kohl, some US presidential candidates (Liddick, 2000) or may use it as clandestine political finance if not bribe money. This appeared to be commonplace among Mayors of Paris, such as Alain Juppé (the former Prime Minister convicted by the trial court in February 2004) and allegedly also including Jacques Chirac (who cannot face trial while he remains President of France). They may also use such funds as contract bribe money that can also be 'dipped into' for personal gain, like Elf and other corporate 'slush funds' most vividly revealed in France, which led to the imprisonment of senior executives in 2002 and 2003. Is the laundered drug money worse or better than the laundered political finance or bribe money?

Given these difficulties, the principle of threat may still be used to create some ordering, if we take that threat as the exercise of an unwanted influence derived from the accumulated drug money. In Van Duyne (2003), the following differentiation has been suggested for the levels of the impact of drug money:

1. *Corruptive permeation: crime-money enters the veins and nerves of the 'control rooms' of the upperworld*

Crime-money enters the upperworld fabric through shareholding in strategic positions and may influence decision making in trade and industry or the administration. Examples from recent decades are Russian banking (Rawlinson, 1996; Burlingame, 1997), Banco Ambrosiano (Cornwell, 1983), BCCI (Adams and Franz, 1992), Banque Crédit Lyonnais – the case of Parretti and Fiorini (d'Aubert, 1993); the results from the 'clean hands operation', for example the Craxi case (Della Porta and Vannuci, 1997).

2. *Criminal upperworld subsidy*

Crime-money is used to establish uneconomic firms or to sustain loss-making enterprises as a kind of bridgehead in the upperworld. We differentiate two variations:

(a) An existing loss-making legitimate enterprise is sustained by money derived from (tax) fraud;

(b) a newly established legitimate loss-making enterprise is maintained for other than rational commercial reasons, like prestige or to provide relatives or friends with a job. (This allegation appears to be one component of the Italian and worldwide Parmalat scandal.)

3. *The once-only crime-money 'impulse': defusion by integration*

The crime-money is invested in a legitimate firm once only, after which the enterprise is able to function on a commercially legitimate rational basis. By full integration of the crime-money in the upperworld order, it loses its potential threat. Hence the label 'defusion by integration', which may also be interpreted as a kind of 'gentrification' of crime-money. As the application of this label is always 'wisdom by hindsight', we can only give a few historical examples, such as the US robber barons; legitimized rum runners (like Joe Kennedy, the former President's father, legitimizing also other obscure funds – Kessler, 1996).[18] Funds returning to drug production countries may be invested in the local economy and boost industry, though it can lead to property inflation. Anderson (1979) also provides examples of such 'gentrification' of Mafia money in New York.

4. *Criminal reinvestment*

Crime-money is reinvested in one's own crime-enterprise for the continuation or expansion of the crime business, whether out of choice or because other avenues of investment are closed off by enforced anti-laundering legislation.

5. *Rainy-day provisions*

However hectic and hedonistic a life a criminal may lead, some may also consider that they may have to retire one day. This may be prepared for by normal savings in bank accounts, hoarding or investment in real estate like a kind of criminal pension scheme, or a luxurious dwelling to which they can retire.

6. *Lifestyle expenses*

Crime-money is used for daily expenses in one's household and ostentatious way of living. This hardly needs explanation, though depending on the social milieu, this spending has also an economic management function, to show off credibility and status.

At first sight this typology provides some ordering, but cannot be considered a linear 'seriousness scale' of the threat of the drug money. For example, the types may cluster, or various types may be observed with the same crime-entrepreneur. Sustaining a loss-making firm with drug money may be used to exert influence on the (local) administration, as the drug dealer provides jobs for the supporters of a political figure or tries to influence the 'correct' voting behaviour of those who depend on his loss-making firm. The 'gentrification' of drug money may not be so beneficial either, when there remain connections with 'the friends of a friend' to whom the, by now legitimate, entrepreneur still owes favours. In addition, this type can only

18 The contemporary Russian 'robber capitalism' may also be interpreted from this perspective, though it is still early to determine the degree of 'gentrification' given the large outflow of flight capital.

be determined by historic hindsight. Lifestyle expenses may socially or psychologically be rated much more seriously if there is an imitation or negative role model effect from the 'made man' that attracts youngsters to climb what Daniel Bell (1964) once termed the 'queer ladder of social mobility' (see also Firestone, 1996). The same may be said of a retired drug dealer (or other crime-entrepreneur) living from his criminal pension fund, which is offensive to the morality of 'crime does not pay'.

Notwithstanding these comments on the idea of scaling these types, from the perspective of potential harm to the upperworld in the sense of corruptive influence, there is a difference between a drug dealer bribing a judge or councillor, or the same person living off his criminal pension fund. The same can be said of the flashy and uncouth big spender, whose materialistic success brings him admiration from 'below', but not the social keys to the upperworld, because of this very success. This may depend on the moral values and wilful blindness capacities of the particular society, which may vary over time, though. The 'absorption capacity' of the city Marbella governed by the late corrupt mayor Jesus Gil will be different from that of The Hague or Cardiff, should the latter be governed by a similar individual.

Investing in the upperworld enterprises, the 'criminal subsidy' has a threatening economical potential of undermining competition, even if the fields of interest and its scale remain limited to such 'classical' areas like the catering business or are otherwise far removed from important political and economic decision makers.[19]

Irrespective of these theoretical considerations, it is worthwhile to compare the categories of this typology with the evidence from the investigations of the twenty-five drug cases, which – according to the police estimates – generated an illegal advantage of at least €450.000.

Table 6 presents the outcome of the comparison. As mentioned above, the convicts could display various types or levels of upperworld penetration. The table also shows that the financial value of the individual transactions or assets involved is not always known. Problems also arose during the classification of the observations as described in the files, which had to be interpreted, during which ambiguities could not be avoided. For example, hoarded money or bank accounts could be 'saving for a rainy day', but they could likewise be considered working capital, or both. This differs little from legitimate people, who may use their savings in some other way.

The summary of the findings in Table 6 must be read with due caution as they do reflect the researchers' interpretations, which in turn are based on

19 In its essence, this criminal subsidy does not differ from other forms of subsidy, like the agrarian subsidy policy of the EU, subsidizing the loss-making farmers. The difference is that the distortion of fair competition by the EU is far bigger and more detrimental to numerous farmers elsewhere, especially in the Third World, though it has a democratic backing and is maintained by EU taxpayers.

Table 6 Levels of penetration of the crime-money in the upperworld

Levels of penetration	*Observations*	*Persons*	*Value €*
Corruptive permeation	3	3	919.027[a]
Criminal subsidy	6	7	559.723[b]
Once-only infusion	8	9	6.979.286[c]
Reinvestment own crime firm	6	12	4.153.355[d]
Rainy-day provision	20	21	14.360.875[e]
Lifestyle	9	–	–

a one (failed) attempt of €450,000
b one observation without mentioned value
c three observations without mentioned value
d two observations without mentioned value
e one observation without mentioned value

police observations, which are also sometimes interpretative. These are again not always the product of hard evidence, like confiscations and direct observations, but may also be derived from statements made by the defendants and informants. The former have every reason for playing down their wealth, while the reliability of the statements of informants should not be taken for granted. Therefore we clarify this summing up with a more detailed description per category.

Corruptive permeation

The cases we qualified as such did not encompass so-called 'executive corruption', like the bribing of customs officers, required for the ongoing crime-business, but 'strategic' penetration, obtaining a position with more long-term potential for exercising influence. Only a few cases/attempts could be identified, though ownership of sports clubs such as soccer teams merges business, criminal, social and sporting interests and has been found in some southern European countries not in our datasets.

- One Dutch middle-level cocaine trafficker (and swindler) obtained an interest in a *bureau de change*, which proved not to be such a stable 'upperworld bridgehead': it was closed down after a killing in the premises.
- Another Dutch cocaine wholesaler (importing from Colombia) tried to invest €450.000 in a car dealer firm. The offer was rejected.
- An infamous British drug dealer[20] residing in the Netherlands, bribed

20 The exploits of this person, Curtis Warren, are described by Barnes *et al.* (2000). This Liverpudlian, feeling too much heat in the UK, moved to the Netherlands. All to no avail:

a senior detective and is alleged to have an interest in an English football club.

- 'Buying power' by acquiring shares and bonds in companies could not be observed. If the drug entrepreneurs ventured financially into this social sphere, they acted just as conservatively as any other wealthy citizen: buying, selling and cashing the dividends, interests and the increased value of the assets, as could be observed in three cases.

Criminal upperworld subsidy

Subsidizing legitimate firms did not appear to be a priority of the drug dealers. Crime-entrepreneurs appeared to take little interest in subsidizing other (legitimate) firms within their control.

- Of a Dutch–Moroccan combination, the Dutchmen invested moderate sums in a restaurant (€68.000) and a sport school (€5.000) in the Netherlands and one of the Moroccans invested in Morocco in a fish-processing factory (€450.000, according to soft information).
- A Dutch hash wholesaler is alleged to have invested in a garage. The amount of money is unknown.[21]
- Of another sport school investment or participation in it the amount of money has not been recorded.

The once-only money infusion: defusion by integration

The establishment of a regular enterprise about which no mention has been made of any illicit operations, could be observed eight times. It goes without saying that this observation is shallow and dependent on the capacity or willingness of the police to scrutinize a legal entity, particularly if residing abroad. On the other hand, without supporting evidence, we should not jump to the conclusion that smugglers cannot set up non-criminal businesses. Nevertheless, a cautious appraisal is appropriate.

- Four Turkish brothers invested in a holding company in their home town, where hotels were exploited: the total value amounted to €4.321.000. A fellow heroin smuggler, related by their common supplier, invested €945.000 in another hotel. Three ethnic drug entrepreneurs established regular companies in their home countries. Little is known about their economic success.

underestimating Dutch surveillance and Anglo-Dutch cooperation, he ended up in a maximum security prison for six years.

21 This investment was apparently disliked by the competition, which fired two grenades at the building. They failed to explode.

- The Dutch hash wholesaler, who had already invested in the garage mentioned above, also took over an international legitimate telephone sex line (the amount of money was not recorded, but the IRS estimated it at €7 million). This company went bankrupt due to over-optimistic management.
- Of the two Dutch hash dealers, father and son, the father invested in a corporation for the exploitation of slot machines and pubs for about €177.000 and bought two other pubs for €95.000.
- A British convict invested €352.000 in a petrol station in Turkey, though its location was not mentioned.

Reinvestment in one's own crime-enterprise

Reinvestment in their own drug-smuggling firm (apart from buying new commodities) concerned mainly methods of transportation: boats and a camper. It was not always possible to differentiate between investment for smuggling or recreation: for example, the yacht could be used for both purposes. Nevertheless, the following could be identified:

- Two Dutch transporters (the previously mentioned 'father and son' and the 'Stutterer', the biggest hash haulier in European history provided for by Abbas (De Stoop, 1998)), invested respectively €533.000 and €2.272.000 in ships. However, after some transports the Stutterer handed the boat to the captain in lieu of cash payment, avoiding the risks of detection for suspicious money transfers.
- One international trucker invested in his fleet of vans, which he hoped to legitimize one day by making a deal with the tax inspector; another transport enterprise invested €726.000 in a touring car operation.
- Three traffickers invested in sales outlets like pubs or coffee shops where, besides coffee or other drinks, the contraband could be sold under the counter; in one case the value, €90.000, could be identified.

Rainy-day provisions

This category also reflects some ambiguity and interpretation. After all, the crime-entrepreneurs do not state to the police that (part of) the observed or confiscated assets were intended as a 'pension' or a 'retirement fund'. In addition, as mentioned before, cash money hoarded at home, at friends or in a bank safe may represent a 'retirement fund' as well as working capital. There is also overlap with the categories of criminal upperworld investment: the hotel in Istanbul is established as a licit upperworld enterprise, but may function as a retirement place after a life of crime. Despite these reservations, we added all the identified savings and hoarded cash plus the real estate, which together can be considered 'capital building'.

- Nine drug entrepreneurs invested in real estate, mainly abroad, one in the Netherlands. In seven cases the countries of investment were Turkey and Morocco. To this effect the Turks exported around €6,6 million. Though the Moroccans exported €3,6 million, there was no demonstrable connexion between these money flows and identifiable real-estate investments. Only in two cases could a real-estate investment with a total value of €1 million be singled out.
- As already stated, the hoarded cash and the money deposited in bank accounts can represent 'capital building', though it is possible that (part of) it might eventually be used for further criminal activities. In nine cases bank accounts in the Netherlands were identified, of which in eight cases the amount of money was determined. In two cases the account was empty or contained little assets. The offenders in six remaining cases had accounts amounting to €463.000. Three of them, with a value of €116.000 also had a foreign bank account.

  In eighteen cases there were foreign bank accounts with a total of €14.604.000, the major part of which was located in Turkey and Morocco: €3.637.000 was exported to Morocco and €5.831.000 to Turkey.
- In three cases, in which Dutch nationals were involved, the offenders bought and sold stocks and shares to the value of €3.138.000.

Lifestyle

The court files were less informative about the lifestyle of the crime-entrepreneurs than we expected. Maybe the investigators did not always think the ways of spending interesting enough to record or learned only from informants about much of the spending. For example, rumours about expensive redecoration of a home, which cost an unspecified fortune. (This lifestyle enhancement is noted in other European jurisdictions also.) Despite this limitation, lavish spending could be deduced from a substantial number of cases, though less or rather, less systematic, than has been stated by Van Duyne (2000). In addition showing off, or refraining from such a display, is a matter of choice, which may depend on various factors. There is the social circle of the crime-entrepreneur and his assessment of the usefulness or the risks of displaying conspicuous spending, as well as personality factors that one should not underestimate, without necessarily subscribing to the general criminological model of offenders as short-run hedonists with poor self-discipline. One of the Moroccan hash-wholesalers, who allegedly had invested heavily in Morocco (a fish-processing factory among others), complained that he could not live according to his considerable means in the Netherlands as he knew that he would attract police attention. Likewise a few other ethnic crime-entrepreneurs allegedly lived a parsimonious life in the Netherlands or in the UK, while going on a spree as soon as they were in their home country.

Otherwise we meet here an abundance of forms of spending: beauty and health farms and expenses for plastic surgery for girlfriends; horses for daughters, (soft) loans to friends and acquaintances; precious objects (crystal, jewellery); an occasional piece of very expensive antique (such as a clock costing €160.000, which may also be interpreted as an investment). Altogether, valuables and expenses for house decoration and lifestyle to the amount of €1.205.000 were identified. To this should be added the expenses for cars, boats and expensive dwellings,[22] insofar as these should not be allocated instead to the other categories of spending. After all, boats and cars may be used as smuggling transports, while collections of jewellery, objects of art and precious metal (including gold, that commodity favoured especially in the Middle East and the Indian subcontinent) can also be classified as hoarded 'nest eggs'.

When we leave the identified means of smuggling aside, the following expenses for 'rolling and floating stock' were determined: ships: €1.992.000; cars: €762.000. The high figure for the ships is for more than 50 per cent accounted for by the hash enterprise of the 'Stutterer': his three yachts were valued at €1.102.000 and within his small circle, sometimes changed ownership, which made it difficult to allocate them to just one offender. One Turkish XTC trader bought a Cessna aeroplane for about €200.000 which proved to be impossible to sell due to the absence of the required logbook. It should be noted that in seven cases the files mentioned that the offenders possessed one or more cars, though without mentioning any value.

Summarizing the financial and economic facets of the interactions of the 'big earners' with the upperworld, we find some tokens of corruptive permeation, of which only one can be considered truly serious. The others did not go much further than attempts. Economically they remained within traditional and socially adjacent circles: catering, real estate, sports clubs, flashy 'rolling and floating stock', in which they could display their wives coming from or going to the beauty farm or plastic surgery. This representation may be considered a cliché, though it must be admitted that more often than not – with some remarkable exceptions – this very wealthy 'subpopulation' lived up to this stereotype.

Comparison with other research findings, like those of Suendorff (2001), are difficult to make, because of differences in methodology. For example the forty cases described by Suendorff are composed of drug as well as fraud cases, though the author does not indicate with every separate example in which category it belongs. However, even if fraud cases are included, Suendorff's description of the economic conduct displayed does not deviate

22 Not all dwellings for personal use were obtained from the illicit profits. Sometimes the house was bought by means of a normal mortgage, perhaps to satisfy any financial investigation that might arise or to indicate normality to a court.

in most cases from that of the Dutch sample investigated (Van Duyne, 2003). The same applies to the comparison with the 'typologies' described in the annual reports of the secretariat of the FATF: with a few rare exceptions (which serve as worst-case exemplars for 'what can happen') known economic penetration in western Europe by drug entrepreneurs remains shallow. This tells us nothing about other types of crime-entrepreneur or about patterns in other countries where displays of ostentatious wealth may be less problematic in terms of attracting law enforcement attention. However, these lie outside the scope of this study.

Drug money and legal entities

Even if wealthy drug entrepreneurs may not display much economic ambition to exploit their large financial potential towards the upperworld economy, they still may have an interest in the legal and other professions, and in corporate entities of the upperworld, for various business objectives. Might these constitute the vulnerabilities through which the drug entrepreneurs eventually 'penetrate' the economy? After all, if they do not have an economic 'dream' and acumen, they have the money to hire experts as 'facilitators', as is often asserted by police officers and prosecutors. Therefore we also scored the extent to which the wealthy drug entrepreneurs displayed this assumed 'brain hiring' conduct.

The drug entrepreneurs investigated used legal entities for the following functions:

- *The regular production of merchandise*: This function is only found with one enterprise which grew cannabis plants alongside flowers. The nursery was a regular firm with a legitimate output, but financially the cannabis production proved more rewarding, while the bookkeeping could be used to co-mingle the various expenses and sources of revenue.

  The other cannabis nurseries delegated or spread the production process to smaller clandestine units in private dwellings and did not work with such a cover. Nevertheless, they still used a legal entity for:
- *The sales outlet*: In the Netherlands sales outlets in the cannabis market are invariably coffee shops. Such firms had the legal status of a partnership.
- *Transport covers*: Four wholesalers, hauling large cargoes, required corporations for importing legitimate goods used as cover and also for exporting the money. This applied to the cocaine wholesalers importing a load of coal, and three hashish exporters, one hiding the contraband in butter, the second (the really 'global' salesman, the Stutterer) putting his ocean-going vessels in the name of various corporations, and the third entrepreneur running a loss-making touring car company as a cover for drug transports.

- *Money-management*: For the management of crime-money (not money-laundering in the comprehensive meaning) some, but not all, drug entrepreneurs used corporations. Shipping the purchase price back to Colombia; making money available for the purchase of transportation; re-investments in the above mentioned touring car firm.
- *Investment and laundering*: Some of the crime-money was invested in corporations, which act was not always accompanied by laundering constructions, like the moderate investment in a sport school and a pool/billiard centre by two Dutch hash-entrepreneurs. Investment *and* laundering through legal entities could be observed with the higher-level dealers, for example by putting assets in the name of (foreign) corporations. The nationality of the corporations and the international scope of the financial relations appeared to be pragmatically determined by geographical conditions of the money flow, which appeared not to be so 'global' as the FATF legend tells us. Some Turkish wholesalers established Turkish corporations; Dutchmen used Belgian and British limited companies.[23] In four cases a larger geographical routing could be observed: one Turkish offender channelled part of his millions through Romania to corporations in Germany; the English offender also used Caribbean off-shore companies; and two Dutch hash wholesalers also used some financial routes through foreign legal entities.
- *Crime instrument*: Only in one case was the legal entity itself the very instrument of crime commission, not for the beneficial owner's drug business, but for the sideline job of long firm (bankruptcy) fraud.

These observations do not support the image of a (threatening) systematic abuse of the legal corporate facilities of the upperworld. Nor do they lend support to a systematic 'expert shopping' to hire facilitators' skills and brains, though in three cases some valuable professional support was lent. In one case (hashish and BMK traffic) a clerk of a law firm provided support in establishing legal persons. A second case concerned a close-knit group of hash traders, who invested extensively in real estate, being supported by a professional real-estate agent, who was their friend for many years.[24] The

23 In this as well as in other research it is interesting to observe that Dutch criminals trying to manage their crime-moneys in Belgium remain north of the Flemish–French language boundary or move on to Luxembourg. Perhaps their lack of knowledge of French makes them feel uneasy. Also laundering has its socially determining factors.

24 As a matter of fact this was one of the few cases in which a very sophisticated money-laundering procedure was displayed. The constructions reflected a fair knowledge of civil law clauses, for example the avoidance of managerial liability (stretching back three years), and complicated multi-bank mortgage constructions, involving Swedish and German banks. The prosecution settled the financial aspects of this case out of court.

hashish wholesaler, the Stutterer, was supported by a shady wealthy veteran money-manager, who the first author observed in previous investigations (Van Duyne, 1997). In some other European countries such as the UK, research indicates the use of lawyers for various schemes, especially the use of clients' accounts as conduits for transfers from offshore companies (Middleton and Levi, 2003). However in those British cases that have been detected, there is little indication of the use of such clients' accounts to deposit large quantities of cash. What is more common is that 'pre-washed' funds are wired into the solicitors who, sometimes knowingly and sometimes naively, allow themselves to be used as quasi-banks when their clients get them to purchase real estate or companies, transfer funds to foreign currency accounts and other acts that seem quite normal to banks when performed by solicitors, bypassing suspicions. At least in cases of which the authorities are aware, elaborate schemes are more commonly part of large frauds such as tax evasion and high-yield investment scams, plus mortgage frauds committed by the lawyers themselves. Whether in a tightly knit group or as a looser network, though, some crime-entrepreneurs are involved in combining these types of activity, and it may be difficult to know the sources of the funds other than that they are probably from some generic crimes.

5.3 The hard core of the scare of drug money

The empirical evidence gathered and elaborated in this chapter provides no conclusive answer to the question of the amount of the drug money or its dangerousness. It rather suggests that the grounds for fear of harm by drugs money *per se* are not as well established as is claimed. In the absence of further evidence, there is thus either self-deception or deception of the public in repeated assertions that have not been evidenced.

We have already mentioned the gap between the proclaimed seriousness of the drug and money issue, on the one hand, and the meagre law enforcement efforts devoted to clarify the extent and nature of this issue, on the other. This gap is not restricted to the drug issue only. In the area of fraud we observe a similar recurring of raising the alarm, while little is done in terms of quantitative information management to obtain insight into the menacing phenomenon (Van Duyne, 1999). A contributory factor to the absence of evidence-led policy may be the normative tradition of the legal and allied professions, in which statistical discipline is valued poorly compared with other disciplines like economics or public health policy. For example, if there is a public health alarm, all professional routines appear to be available for a quick epidemiological survey and a follow-up statistical programme, whether it concerns influenza or a rare disease like SARS. Within the law enforcement area – ranging from the police to the departments of Justice and Internal Affairs – we have repeatedly experienced the low interest in and valuation of quantitative information management (internationally), at least until recently in the UK.[25] It is important to understand this background in order to understand the easy spreading of fear, in our case the fear of drug money, which is not countered by empirical evidence or translated into a rational fact-finding assessment.[26]

Fear and facts

The fear of drug money should not be brushed aside as a hallucination or a cynical mind manipulation of policy makers. It is firmly based on the fear of psychoactive substances and on the fear of social domination by evil groups. This has been elaborated in the first chapter. However, there is more to it, as the story has somewhat of the characteristic of an old saga: much narration around a truthful core.

The truthful core of the saga of the threat of the drug money is a simple one: a large-scale criminal drug economy combined with weak and/or corrupt governance. In a number of cases, this has been compounded by the foreign policy requirements of covert operations. In this regard, there is nothing special about the role of drug money which differentiates it from the illegal wealth accumulated in any other criminal or unregulated market. Let us look at some historical and contemporary examples, for which we had to look outside Europe.

A properly documented example is the case of Colombia. Without pretending to write a concise history of Colombia, we find here the combination of a historically badly governed country, a high level of tolerance of violence, an industrious entrepreneurial class, a smuggling tradition and a geographically well-situated position with coastlines facing the Caribbean and the Pacific Ocean (Visser, 1991; Thoumi, 1995; Crandall, 2002). These propitious circumstances accelerated the growth of the Colombian foreign drug trade. The cocaine boom of the 1980s was preceded by extensive marijuana smuggling to the main market, the US. This did not (yet) turn Colombia into a 'narco state', though it already raised the concern of the US even without the later association with communist insurgents (FARC). However, the success of the American-induced marijuana-eradication programme and the increasing demand for cocaine in the US caused a shift to the better yielding cash crop and related industry: coca leaves and its processing into cocaine (Perkins and Gilbert, 1987). The pioneering

25 Emphasizing the need for quantitative fact-finding was usually met with little interest, if not a sullen resistance expressed in the repeatedly asked questions like: 'Why should we know all that?', or: 'If we know, does that help the detective or prosecutor in his daily tasks?', or worse: 'If all that becomes known I will have to answer a lot of nasty questions'.

26 It remains to be seen whether the higher seriousness which has greeted the struggle against terrorist finance, will generate more systematic data analysis over the longer term.

Lehderer, Escobar and García did not detect the open doors to their main North American customers, but did find out the efficient sneaky ways through the Caribbean, after which the shipments became seriously wholesale (Strong, 1995; Sabbag, 2003). The ever-increasing return flow of drug income saturated the economies of Colombia, as well as its neighbouring countries which were the main providers of the raw material. This flow of drug money reinforced the already existing Colombian tragedy of rampant corruption, civil war (Visser, 1991) and local oppression of the farmers by either death squads or the revolutionary movements (Verbeek, 2001).

Apart from the unsavoury characters it attracted, the enlarged smuggling economy brought mixed blessings. Undoubtedly the buying power of wide circles of the population was increased, though this seldom if ever benefited the local markets in legitimate products. As with traditional elites in South America, the newly acquired buying power was used for foreign luxury articles, like household articles, clothes and cars. This increased imports, creating trading deficits and a shortage in import tax revenues, because within such a smuggling economy it is 'normal' to use the smuggling routes both ways (Kalmanovitz, 1991; Verbeek, 2001). Neither the preference for foreign prestige import articles nor many forms of wasteful investments by the drug elites helped the development of the national economy or local industries.[27] The huge investments in real estate and large stretches of landed property were often ruinous to city dwellers and farmers alike, who were priced out of the market. The drug elite itself consisted not just of wealthy entrepreneurial ruffians like Escobar, but also of a new well-educated 'drug bourgeoisie' which challenged the old Colombian bourgeoisie. This challenge brought violent encounters as well as a symbiosis, motivated by the forced choice between 'lead or silver'.

However, not all drug barons squandered their capital, which could only partly be absorbed by the local economy anyhow. Having become large landowners they kept not only fancy, exotic animals, but continued their entrepreneurial conduct. For example, they introduced improvements to cattle rearing and to the meat industry, which had a stabilizing effect on meat prices (Kalmanovitz, 1991). As only part of the money could be turned into local production factors and luxury items, much of the drug money remained in foreign banks. It is difficult to state that these institutions were victimized, as they did not stash the money in their vaults, but did what any proper bank should do: made money from money, to the delight of the

27 The UNDCP 1997 report on the economic and social consequences of the drug trade points at this one-sided concentration in relation to the 'Dutch disease', which consisted of the Dutch policy of expanding the welfare state made possible by the sudden large income from the discovered reserves of natural gas in the 1970s. As the report refers to the Dutch gas production, it is clear that this economic one-sidedness does not pertain only to the drug boom.

borrowers and shareholders. Last but not least, an undetermined part of the huge circulation of drug dollars in Colombia, as in the whole Andes region, was used to pay off the high foreign debt to European and American banks.

A somewhat more elaborated account is given by De Mas (2001) in his description of the economic development in northern Morocco, the Rif region, which is the main provider of the kif or hash consumed in Europe. From a poor mountainous and unruly area it has grown into a wealthy province due to the export of hashish, the smuggled import of consumer goods and – last but not least – the licit repatriated funds from 'guest workers'' savings in north-western Europe. Real-estate prices have soared, the rural population has moved to the new towns and the three old towns (Tanger, Tetouan and Oujda), which have expanded tremendously. The power structure has not remained unaffected either: authoritarian, arbitrary and corrupt, the threshold separating the old power elite from the new 'smuggling bourgeoisie' was easily levelled and replaced by a profitable symbiosis. Comparing these findings with the documentation on the economic and social aspects of the drug economy in other jurisdictions, compiled by the UNDCP in 1997, reveals little contradictory information, though the statistics it contains on laundering are debatable (see UNDCP, 1997; Keh, 1996).

In Morocco as well as in Colombia, the power of the new 'drug bourgeoisie' was not unassailable. The influential, more 'bourgeois' Cali 'cartel' was incarcerated too after the demise of Pablo Escobar in 1993, though their lot was softened by the privileges they could buy in the prison (Verbeek, 2001). The bloody war between the Colombian government (assisted by paramilitaries not without an interest in control over drug production and distribution) and the neo-Marxist FARC still goes on. The erstwhile Moroccan King Hassan II clamped down in 1993 on the northern drug barons as soon as they threatened to destabilize the equilibrium of the region by arms dealing and engaging in hard drug trafficking.[28] These successes did not stem the tide of drugs, though.

Looking at the histories of these two regions (which may be complemented with other drug-producing regions), there is an undeniable kernel of truth in drug money sagas. However, it should be noticed that there is nothing peculiar about it: the illicit profits of the drug exports was just one aspect of a widespread underground smuggling economy, though it proved to be the ultimate bonanza deriving its impact from its massive scale and its artificial price-wedge created by illegality. In addition to its illegality, its economic

28 Another reason was foreign pressure combined with financial aid. However, as soon as the central authorities were no longer challenged, the hashish export continued unabated to satisfy the European consumers.

one-sidedness should also be considered negatively, in which regard it does not differ from 'legal bonanzas' combined with bad governance, like the oil booms in Angola and Nigeria, bringing corruption and criminality in their wake too. To the indigenous Nigerian there may be little difference between drug money and oil money: he will only get a pittance from the large profits, most of which leave the country for trustworthy western banks anyhow.

The above elaborated examples may be considered a 'far away' scene, not really touching the European industrialized countries, except for the import of drugs and the export of currency. Whether that is disadvantageous in terms of causing a kind of (criminal) trade deficit is unknown. Despite all its momentous concern and monumental figures in terms of global turnover, the FATF has never addressed this question. In one ironic sense, it redresses the chronic trade deficit of the drug-producing countries with the affluent drug-consuming countries. However, part of the exported currency may be spent again on luxurious consumer goods imported from the consumer countries, on which import taxes may be evaded, indicating the lack of need for legitimation of capital.

Apart from that question, there are other ways in which the drug economy did affect the Western world: it has been a steady accompanying factor in (cold war) foreign policy matters as we have seen in Chapter 2. The expenses of covert warfare in Indochina, first by the French and subsequently by the US forces, were (partly) covered by the yields of the opium traffic, as the secret services needed resources outside the control of the French Parliament or the US Congress (McCoy, 2000; 2003). This formula was (with variations) repeated in the Afghanistan war in the 1980s and in the Iran–Contra affair (Chambliss, 1994; Scott and Marshall, 1998). In the weighing of the interests of the war against left-wing or communist insurgents and the 'War on Drugs', foreign policy interests usually tipped the balance, while the locally generated drug money provided the intelligence agencies with the financial latitude for its operations. While saving Western budgets, the real sufferers from the application of the drug money were the countries that were the battlefields of the left- and right-wing ideologies, and those victims of predatory crimes in the West motivated by the need to obtain money to pay for overpriced illegal drugs.

Absorption and bad governance

The above examples from recent history can be considered the factual basis for a reasonable concern about drug money. Granted, there should be more concern about the ill effects of the drug money on the fragile economies of the production countries than on the industrialized world. Though the industrialized countries raised the alarm, their economies are more diversified and better equipped to absorb the often floating reserves from the underground economy. Despite the 1990 picture of an economy allegedly on the verge of succumbing to the evil of crime-money, very little has happened since. The anti-laundering and recovery weaponry is practically globally in place, but the recovery squads are almost everywhere as slow in producing results as they are defective in providing proper analysable statistical insight (Kilchling, 2002). While the drug markets continued to thrive, there has been a gradual decline of the drug price, with the exception of hashish (Paoli, 2000) and financial scandals involving economic losses are normally white-collar matters with no drug money involved (Van Duyne, 1999; Levi, 1997; Levi and Pithouse, forthcoming). One can say: '*Im Westen nichts neues*' ('All quiet on the Western Front'). On the other hand, given the drug consumption habits of the industrialized world, we have to face the prospect of a continuous flow of drug money to the production countries, with the exception of designer drugs. What negative financial-impact scenarios do we have?

The previous section described some negative-impact scenarios in Colombia and Morocco. Because of the widespread popular involvement, these countries are sometimes called narco-democracies (though the denotation democracy does not apply to Morocco). To what extent are these economies 'addicted' to drug revenues? This question may presuppose a too gloomy and static picture of the dynamics of the (criminal) economy as much depends on other economic and social developments. Various examples may be put forward to counter a too pessimistic view. The most recent concerns some of the coca-producing countries like Bolivia. The share of the cocaine proceeds of the Gross Domestic Product of the Andes countries has declined as their economies expanded and the price of cocaine fell (UNDCP, 1997). This does not mean that the drug trade has passed. The trafficking continues unabated alongside the US-militarized *Plan Colombia*, allocating $860,3 million of aid to Colombia (Crandall, 2002): 60 per cent for military assistance and 14 per cent for police support. Many farmers are still dependent on coca cultivation and offer motivated resistance against government campaigns to eradicate their crop, like the farmers in Bolivia. However, this may rather be interpreted as a failure to provide a profitable substitute cash crop than as a drug revenue addiction.[29] How much drug money has been absorbed by the legitimate economy remains unknown. There are no detailed

29 The history of the crop-substitution programmes is as sad as that of the 'War on Drugs'. In 1990 the coffee prices plummeted because of the lapsing of the coffee and cocoa agreement in 1989, mainly due to US pressure. Many farmers who had been persuaded to cultivate this crop instead of coca, suffered economic hardship, got deeply into debt and were even evicted. For other substitution crops, started enthusiastically, there were no buyers. The way out of this misery of debt was to cultivate the only crop for which there was a market: coca. It goes without saying that this history did not contribute to make the US 'War on Drugs' particularly popular with the local population (Oomen, 1991).

reports of these economies cracking under the weight of drug money, though a substantial part of these illegal incomes finds its way to the paramilitary militias and their left-wing opponents. Maybe – within certain boundaries – economies are sufficiently flexible to cope with the existence of a drug economy.

Another historic example of a country successfully coping with an equivalent of drug money is the American 'real life' experiment with the total prohibition of alcohol from 1919–1933. If the Andean countries have been called 'narco-democracies', would the US in this period deserve the description 'alco-democracy'? There are differences and similarities. The role of the narco-traders in the rule of the Andean countries was intermittently far greater than that of the US bootleggers. On the other hand, during the Prohibition there was widespread law breaking, the situation of the country was characterized by a similar full-scale disregard of the law, corruption and the rise of an aggressive professional class of criminal entrepreneurs, which encompassed more than 'La Cosa Nostra'. The illegal booze trade was not only a matter of the criminal gangs, which entered the annals of 'organized crime', but also of many normal citizens and not only in their role of consumers (Gerritsen, 1993). Along the long Canadian–US border, alcohol smuggling had become as common as butter smuggling between Belgium and the Netherlands after the Second World War or the present cigarette traffic between continental Europe and the UK. Apart from professional smuggling, the US home production of alcohol was enormous and destined to quench the domestic thirst as well as to be exploited professionally by crime-entrepreneurs. Home brewing was often part of a putting-out system, reducing the risks for the crime-entrepreneur if one or a few such breweries were closed down.

The intriguing questions for our investigation concern the amount and whereabouts of the 'alcohol money'. Analogous to the drug money questions, we may ask: how much 'alcohol money' was flowing around – if that could be identified at all – and where did it remain after the abolition of the Vollstead Act? There is little empirical evidence to answer this question. Perhaps most of the surpluses of 'borderline' criminal bootleggers were quietly absorbed in the American economy: some well-connected wholesale bootleggers settled their differences with the IRS (Abadinsky, 1991; Fox, 1989). However, the crime-families, who could provide employment to the young aggressive bootleggers, did gain enormously. They had learned how to handle upperworld trading connections and, last but not least, had amassed much money. Whether all these assets were turned into positive production factors is unknown. The saga of Meyer Lansky gives us a glimpse of fruitful investments in gambling and other more or less traditional criminal investment areas (Lacey, 1991). Indeed, the 'world of Meyer Lansky' is a model for the combination of crime-money and bad, corruptive governance (Lyman and Potter, 2000). It teaches us that we cannot sketch out any crime-money doom scenario without taking into account the upperworld environment: the morality of the political elite and of the public administration. See also Thoumi's (1995) analysis of the state of delegitimation of Colombian society preceding the emergence of the drug market, which was exacerbated by the drug trade.

Given these elaborations, what should really be the object of the concern about drug money? Of course, the existence of unaccounted 'black' money, like all revenues derived from crime, should be sufficient reason to halt and reduce it because of its illegality, which is mainly a moral issue. It may have also a destabilizing impact, though that depends on other circumstances. It is a commonplace that most countries have experienced at some stage of their histories a period of a thriving black economy, for example stemming from times of unrest and/or from bad laws and inefficient (fiscal) law enforcement. However, most economies have shown a remarkable resilience: improvements of governance were often accompanied by recovery and successful absorption of unrecorded crime-monies. Maybe the real object of concern should be the symbiosis of bad government, living on the proceeds of crime, and a structural interest in doing nothing about it.

6 The craft of laundering and the counter-reaction

Before being partially replaced by the even more fearful term 'terrorist finance' (Levi, 2003b), the phrase 'money-laundering' had generated an emotive value of its own, especially if connected to the phrase 'organized crime' (Van Duyne, 1998b). We have already recounted the image of the world swamped by drug money stemming from an evil industry. According to the (erroneous) traditional UN claims, the global trade in illegal drugs exceeds that of iron and steel (see Reuter and Greenfield, 2001).[1] Against this threat, law enforcement agencies have been mobilized world wide, though more in rhetoric than in resources. Irrespective of the validity of the claims concerning the real volume of the crime-money or the urgency of the threat, the FATF did succeed in cajoling (or coercing) and imposing its recommendations on virtually all the industrialized countries of the world and non-industrial off-shore financial centres. It would be a mistake to see this as a crude imperial venture by the G7. Some measures were welcomed by some public- and private-sector elements in most countries who were in favour of greater social responsibility in commerce (see Levi, 2003a). However, it would be an even greater mistake to believe that these measures would have been arrived at as a purely voluntary arrangement. The most important elements of the recommendations have been put into place. Among others, these concern: the penalization of money-laundering, the recording of account-holder and account details, and obligation to pass these on to properly constituted requests for mutual legal assistance; the training of financial institutions and other regulated staff with a duty to report 'suspicious transactions' to the authorities;[2] and the

1 Reuter and Greenfield (2001) compared the trade flow of illegal drugs with that of most agricultural products to conclude that the drug trade remains approximately within the range of licit agricultural products: about $25 billion.

2 Gold and Levi (1994) sought to persuade the authorities to change this terminology to 'suspected transactions' on the grounds that this more fairly represented the cognitive process. This proposal had no effect on the use of the term that misleadingly gets us to think of these transactions as inherently suspicious, making the enforcement yield from them even less impressive than they would otherwise be.

establishment of properly trained financial intelligence units to deal with those reports.

Some recommendations, which went too much against the interests of the (Western) financial institutions, were not implemented, though. For example, it was recommended to monitor the cash flows between jurisdictions, which no member country heeded. The first author was privately told that the banks considered this information about the cross-border cash money flows too sensitive, though such reservations were never stated in public. This recommendation was either not referred to, silently passed over as 'not interesting' or considered 'not our responsibility'. The research of Van Duyne and De Miranda (1999, 2001) demonstrated that this show of non-interest or non-responsibility was ill-founded or even irresponsible. Mapping the cash flow between the British Isles, the Netherlands and Belgium, and the related currency exchange, revealed an interesting pattern which reflected the 'criminal deficit' in the drug market between the drug-exporting Netherlands and the importing UK and Ireland. Whereas hardly any Scottish banknote is found south of Hadrian's Wall, there were millions of them offered for exchange in the Netherlands and Belgium. Since the UK remains for the time being outside the Eurozone, this is still the case. The statistical data also showed the interaction between the law and the crime-entrepreneurs. At the beginning of the 1990s, the Dutch and UK traders still felt safe to change money in the Netherlands. After the police had clamped down on the bureaux de change in Amsterdam, many 'money movers' went to Belgium to change their currency there (Van Duyne, 1995). Whether or not anti-laundering enforcement actually was weaker in Belgium than in the Netherlands, criminals *perceived* that it was safer to cross the border. Despite that, most of them were smart enough to reduce their risks by sending an errand boy, often on the unemployed register (Van Duyne and De Miranda, 1999), to do the job.

This example illustrates the interaction between the fight against drug money and the nature of the 'money management' of the drug-entrepreneurs. The question is whether the crime-entrepreneurs (not only the drug traffickers) effectively learned from the law enforcement efforts and became more sophisticated, more international and more probing a 'global' scale to launder their ill-gotten profits. We find many statements of this nature and much rhetoric to underpin the necessity for more severe law enforcement. However, the facts remain scarce. It is still uncertain whether and to what extent this interaction is a matter of perception instead of facts, or reflects a genuine spiral of law enforcement measures and criminal sophistication. The results of the research discussed in the previous chapter do not provide much support for the sophisticated globalization of money-laundering on the part of western European drug traffickers. One key question that arises from that is whether this is the result of our poor intelligence-collection policies and capacities, or whether there is less need for laundering sophistication than is generally imagined. The assumption that improvements in enforcement information management may have driven laundering into such sophistication that it escapes detection altogether, may lead to the strange outcome that we believe its existence because it cannot be observed anymore. We think we should leave this variation on *credo quia absurdum* of Tertullian to the realm of religion.

6.1 The law unleashed

The drive for drug money – and in its wake, for all proceeds of crime – did not arise overnight. A number of tributaries came together in the main stream, which after the late 1980s became the ever-broadening global anti-money-laundering policy. These tributaries mixed real and perceived threats and included:

- the enormous expansion of the drug markets in the 1980s, mainly caused by US cocaine imports
- the huge capital flow from the US to other jurisdictions, particularly offshore banks and tax or financial-secrecy havens, much to the dismay of the Internal Revenue Service
- a criminal asset-stripping drive, stimulated by the activation of US racketeering legislation (RICO) passed in 1970, but shaped particularly by the Presidential Commission on Organized Crime established under the Reagan Presidency
- European 'policy-learning' from the US and concern about the new threat from post-communist central and eastern Europe, plus some specific national concerns, normally connected with the growth of the drugs trade. The fear of organized criminals 'buying power bridgeheads' with crime-money was voiced. The protection of the 'integrity of the financial institutions' was put forward as the 'legal good' ('Rechtsgut') to be shielded.
- the policy perspective of 'hitting the criminal where it hurts the most' gained increasing ground, combining populist punitiveness, restorative justice and incapacitation justifications.

All these tributaries fed the mainstream of the anti-laundering policy, leading to the establishment of a system of 'financial Maginot Lines' and a 'Locarno Treaty' of international cooperation.

The pernicious role of crime-money in any constitutional state is certainly no novelty. Despite that, many jurisdictions, not the least the US, have actually learned to live with it, albeit somewhat uneasily. In many (allegedly) rigged elections, ranging from mayors to presidents, the 'mob' is said to have contributed handsomely to the re-election coffers (Peterson, 1983; Lyman and Potter, 2000). The 'mob' was not the only group who tried to exert financial influence to get 'their' man in high offices. Legitimate entrepreneurs likewise illegally invested heavily in election campaigns. Their donations did not stem from criminal funds, but were 'white' money, which had to be diverted through shady alleys or become 'black' before it could surface again from a 'white' source (Liddick, 2000). One may call it 'perverted' laundering, to which we have referred already in the context of some leading European statesmen.[3] Granted, that is not considered fashionable, and 'something had to be done against such an abuse', but in this field the full weight of the law and law enforcement was never put into place, let alone felt. The international bodies concerned with money-laundering and corruption hitherto – for example, the FATF and OECD – have put political finance in the 'too difficult' category. It was the worrying upswing of the drug market and the ensuing staggering flows of money to a few drug-production countries, which brought American policy makers into action.

The drug or scare wave

The fight against crime-money was not an American innovation, as the Italian legislature took the lead by penalizing laundering in 1978, four years later strengthened with recovery laws of illicitly obtained advantages and objects which related to the predicate crime (Paoli, 2002a). These laws were part of the general fight against the *Brigate Rossi*, the Mafia and Mafia-type associations. Though this penalization was an important step, it had still little international impact. At that time, most countries thought they had little to fear from the Mafia or Mafia moneys. The wave of panic would spread later over Europe after the Mafia-killings of the judges Falcone and Borsellino in the early 1990s. Investigators started to collect information, and some scattered Mafia presence was observed in southern France, Walloon Belgium and Germany, raising huge alarm (Fijnaut, 1993; Van Dijk, 1993).[4] However, it was not such Mafia fears, but the concern about the steep influx of drugs in the US which gave the fight against the related drug money and the laundering thereof its *international* drive from the mid-1980s onwards (Levi, 2003a).

3 The author Liddick (2000) qualifies the illegal funding in the US presidential elections as 'laundering', which should also apply to the handling of illegal funds by the cronies of erstwhile German Chancellor Kohl. Actually this qualification does not apply when the money does not originate from law breaking.

4 The debate on organized crime in north-west Europe was very much fanned by the supposed threat of the Italian Mafia, which was 'stretching its tentacles' all over Europe. The killings of the judges and other atrocities intensified the fear of the Mafia in Germany and the Netherlands (Van Duyne, 1995; 2002). Actually, there were (and still are) Mafiosi doing business in Germany and occasionally the Netherlands, but their presence is thin and widespread, not presenting a build-up of power. The German BKA report on the Mafia in 1993 revealed little evidence of Mafia importance and remained secret.

Was there compelling evidence to warrant this new US and subsequent world-wide mission? Without declaring the whole drug issue as a matter of a Schopenhauerian '*Wille und Vorstellung*' (will and imagination), the existing data reflect too much ambiguity for an objective and compelling deduction of a continuous and overwhelming drug threat and related drug money menace. The sources of data are diverse, which makes it difficult to amalgamate the pieces into a coherent pattern. But this incoherent diversity raises doubts about the validity of the imagery of society under siege, to which controlling the money trail was a purported solution. On the one hand, there is the undeniable accumulation of wealth by a small number of drug 'barons' in Latin America or the Far East, by politically well-connected middlemen in the Balkans, and of more modest wealth by crime-entrepreneurs in Europe and the US. On the other hand, there are the long-term users' trends surveyed by research institutes like the US National Institute on Drug Abuse (NIDA) as well as the price changes in drugs. Briefly summarized, the following trends are observed in the US, mainly based on the surveys of the NIDA and the UN reports.

In the first place there are the prevalence figures for secondary school students, which reveal an interesting steady downward trend for all illicit drugs from 1979 till 1992. After that year prevalence increased again only to level off after 1997. Interestingly the prevalence data of drug *use* do not correlate with the *perceived availability* data, but inversely with the valuation by students of the health risks of drug use. The availability figures for marijuana remained more or less the same from 1976 onwards. The same applies to the availability of crack in the time span of 1986–2001, though that of cocaine powder dropped somewhat. Only the use and availability of MDMA (ecstasy), for which only recent data are available, increased sharply since its recording in 1995 (though recent UK data suggest a falling-off in use).

Though these figures may seem reassuring, they have to be projected in an explanatory framework. Rasmussen and Benson (1994), discussing the period before 1994, commented that the findings concern interviewees in *households*. Persons who are not part of a stable household may be heavy users, causing a biased distribution of the prevalence of consumption. Despite this gap, the number of more frequent users in the surveys increased slightly between 1985 and 1990. It is estimated that about 11 per cent of the users account for about 60 per cent of the cocaine use (Rasmussen and Benson, 1994). This may be reflected in the sharp increase in the number of hospital emergency-room cases. On the other hand, the *daily use* figures of the twelfth-graders followed (with lower percentages) the same trend.

Comparing these historical figures with the law enforcement 'war efforts', it seems to be a plausible hypothesis that the use of drugs in the US has less to do with these warlike exploits, including the fight against drug money, than with the users' perception of the risks involved. The perceived availability did not reflect drug war successes either, as illustrated in Table 7.

Table 7 Long-term trends in thirty-day prevalence of various drugs for twelfth-graders

	1975	*1980*	*1985*	*1990*	*1995*	*2000*
Any illicit drugs	31	37	30	17	24	25
Marijuana/hash	27	34	26	14	21	22
Hallucinogenics	5	4	3	2	4	3
Cocaine	2	5	7	2	2	2
Heroin	4	2	3	2	6	7
Amphetamine	8	12	7	4	4	5

Source: Adapted from: http/monitoringthefuture.org

Despite methodological comments, these findings seem to convey (by way of plausible hypothesis) a 'good message': education and insight appear to have a stronger effect than unleashing wars. Nevertheless, it was not considered to be a reason to loosen the reins. Instead, once set in motion, the arrest rate in the US continued to rise sharply until 1989, only to decline after 1990, though remaining well above 1984, while it is on the whole negatively correlated with the downwards trend of drug-prevalence in the second half of the 1980s, when it dropped again when drug consumption increased somewhat. If the arrest rate mirrors the police efforts and the drug prevalence figures are taken as (one of) the indicators of the threat of illegal drugs against 'established society' one may tentatively conclude that the police efforts are stepped up, while the drug 'threat' varies independently: receding and returning as another fashion sets in, while remaining uncorrelated with availability.[5] The only thing which did not vary appeared to be the rhetoric, according to Rasmussen and Benson (1994).

An interesting phenomenon is the international price and production development: the price curves reveal a decline for the heroin and cocaine, while the production of opium has tripled since 1985 and the production of coca leaves more than doubled in the period 1988–1991, dropping and rising again through the first half of the 1990s. The downward trend in retail and wholesale prices for heroin and cocaine can be observed in the US as well as in Europe.

Is this combination of price development and production (declining prices and stabilizing production) an indication that the drug industry is in a slump? That would be a too hasty conclusion, in view of the availability figures mentioned above and the lack of sufficiently precise insight into the cost price structure of the chain of transactions. The few indicators suggest that the changes in the prices of drugs in the supplier countries have no

5 Mid-2002, the XTC fashion appears to have been amplified with the addition of viagra to boost the sex drive, which combination is called Sextacy.

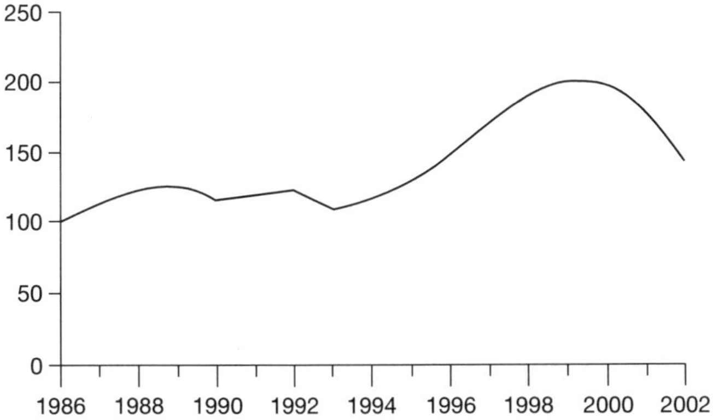

Figure 5 Development of DEA drug arrests 1986–2002
Source: Adapted from the 2003 DEA annual report

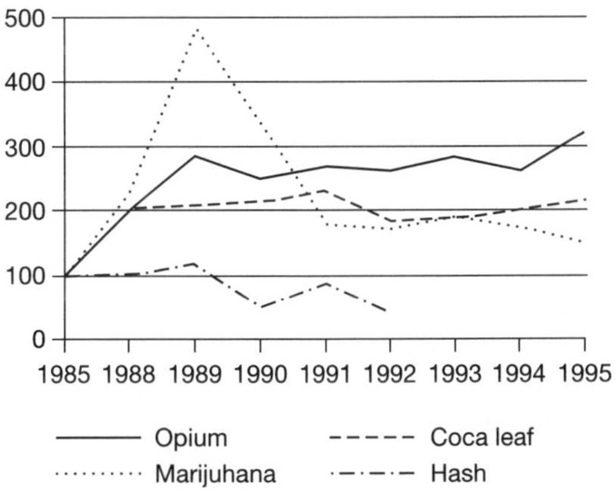

Figure 6 Illicit drug production: trends in global drugs production
Source: Adapted from annex II of the UNDCP technical series report 6: Economic and social consequences of drug abuse and illicit trafficking

direct or only a minor influence on the retail prices in the main consumer countries in Europe and America (UNDCP, 1997). The price margins between the successive chains of transactions appears to remain attractive enough to seduce ever-new 'risk takers' to try their entrepreneurial luck, as illustrated by Zaitch's (2002) overview of the cost (= income) distribution for the wholesale cocaine market.

Most interesting – if generalizable – is the big 'slice' in the costs structure of the financial risk takers, most of whom we may assume reside in the

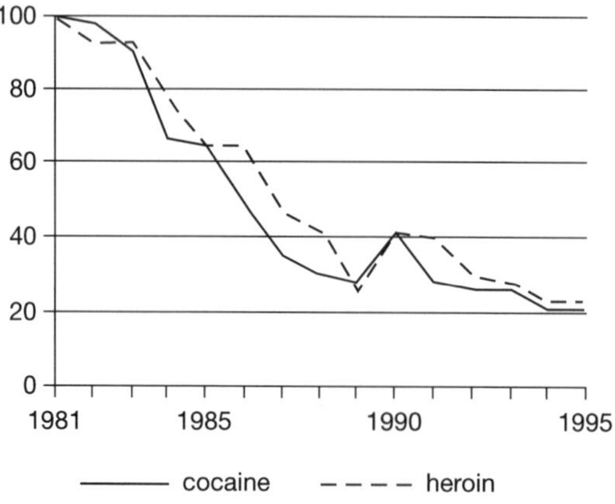

Figure 7 Development of real (inflation-adjusted) cocaine and heroin prices in the US

Source: Adapted from table XII, UNDCP technical series report 6: Economic and social consequences of drug abuse and illicit trafficking. The prices are for pure substances, deflated by US Consumer Price Index.

consumer countries. The figures may also partly reflect another economically grim reality as far as the producer countries are concerned: the prices of legitimate cash crop still lags behind the prices of poppies and cocaine plants. In the absence of more rewarding alternative opportunities, farmers continue to sow and harvest the same products and will continue to do so until the prices for drugs cash crops equal or become lower than that of the legitimate cash crops.[6] However, even if trading conditions for the latter improve, farmers still may be little interested in changing to licit crops if other conditions are not met. For example if the tenure of the land they till is insecure, they will have little incentive to spend money and efforts on crop substitution (Rasmussen and Benson, 1994). In many production countries, the land tenure for small farmers is far from settled.

Like all data about the underground economy, the figures in the previous sections have wide margins of uncertainty. There is also a huge variability over time and space, which makes it even difficult to detect national price parameters (Caulkins and Reuter, 1998). Also the price development of cannabis and the varieties of synthetic drugs are not taken into account. It seems that the prices of cannabis products have remained fairly stable (Paoli

6 The impact of this grim economic reality should not be underestimated politically: in Bolivia, one of the poorest countries of South America, the leader of the coca farmers, Evo Morales, got 21 per cent of the votes in the presidential election in 2002, just 1,5 per cent less than the liberal candidate Gonzalo Sánchez de Lozada.

Table 8 Costs for delivery of wholesale distribution in consumer markets, per kilo of cocaine

Costs	*US$*	*Destination*
Raw material	600–800	Columbian, Peruvian and Bolivian coca growers and labourers
Transport to laboratories	100	Carriers (Colombians)
Chemical precursors	200	Local and multinational chemical industry
Refining costs	200–300	Colombian cooks and labourers
Transport to consumer markets	3200	Carriers (Colombians) and other organizations (Mexicans)
Vigilance, security and bribes	500	Weapon dealers, Colombian security staff, Colombian politicians, national and foreign customs and police officers
Money-laundering	1700–3400	Intermediaries, financial advisers, banks
Other	200	Lawyers, rents, etc.
Total	6700–8700	

Source: Zaitch (2002)

et al., 2000). Reliable figures about the price developments in the field of synthetic drugs are scarce, but also in this market the price differences are interesting enough to stimulate a thriving international trade in the precursor substances and the end products.

How can we interpret these contrasting data against the background of the fear of the drug money, particularly concerning the industrialized world? It remains difficult to square the prevalent threat image with a market of diminishing market prices. Granted, the profit margins have remained attractive enough for newcomers (or experienced middle-level dealers) to replace those established wholesalers eliminated via the criminal justice process. If the costs of the drug business are rising, due to more professional transport and (sometimes) financial services, there still remains sufficient profit margin to hire those services.[7] It is even more difficult to reconcile the absence of evidence of extensive drug money investments in the industrialized world with the supposed wave of drugs and drug money. All the documented large-scale investments of drug moneys in the upperworld of legal trade and industry concern *developing* countries. However, one should seriously question how much of these hundreds of billions these countries are capable of absorbing. Perhaps only a portion? Where has the remainder of the drug

7 Keh and Farrell (1997) provide a sketch of drug trafficking against the background of ever-intensifying and cheapening transport and communication structures in the 'global village'. Despite that gloomy perspective, the technological improvement and control density may offset this trend.

money wave gone? Given this lack of evidence and coherence, we have to end inconclusively: is there a drug and corresponding money wave or is there a scare wave? The latter is clearly manifest, but the former is 'measured' mainly by scattered, frequently recycled examples in a rather artificially maintained consensus shared by law enforcement and scholars alike.[8] Indeed, a world of '*Wille und Vorstellung*' (will and imagination).

6.2 The hazy criminal response

We have already mentioned the law enforcement or criminological dogma, which states that there is a kind of arms race between the law and the criminals. According to that dogma, criminals are induced to act in an ever more sophisticated way, easily finding new loopholes and therefore always being 'ahead of the law' or reacting perfectly to the latest legal changes. Frequently this belief is put forward – together with flaws in the legislation – to explain the moderate or meagre results of the 'dirty money chase' (Kilchling, 2002) and of course, to proclaim the need for more legislation, including more police powers and more involvement of the private sector to supervise its fellow citizens.

This section will compare this thesis with the empirical evidence. It will expand on the point of the techniques of laundering and describe what kind of money-laundering conduct or money-management is actually observed. This topic will be addressed by summarizing the available data, among them the figures from the Dutch police research mentioned in Chapter 5, the research carried out by the Max Planck Institute and the University of Würzburg, as well as the typologies presented in the annual FATF reports.

Criminal financial managers in action

The criminal money-management of the twenty-five high-profit Dutch drug enterprises can be analysed from different angles. In the first place we can address it by means of the money-laundering pattern or categorization, as has been introduced by the FATF and which has been adopted dutifully by most of the academic, bureaucratic and popular writing community, though with minor variations (Van Duyne *et al.*, 2001). For convenience we summarize this pattern as follows:

8 This state of affairs is amplified by assumptions-recycling research projects in which researchers subsequently interview law enforcement 'experts', actually the 'assumption bearers', about their view on money-laundering and organized crime. The resulting research reports are subsequently used by policy makers as 'scientific' evidence. See as a methodological example Savona and Manzoni (1999).

- *placement*: money is put into the financial system.
- *layering* and *criss-crossing*: the sum is divided into smaller amounts for smooth handling and criss-crossed between numerous bank accounts.
- *integration*: the smaller amounts must be put together again.
- *justification*: the crime-money must be justified.
- *embedding*: the money is woven into the upperworld economy.

The outcome of the comparison of this categorization with the findings of the criminal files is summarized in the following table. It should be noted that the observed categories are not mutually exclusive, nor do they represent a necessary *sequence* of transactions. In the course of handling crime-money, the criminal may follow fanciful paths: the money may first be deposited in a bank account, after which it starts to 'travel', to be (partly) withdrawn later on to be deposited in another bank, after which it may be criss-crossed over numerous (foreign) bank accounts, to be finally put (partly) together to form one big sum of money (integration). All this concerns the *handling* of the money, during which it is still as 'black' as it was before: in the eyes of many criminal justice systems, each one of these stages may constitute a separate act of money-laundering, but from the point of view of our analysis, this is irrelevant. *Justification* relates to the proper construction of laundering in the sense of pretending a legitimate source, while embedding the money in the upperworld. It is the final destination or 'white-wash' phase of the successful carrying out of the previous criminal money-management.

Theoretically, all these stages of criminal money-management may be observed in one single case with the same amount of money. That would constitute the ideal pattern of laundering, though it is likely that the real life of criminal financial management will look less neat. After all, criminals need to develop only as sophisticated a model as the control process requires them to do. Moreover, criminal skills, knowledge and discipline vary, and sometimes this generates a 'natural selection' process for those who survive *with* their 'white', legally accepted assets. Apart from rumours, they attain the desired respectability, because successful laundering, by definition, means that no-one knows that their funds have a criminal origin.

As is to be expected, we did not observe such neat ideal patterns. The reason for this outcome is not only the disorderly, murky reality of the criminal business, but also the highly opaque ways in which the Dutch police handled the financial information during a criminal investigation. Most files provided only a few 'slices' of the potential sequence of transactions, while a number of files did not allow any insight into the financial conduct of the criminals. This was – in about five cases – due to the stubborn taciturnity of some suspects, but otherwise the result of the selection process while composing the criminal file, which is mainly oriented to the production of forensic evidence (i.e. for the decision-making of the court). When there is sufficient evidence for conviction, a forfeiture order and substitute

Table 9 The handling of the drug moneys[9]

	Observations
Cash phase: placement/withdrawal	14
Layering/criss-crossing	2
Integration	2
Justification	12
Embedding	21

imprisonment, there is little motivation to obtain more insight into the criminal's financial exploits.

It is not surprising to observe a high frequency of cash handling of the drug money: after all, except where it involves barter, the drug trade is a cash-based economy. As a rule, the observations ended with this phase, for the simple reason that (part of) the money was still in the bank accounts at the time of arrest and was consequently confiscated. The more complicated forms of money-management, like criss-crossing between numerous foreign bank accounts and subsequent integration, were much less often observed. Whether 'justification' represented the real sophistication of the high-level crime-entrepreneurs will be investigated below. In twenty-one observations, the drug money had been 'embedded' in the upperworld, as has been discussed in section 5.2. This embedding ranged from buying securities, like ordinary shares and bonds, to the usual tangible assets like pubs, restaurants, small sport schools and real estate, either as an investment, but more often as their own dwelling. To this should be added the expenses of a luxurious lifestyle, which could not always be qualified as ostentatious (Meloen *et al.*, 2003). Granted, by including this category, the meaning of 'embedding' becomes somewhat tautological, as all money spent on the acquisition of (legitimate) goods or services becomes automatically embedded in the upperworld: it is a component of the GNP.

This analysis, based on the FATF categorization, demonstrates more its limited usefulness than any light it sheds on the financial conduct of criminals. The reason for this may be that this categorization has been designed from the perspective of law enforcement, not to classify the financial behaviour of criminals. From a financial *behavioural* perspective the classification in Table 10 may be more appropriate. The classification aims to map the ways the perpetrators attempt to hide the crime-money itself, or the illegal ways of shielding from law enforcement, whether the police or the Inland Revenue Service.

9 To these scores no figures of money totals could be added. The files were very unsystematic in connecting observed ways of handling money with the amounts of money involved.

Table 10 Ways of disguising and laundering crime-proceeds

Forms of disguise	*Frequency of observations*
Export of currency	31
Disguise of ownership	10
False justification	
loan back	3
payroll	2
speculation	1
bookkeeping	7
Untraceable	4

From our strict interpretation of the meaning of money-laundering – which is much narrower than the legal denotation of that term – only the category 'justification' is considered 'white-washing': claiming a legitimate source for the acquisition of the money or assets. The categories in Table 10 again are not mutually exclusive, as in the same case and with the same money more than one way of handling the crime-money may be performed. For example, a portion of the money may be exported, part of which is subsequently brought back by means of a loan-back construction, while the expensive car is paid for in cash, to be subsequently put in the name of a relative.

Bearing in mind that these observations derive only from identified cases, and that in at least some cases, they may have derived from an era in which it was expected that money hidden abroad was safe from the clutches of the courts, we give the following comment.

Export of crime-money

As can be observed in Table 10, in most cases the money was simply exported: the thirty-one observations, covering seventeen cases, concerned €16.644.000 which had been found in foreign bank accounts (over a time span of eight years). In four cases, there was evidence of money export to foreign bank accounts, though either these accounts were already cleared before the police arrived or the files did not mention any figures. According to these observations, the Turkish/Kurdish drug entrepreneurs exported the largest amount of money: €6.747.000. The Dutch drug entrepreneurs' money exports accounted for €5.689.000, while the Moroccans exported €3.674.000. In the cases of Turkish or Moroccan drug entrepreneurs, this export appeared to be an obvious option, given their country of origin. Either through exchange offices or by physically transporting the cash, the crime-moneys were brought into safety in their home countries. In one attempted case of money export, about €190.000 had been hidden in the elevated heels and soles of shoes the courier was wearing. The awkward walking movement appeared to draw the attention of the customs to this smuggler, who was subsequently brought down to size.

Disguise of ownership

The second most frequently observed form of safeguarding assets while still being able to use them is the simple *disguise of ownership* by putting them in someone else's name. The ways this construction was used reflected only in a few cases some sophistication or preparation, for example when corporate structures (legal persons) were used. The usual defects were (a) the closeness of the relationship between the nominal owner and the beneficiary and (b) the difficulty of the nominal owners to prove that they actually possessed the means to acquire the assets in the first place. Nominal owners were frequently acquaintances or relatives, some of whom apparently found themselves to be the involuntary owner of unknown property. For example, the mother of one middle-level Dutch cocaine trafficker, who only received a meagre pension, was dismayed to learn that she owned a villa. Also in other cases, relatives were (ab)used by putting (moveable) assets or bank accounts in their name. In these cases, natural persons (instead of 'legal persons') as nominal owners appeared to be used by default or as an emergency measure.

Though pre-existing legal persons were used to channel the drug-money, few of them were actually set up for the purpose of disguising ownership. For most crime-entrepreneurs in this sample, this method seemed to be beyond their mental or entrepreneurial scope. The (notable) exceptions were a British crime-entrepreneur, two Dutch cannabis traffickers and a Turkish heroin wholesaler, all of whom invested in real estate using legal persons for the beneficial ownership. Another Dutch hash trafficker established an extensive network of legal persons to disguise the ownership of cash, bank accounts and vehicles. It should be remarked that these corporate constructions to *disguise* real ownership overlaps with the laundering (*justification*) category discussed below: tampering with paperwork and with other evidence.

False justification

From the point of view of 'real' laundering, the successful *justification* for the ill-gotten moneys or assets is the core craft: providing documentary evidence that the increase in wealth, whether in terms of money, assets or valuables, has a legitimate source. One of the methods most frequently used is the often mentioned, well-trusted *loan-back construction*. Given the frequent references in the literature to this, it is surprising to learn that (a) its observed frequency was low and (b) its sophistication was extremely shallow. Van Duyne *et al.* (1990) described a professional provider of loan-back constructions, who designed professional loan contracts, complete with related correspondence and a real money flow of interests and repayments to the lender corporation abroad in order to imitate perfectly real loan transactions (and deduct the paid interest from the rate of income tax). The loan-back provider saw to it that his clients did pay the required monthly interest and repayment.[10] Except for one case, such professional conduct could not be observed in the cases of this study. Loan contracts were sometimes missing, or the apparent 'contracts' did not mention the repayment and interest terms, nor was there any record that the required demonstrable 'flow back' of interest and instalment payments were carried out.

In one case, a thorough loan-back construction running through a number of banks in European jurisdictions like Sweden and Germany – none of them financial secrecy havens – could be observed. In this case, the drug-entrepreneurs were aided by a real-estate developer, who meticulously applied all clauses and time limits of the Civil Code to prevent the invocation of managerial liability, for the acquisition of real estate through loans (from a Swedish bank) guaranteed by collateral in a German bank. As much real estate was bought and sold for increasing prices, the profits could be declared as untaxed speculative gains.[11]

In two cases, the laundering of a monthly income by means of the paying of a salary could be observed. In one case a moderate sum of €75.000 was loaned to an independent but friendly small firm which subsequently handed out a modest monthly salary. Obviously, this laundering was not intended to justify the millions of proceeds, but to placate the Inland Revenue Service and create the illusion of a genuine income.

'Real' laundering by setting up *phoney bookkeeping* to make the money really 'white' appeared to be a craft mainly used by *residential* drug-entrepreneurs. This form of money-laundering related to the way in which their firm functioned as a cover for the illegal activities. For example a florist, using his floriculture as a cover for growing cannabis plants, had to obtain invoices to cover expenses as well as the income from the cannabis sales. In the cocaine traffic with Colombians, certificates of transportation of goods and accompanying phoney paperwork with commodities (sugar) on the parallel market was carried out to justify the return flow of the money to Colombia. Such cover stories were easily busted.

10 The exploits of this money-launderer were not detected because of laundering (not punishable at that time) or fiscal fraud, but because he cheated pensioners.

11 The public prosecutor, not being able to charge for drug trafficking and having made other procedural mistakes, did not press the charge for fraud underlying the constructions and settled the matter out of court.

The untraceability of crime-profits

This is a 'default' category of the supposed moneys which could not be found. This may be attributable to the cunning of the drug-entrepreneurs as well as to shortages of resource and skill among the investigating squads (including the stage at which they were brought in to look at the financial issues). Evidence of criminals trying to get their crime-profits not only beyond the reach of the law but also beyond tracing was derived from telephone taps and sometimes from interviews with co-defenders. They showed that the main concern was not laundering as such, but keeping the money out of the hands of the police and tax man.

Worldwide laundering?

A frequently recurrent refrain in money-laundering literature and political speeches is the transnational dimension: money trails around the world through impenetrable accounts held in sunny, faraway resorts. Such far-flung hideaways do exist, but the question remains of the extent to which wholesale drug entrepreneurs are customers of these facilities. Our wholesalers were certainly not: the exotic 'financial secrecy havens' or – in the terminology of the FATF, 'non-cooperative territories and jurisdictions' – did not figure as frequently as target countries for depositing drug money as was expected. The frequency distribution over the foreign countries clustered around the *neighbouring* countries: Belgium, Luxembourg, Germany and (depending on the nationality) Morocco and Turkey. For other jurisdictions, the frequency distribution was very thinly spread: bank accounts in Panama, Gibraltar, Liechtenstein, Jersey, the British Virgin Islands and Dubai did occur, but in only six cases. It seems that the Dutch drug-entrepreneurs favoured Belgium and Luxembourg, and the Turks and Moroccans their own countries. A Dutch-Thai couple held bank accounts in Thailand because of the nationality of the partner and possibly because at that time, Thailand was judged to be inactive in combating laundering.

This finding does not appear to fit the usual image of 'transnational' criminals spreading their ill-gotten profits worldwide over the 'bad' financial secrecy havens. Instead, it rather seems that the choice of banking jurisdiction is to a large extent determined by proximity to the drug-entrepreneur's 'economic home'. Even in the 'global village' most villains do not venture further than familiar territory, while 'financial brains' like the legendary Meyer Lansky have always been thin on the ground.[12] An alternative explanation

12 The alleged sophistication of Lansky's money-management was less than is attributed to him: much cash transport during the skimming of gambling enterprises in Vegas and otherwise an anonymous account in Switzerland. One message here is the familiar one that one needs to be only as sophisticated as the authorities force one to be.

may be the very uncooperativeness of the financial secrecy havens themselves in the period to which these data relate, which the investigators second-guess by making no further efforts to find the money. That would turn this outcome into an artefact of the actual or perceived investigative possibilities. As we also counted the mere mentioning of foreign bank accounts, even if the balance was unknown, this argument remains pure conjecture. All we can determine is that financial secrecy havens are important, though the frequency of their use was not reflected by our affluent drug-entrepreneurs.

Comparison with other research

The findings of the Dutch research project do not seem to be in agreement with the usual threat image presented by the law enforcement agencies, nor with the regular press reports about the enormous wealth of drug barons. Of course, the existence of a number of extremely wealthy drug barons should not be dismissed as a mere media effect, nor should they be considered representative of the economic landscape of the drug-entrepreneurs. The same applies to their financial sophistication and their economic impact. Nevertheless, the empirical findings in one country should be considered too narrow to allow broader generalizations. What comparisons with findings in other jurisdictions can be made?

To answer this question, we searched for comparative material. This proved difficult for the simple reason that no comparative research has been carried out thus far. Even where there are some scattered data, the different ways of collecting and processing them renders a direct comparison well-nigh impossible. As a matter of fact, all we have are the 'typology reports' of the FATF and a recent modest German study on money-laundering in which the empirical data (experts' statements) are more or less a by-product (Suendorff, 2001). For good or for ill, neither of these rely on conviction of the alleged money-launderers or their principals.[13] In addition, neither the data from the FATF nor those from the German study focus on the relation between drugs and money: the laundering data concern the profits from all sorts of crime.[14] The more thorough research of MacCoun and Reuter (1992) on

Considered the 'accountant' of 'La Cosa Nostra' and alleged to be a man 'worth' $300 million, he lived a modest life. After his death his legacy proved to be almost empty (Lacey, 1991).

13 We recognize that our disciplined adherence to conviction as a criterion may be open to criticism of a kind familiar to corporate crime researchers since the Sutherland era of the 1930s (Weisburd *et al.*, 2001). The appropriateness of methodological standpoints on this issue remains a matter for proper scientific debate.

14 The same applies to Kilchling's reader on the application of crime-money recovery in Europe (Kilchling, 2002), which consists of a selective survey of eight European countries, which because of the diverging methodology of data collection is even more difficult to

drug earnings concerned street-level drug dealing. It revealed interesting income distributions, but at this level of the market, money-laundering equates to daily spending.

Despite this difficulty, we inspected those data from the question: 'if, in this field of drug-money, there is so much money laundered so widely and so professionally, what do the presented examples tell us about that phenomenon?' Underlying this question is a 'surfacing of scale' assumption, namely that if (organized) criminals do succeed in acquiring such predominant (financial) positions in the upperworld, it will not take long before they surface, become spotted, to be subsequently included in the semi-public 'threat catalogue' of the law enforcement agencies. These 'threat catalogues' can subsequently be compared with the outcomes of the Dutch research project.

The study of Suendorff (2001) of the state of affairs of laundering in Germany contains some forty examples of money-laundering in the broad juridical meaning of the word: i.e. every subsequent disguising handling of illegal profits. The examples were provided by interviewed expert law enforcement practitioners and cover a time span of almost ten years (like the Dutch research project), though one example stems from the mid 1980s, suggesting that in practice, a rather more expansive view was taken by respondents.

From this set of examples over this broad time span, *two* cases can be considered to be thoroughly organized money-management: the *Bosporus* case and the *Mozart* case. Both cases concerned organizations established with the purpose to move the crime-moneys of heroin wholesalers to their respective home countries. In the Mozart case, about DM60 million had been transported.

Bosporus and Mozart case: The *Bosporus* case consisted of an extensively ramified network of money-exchange bureaus directed by an Iranian entrepreneur, who served a Kurdish heroin wholesaler. In a well-organized way the moneys were collected in various cities in Germany, carried to branches of the Iranian or associated independent bureaus de change. Subsequently the cash was placed in German banks and transferred to bank accounts of allied money-change offices in New York. From these accounts the moneys were diverted to Dubai and – if required – back to Germany or Turkey. To fool the German police, the bureau de change submitted occasional suspicious transaction reports.

The *Mozart* case represents a similar network of money-change offices working on behalf of Turkish heroin wholesalers, which were fed with crime-money from Italy and Spain. The handling of the crime-money appeared to

compare. But also this survey does not reveal much of 'big crime-money' surfacing in the upperworld.

be even better integrated in the legitimate cross-border trade system of Turkey with Europe. Turkish traders, who were in need of EU-currency, could circumvent the valuta restrictions by balancing their payments in Germany (made through the exchange office in Germany) by the placement of Turkish money in Istanbul. These legitimate moneys (apart from valuta regulation violations) could be intertwined with the crime-moneys.

These examples, which represent quite professional money transport schemes, still do not clarify what is actually done with the crime-money, let alone the ways in which the money is 'cleaned' and integrated as 'white' in the legitimate economy.

When we inspect the examples provided by Suendorff of investment in the upperworld, we get the following picture. In eleven cases there was (an attempt to make) an investment in the upperworld, though with variable success and degrees of professionalism:

- Real estate: three examples of insolvent enterprises, including a construction firm which obtained a suspicious Italian money infusion, but nevertheless went bankrupt. No relationship with drugs is mentioned.
- A greengrocer, whose son was involved in heroin traffic and who invested part of the proceeds in his father's firm, which expanded quickly;
- Some small, unspecified enterprises obtained suspicious money; one was misused by Russians who acquired a share of 10 per cent. The owner succeeded in buying them out. No relationship with drugs is mentioned.
- A bathroom-design store, where the licit Russian owner was pressured to accept a compatriot as manager. Money-laundering is suspected. Also no drug relationship is mentioned.
- Attempts to take over ownership of banks: three attempts were mentioned, among others by the suspects of the above-mentioned Mozart case, who tried to establish a loan firm (*Teilzahlungsbank*), to no avail;
- A pizza bakery, established by a Mafioso family who had fled to south Germany because they had been threatened by fellow Mafiosi. The firm expanded quickly, due to its extortion of the local restaurants and pubs, but was otherwise not drug-related.
- A steel firm with a female manager, who indicated that she 'did not understand much of economics', which was clearly manifest from her very suspicious transactions. No drug relationship is mentioned.
- A car dealership which is supposed to have grown due to Italian crime-money investments, but no drug relationship is mentioned.

These case descriptions recorded in interviews with German investigators should be interpreted with great care. Only in a few cases is it clear that the description is based on a finalized investigation or trial. In many cases, it is not at all certain that any court approved the analysis. In addition, in many cases, it remained unclear whether the moneys, which were supposed to be invested, had been really 'cleaned', i.e. fully laundered. Most of the other examples concerned only the channelling of suspected moneys. The sophistication and professionalism displayed did not look over-impressive (with the exceptions mentioned here).

This picture seems to underline the common statement by some law enforcement officers that 'only stupid criminals are caught' in this context. However, irrespective of the unproven validity of this argument, if every law violator, including the clever ones, has a certain statistical chance of being caught, which increases with the amount of his wealth and the time span of operation, why do we not find more examples of those 'clever guys' after ten years of chasing after the 'big money'? One cunning elusive 'Scarlet Pimpernel' may dodge the law, but a supposed host of golden Pimpernels? Is this absence only due to the difficulties of gathering court-usable evidence in so many different jurisdictions, each with their own regime of evidence finding? Despite the above-mentioned problems of comparability, these findings certainly do not contradict the results of the Dutch research project.

In its annual reports 1997–2002, the FATF has presented various 'typologies' of 'laundering', again in the broad legal meaning of the word. These typologies, hardly deserving that term, consist of a diversity of case descriptions, which are actually intended as instruction material. For a direct systematic comparison they are not useful. This is partly due to the way these examples have been collected. The cooperating countries of the FATF are requested (through their representatives) to submit striking examples from which the secretariat of the FATF can compose its annual selection of laundering cases. The emphasis is on those suspicious transactions which may contain some educational value for the financial institutions, to which are added explanatory and warning notes including 'penetrating' comments like: 'In this way legal persons may be abused for laundering' or 'more cooperation is needed'. The cases concern mainly the *movement* of suspected moneys through the financial system. Only nine of the 'types' or case descriptions mentioned the 'cleaning' of the crime-money in the sense of legitimation or the economic embedding of cleaned money in the upper-world economy.[15] Close reading of the collected typologies over ten years may again raise the questions: 'Where are the really sophisticated "trans-national" drug-entrepreneurs and their launderers? And if there is so much crime-money around that threatens our upperworld economy, where is it, and why are there only anecdotal examples of that global menace?'

Other research findings do not provide us much material for direct comparison either, though they did not contradict the image conveyed by

15 A number of cases actually did not concern money-laundering, but fraud (e.g. VAT evasion in the gold trade), which demonstrates again the overlapping of money-laundering and fraud.

the studies mentioned above. The studies concern the summary and survey of official statistics, such as maintained in England and Wales (Levi, 1997), the US bureau of judicial statistics (Tonry, 1997) and the Central Directorate of the Judicial Police in Italy (Paoli, 1997; Vettori, 2003). The articles show that the researchers had to rely on rough descriptive statistics with very little distinctive features or variables. The gross totals reveal enormous catches by the US Customs and the DEA ($520 million by the customs and $60 million by the DEA). Compared to this, the amounts in England and Wales (£12 million in 1993 and under £8 million in 2001) have been very modest until the legal and resource shift following the Proceeds of Crime Act 2002. However, from these figures, little or nothing can be deduced in regard to criminal financial management, the amount of drug-related moneys or the relationship with the upperworld. For example, in the US, the fact that something has been confiscated does not necessarily imply that it had been acquired with crime-money. Objects can be forfeited if they have a relationship with a crime, even if they have been purchased with 'clean' money. For the forfeiture of a car or house it is sufficient to possess a small amount of drugs while driving that car or to make telephone calls from a house to a buyer of drugs. The American data do not allow us to disaggregate the amounts forfeited after being cleaned from criminal sources, nor sums forfeited from financial and other intermediaries related to primary offenders themselves.

What do these fragmented insights from ten years of combating money-laundering reveal as far as the drug market is concerned? Is there a law enforcement–criminals 'arms race' going on? Do the crime-entrepreneurs respond by updating their money-management skills? Apart from a small number of cases (referred to time and again), there is little evidence for such a 'criminal financial social Darwinism'. Or is there simply less laundering (in the narrow meaning of the word) going on, while most of the drug-entrepreneurs are already satisfied if they succeed in keeping their crime-profits out of the reach of the law? It seems likely that – for the time being – this question has to be answered affirmatively. This implies a less perfect interaction between the law and the criminal community than is implied in the proverbial 'the criminals are ahead of us', which is frequently heard after the introduction of new, more severe legislation fails to stop the drug market or predatory crimes.

There are, of course, other issues highlighted by this analysis. Conviction-based crime-money analysis does not tell us much about the general effectiveness of the anti-drugs trafficking strategy. There may indeed be difficulties in getting evidence linking offenders at the top of the crime networks or hierarchy to the offences, due to corruption, skilful criminal management or lack of law enforcement capacity. Legal professional privilege and restrictions on telephone intercepts and bugging of legal premises can sometimes inhibit the development of better insights into the money-movement process (Middleton and Levi, 2003). However, it seems curious that given the ubiquity of the drugs trade and the resources devoted to investigating it, so little is known in an organized form about how such large quantities of money are inserted into the financial or commercial systems.

6.3 Legislative automatism and tunnel vision

The image of an arms race between the law and crime-entrepreneurs is an emotive metaphor with little descriptive value. It assumes two rationally calculating opposing parties, reacting to each other like superpowers, which conceals the enormous variation between criminals as well as between national law enforcement systems. Actually, proportionately little rationally calculating conduct can be observed: rather, with exceptions, there is a chaotic and whimsical interaction between criminals and law enforcement. From what has been discovered and analysed, as contrasted with hypothesized, criminals have only a very imperfect insight into the law enforcement risks. Their often overstated ways to circumvent these risks reflect a mixture of sheer luck and a bit of cunning based on experience and hearsay. We think it plausible that the interaction is to a large extent characterized by 'trial and error' and learning by doing, alongside some tokens resembling the arms-race metaphor. The criminal's operational economic perspectives and aims are usually narrow too, directed primarily at improving the living conditions of himself and those whom he wishes to care for.

On the part of law enforcement overall, despite gradual improvements in the course of preparing national 'threat assessments' and 'organized crime situation reports', the perspective on the criminal reality is equally imperfect, given the sparse data and surveys, while according to an internal policy paper of the Egmont Group, the targets are set very high: 'rooting out money-laundering'. These often limited insights are usually a kind of compilation of everyday – often recent – experience and a few striking criminal cases or some failed prosecutions because of a divergent opinion of the (appeal) courts. As a rule, when such verdicts concern a matter of evidence or the interpretation of the law, grave concerns arise that the criminals will have an unconstrained set of opportunities. Consequently, unless there is some reason for political opposition or identified incompatibility with the European Convention on Human Rights, initiatives are taken to tighten the law such that the courts are bound to come to the desired decision (from the crime control point of view). Though there are some signs of interest in evidence-led policy making in some European countries and at the European Commission, the impact of new legislation on the small section of actually affluent criminal earners is often unknown and not of primary concern to administrators focused on 'filling the gaps'. The same applies to the potential impact on the crime markets, or, as in this case, the drugs markets. In the previous chapters we have depicted the resilience of these markets. It is not that it is not sensible to conduct a 'gap analysis' or to examine the potential for system arbitrage by offenders arising out of disparities in law, regulation and enforcement practices. However, to show that there is a gap capable of exploitation is not to show how often or under what circumstances it is actually exploited.

Is there a kind of legislative automatism or self-propelling momentum, continuing within its own legal space once it is set into motion, irrespective of the mundane criminal reality? An affirmative answer may be challenging for a debate, but would be a gross simplification. On the one hand, the 'famous cases' are frequently more than sensational incidents, reflecting ongoing developments in the (higher echelons of the) criminal economy as well as serious defects in the system of law enforcement. The remarkable BCCI affair is in this regards a telling example (Passas and Groskin, 2001), which showed some structural issues in the facilitation of serious crime and terrorism – even if monitored by some intelligence services – beyond 'mere' money-laundering.[16] On the other hand, the development of the anti-laundering movement also reveals a momentum of its own towards ever-widening application of the penalization of the handling of *unrecorded* money, which is supposed to be derived from crime. As a matter of fact, financial secrecy is equated to criminal stealth, though some of the grounds for the demand for financial secrecy may be quite honourable (Walter, 1989).

An important driving force proved to be the scare of organized crime in the 1990s, which absorbed much of the driving function of the drug (money) scare. Fighting money-laundering as an aspect of 'hitting the (organized) criminal where it hurt most', became a self-evident dogma, irrespective of the fact that the very concept of organized crime is anything but clear, while proper research based on empirical data other than 'experts' opinions' still remains scarce (Kleemans *et al.*, 2002; Van Duyne *et al.*, 2001; Paoli, 2002a). Subsequently most jurisdictions included all sorts of 'heavy' crime enumerations in the lists of predicate crime. This qualification as 'heavy' or 'serious' does not clarify much, as this is a value term, for which jurists tend to provide some baseline by determining that all crimes are serious if they are punishable with a maximum imprisonment of 'at least . . . years'. In the UK this even includes non-indictable, relatively trivial crimes in the Proceeds of Crime Act 2002. Given the political pressure to be 'tougher' on

16 Though the Tampa sting operation (Adams and Franz, 1992) against the alleged laundering of coca dollars attracted most attention, being sensational and easily fitting into the 'bad guys' image, equally or even more disturbing was the widespread and long-lasting awareness of the shady financial management, benefiting more than one Western secret service, though this does not mean they realized the bank might go 'bust'. The issue of whether the Bank of England was culpably negligent in allowing BCCI to continue to operate is the subject of a civil lawsuit by the liquidators in 2004.

crime, an increasing number of offences are pushed over this penal border into the list of 'predicate crimes'. An increasing number of jurisdictions, like the British and the Dutch, have taken the logical step implied in the dogma 'crime does not pay' and have penalized the handling of *any* money derived from crime, including tax evasion, as money-laundering. After the launching of the fight against drug money, one can observe a policy development, which attempts to eliminate excuses from which those handling suspected (drugs) moneys can exculpate themselves. Gradually the policy has evolved to using the system of financial surveillance to fight 'black', unrecorded money, whatever its source. What is unrecorded tends to be considered criminal, unless the reverse is proven by the identified beneficial owner, either post-conviction or to the tax investigator or civil courts. The circle of the regulated sector, which must report unusual financial transactions to the FIUs, has also been broadened. In the EU and to a variable extent elsewhere, not only financial institutions but also lawyers, notaries, house agents, car dealers, jewellers, and vendors of antiques and precious metals have to report unusual and/or suspicious (cash) transactions, according to the second EU directive 2001.[17]

After the terrorist attacks on 11 September 2001, the scope of the attention to unusual/suspicious transactions has obtained a new global dimension and justification: *terrorist financing* (Levi, 2003a). This tragic event and the subsequent declaration of the war against terrorism seems to have absorbed much of the energy and scarce resources of the other still ongoing 'wars against . . .': drug money, organized crime, corruption of the financial system and other 'global' menaces. Yet none of these 'wars' has ever been terminated with a victory. All we can observe is a continuing unfolding of (penal and fiscal) law enforcement energy and a strengthening of the authorities' hold on trade and industry against the centripetal forces of deregulated globalization. In the process, increasingly more entrepreneurs are designated to act unpaid as updated financial contemporary deputy sheriffs as the price of being allowed to trade. Meanwhile, the criminal reality seems to run its own course, adapting itself to new market opportunities, which are to a large extent developing quite autonomously. This certainly seems to apply to the swings and fashions in the drug market. In our introduction, we presented the human being as the only 'boring animal'. In accordance with this state of affairs, the various modes of drug consumption appear to be addictive as well. Heroin has become a 'loser's drug', hashish is now the beer of the drugs and at present, the popularity of ecstasy is connected to the techno-music scene and may be waning with changing musical fashions. A combination

17 Since January 2002, in accord with the Second EU Directive on Money Laundering, the Dutch law on the notification of unusual transactions (Wet MOT) has been extended: dealers in objects with a high value have to report unusual transactions too.

with Viagra pills may prolong its popularity (and its working life). One does not need much imagination to speculate about the emergence of some 'erection Mafia'. However, if the Viagra industry, stimulated by an increased turnover and profits, turns as blind an eye to unusual routing diversions as do parts of the tobacco industry to the parallel cigarette market (Beare, 2002), we will encounter new connections of drugs and money, this time right in the upperworld. Just as there is counterfeit as well as genuine contraband tobacco, there is already a flourishing online market for Viagra and similar products whose purchasers cannot judge the authenticity of the product until it fails to have the desired effect. A new issue of concern in our 'drugs and money-laundering catalogue'.

7 Haunted by drugs or money?

During the writing of this work, the issue of drug money became overshadowed by the greater scare of terrorism (against Western multinationals and against nations with a military presence in Islamic countries) and the concern about its financing. Does this mean a silent easing of the 'war' against drugs and drug money? Not necessarily and certainly not permanently, as is demonstrated by the ever-increasing DEA budget, reaching $1,9 billion in 2003.[1] In Colombia, the war against drugs efforts have been stepped up again and combined with the fight against guerrillas, who have been declared terrorists (Ronderos, 2003). Given the history of this 'Hundred Years War' against drugs, and the way it has remained a steady component of the US foreign as well as its domestic crime-control policy, it is not very likely that the combat will be over soon. Indeed, a new pragmatic dualistic policy may emerge because of the war on terrorism, as it seems to be evolving in Afghanistan. As in the days of the Cold War and despite the severe governance problems in Afghanistan, the poppy-growing warlords may be left alone as long as they are the allies against the enemy – this time the still surviving Taliban resistance and Osama bin Laden's allies. Opium revenues are not easily abandoned, as the history of the region has shown (Meyer, 2002). The old combination of drugs and money in wartime may again contribute to a tacit understanding: drug entrepreneurs siding against terrorism may be left alone; drug money flowing into the war chest of terrorists is proclaimed the worst-case scenario.

Nor do many European or non-European countries feel particularly tolerant towards the flourishing drug problems in their midst. As other

1 DEA Staffing and Budget. The increase in total number of employees appears to be more gradual than the total budget: since 1993 the increase in staff was 33 per cent, while the budget more than doubled from $921million to $1.897 million. To this should be added the drug budgets of local law enforcement as well as for special foreign programmes, like *Plan Colombia*. There is no easing of the US 'War on Drugs'.

criminologists have noted, it is a common though not universal cultural reflex for governments to react to social problems in their midst by using criminal justice systems to repress criminals rather than to look for more creative approaches such as restorative justice or situational opportunity reduction to lower crime rates.[2] Apart from that, there is an oversupply of crime: illicit transportation of people and goods, fiscal fraud, organized crime, people (especially women) trafficking and terrorism. The enforcement system in practice is forced to prioritize what it is going to spend time on, even as new generic law enforcement bodies are established to orient intelligence-led policing more in the direction of multiple crime-enterprises than against particular offences (see, e.g., the UK's proposed Serious and Organized Crime Agency, Home Office, 2004).

Another historically important determinant is the consolidation of the anti-crime financial policy and concomitant international bureaucratic establishments. These are embodied in the Council of Europe, EU, IMF, FATF (and regional bodies), OECD, United Nations, World Bank, and all the national institutions executing their 'recommendations' to which the more powerful nations contribute disproportionately. For example, the FATF and its policy is served by a worldwide network of institutional 'problem owners'. Institutional rivalries remain important and a source of heavy bureaucratic burdens on jurisdictions who are reviewed by multiple international bodies, but together they have obtained a momentum of their own. After an initial push and having acquired sufficient political mass, such a momentum continues or increases in speed, as the rhetorical goals of reducing levels of criminality (particularly drugs and drug-related criminality) become displaced in practice by more bureaucratically convenient and internally measurable phenomena such as the extension of anti-laundering provisions and the creation of Financial Intelligence Units.[3] The momentum of drug policy and of anti-laundering policy have fused, reinforced by the fear that 'terrorists' (of whatever denomination) might use drug money to finance their evil deeds. Given this double momentum and the not very convincing

2 Statistics are often marshalled to show that x per cent of property crimes are committed to pay for drugs. The difference between reducing burglary and reducing drug *use* is that there are no direct victims of drug use, though there is a proportion of cases where crimes against others would not have been committed if it had not been to pay for drugs. Some of the crimes committed by some of the offenders to pay for drugs would have been committed anyway, because of the values and personalities of the people involved. Drugs can be what offenders choose to spend their money on, rather than a necessary and sufficient 'cause' of their burglaries, frauds, robberies and thefts.

3 Though demonstrating the counterfactual – what would have happened if crime-money confiscation was absent – is far from easy, it is seldom clear whether the goal is the reduction in criminal behaviour or the reduction of the importance of a particular individual or crime group targeted.

past performance in the two adjacent fields of drugs and money, how should we assess these policies? Let us briefly look back at our findings and the history of anti-drug policies.[4]

7.1 Fighting sin, foreign policy and public health

Describing the historical inception, roots and development of anti-drug policies in broad outline, we have reviewed a multitude of interests and values propelling policy makers, politicians and law enforcement agencies towards a war-like approach or at any rate a war-like rhetoric revolving around worldwide controls. This approach did not originate in the European jurisdictions, but in the US before the First World War, which due to American dominance, developed into a worldwide repressive penal law system (Bewley-Taylor, 1999). It had deep roots in the politically important White Anglo-Saxon Protestant conservative rural constituencies, where intemperance and in particular the consumption of alcohol, succeeded by other psychoactive substances, was considered an evil, ungodly sin to be rooted out rather than dealt with on the more gradualist containment model more common in Europe. American moral crusaders overcame industrial interests as well as drinkers and drug users to achieve full prohibition, maximizing and sustaining fear of the consequences of toleration. Part of this struggle involved the bending of statistics to scare Congress into passing the Harrison Narcotics Act. In the evoked climate of fear, false trend statistics lingered on as received wisdom, influencing subsequent regulations, perceptions and the nature of enforcement. Accurate data about the incidence and prevalence of harm were considered subordinate to such higher moral aims and the need for action. A similar approach was observed by Bruun *et al.* (1975) in the international forum of the League of Nations and in the UN in relation to drugs.

Another facet of momentous importance was the ways in which the anti-drug regime played a role in the shaping of a criminal foreign policy, not least that of the US (Woodiwiss, 2001; Bewley-Taylor, 1999; Nadelmann, 1993). Beginning with a foreign policy centred on opium and China, it entered world politics with the establishment of the League of Nations in 1919, to be inherited by the United Nations. The international prohibition agreements entailed ever-increasing international law enforcement cooperation, from which no jurisdiction should escape, though for varied motives, sometimes humanitarian, many countries embraced the social movement against drugs, requiring no pressure from the US. It implied the acceptance of important inroads by penal law enforcement into national sovereignty, encompassing

4 See MacCoun and Reuter (2002) and the articles in their edited collection, for some insights into contemporary drug policies in Europe and elsewhere.

legislative harmonization as well as inter-agency co-operation. Which foreign jurisdiction, aiming to be respected in the international community, could say 'no' or remain blind to the call for the common fight against the international drug fiend? The US alone could afford to grant itself such toleration to anti-communist allies in south-east Asia, Afghanistan and Latin America, aggravating the existing drug problem in the US as well as western Europe.

This display of ambiguous *realpolitik* and the widely publicized scandal of the Iran–Contra affair made no impact on the national or international forum of policy makers. The demonology of drug sellers and the personalization of harm in the form, for example, of the deaths of young people, combined to subdue any statistical evidence of the harms and prevalence of opiates. When about a century ago, the drug problem was put on the agenda of legislators, there were medical problems to which opium and later morphine was a palliative, as well as their use for distraction and recreation. The problem had certainly not yet reached the dimension of an epidemic, but it was given a 'face' and a demonology. This was not without racism, whether openly, as in the first decades of the anti-drug policy,[5] or more implicit in its effects, as reflected in the heavily skewed drugs-related arrest rates of black and other people of colour versus whites in the US (Rasmussen and Benson, 1994; Human Rights Watch, 2000). Nor was it without reinforcement from allied concepts such as organized crime, also usually depicted as an alien conspiracy.

In one combination or another, the moral perspective of addiction to the prohibited psychoactive substances (the 'sin' perspective), public health concerns and foreign policy pressure formed compelling mechanisms. As we have elaborated in section 2.1, the drug issue provided the leverage by which the US could successfully widen and consolidate its international law enforcement reach: 'the ['War on Drugs' has] provided the crucial impetuses for a host of actions and agreements that otherwise would never have occurred' (Nadelmann, 1993, p. 470). Together these pressures kept the drug issue on the international political agenda, in Europe also. However, there are inherent frictions because of the ambiguities in the ultimate public health foundations of the prohibition policy on the one hand, and the apparent lack of success in weaning (young) people off using psychoactive substances, on the other. Though we are *not* arguing that prohibition policies had no effects on drugs consumption, as time went by, the volume and variety of drugs supplies increased in defiance of all law enforcement efforts. Hence calls in some (minority) European law enforcement circles for a shift away from

5 In this regard the testimony of Anslinger (Commissioner of the Federal Bureau of Narcotics) before Congress in the 1930s is telling: 'Colored students at the University of Minnesota partying with female students (white) smoking (marijuana) and getting their sympathy with stories of racial persecution. Result pregnancy' (Woodiwiss, 2001).

penalization, in despair at the perceived lack of impact of policing and interdiction.

7.2 The uncertain grounds of the public health foundation

Public health is a 'public good', which should be cherished at all times. However, is it the firm and indisputable foundation for a penal law regime against taking substances for reasons other than medication?[6] What level of harmfulness (as opposed to popular alarm whipped up by a sensationalist media) is sufficient to merit rational criminal law controls, and how might such rationality be manifested?[7] To answer this question we have to solve two practical difficulties to determine the harm criterion. In the first place, even outside populist politics, people often confound the physiological effects of substances with the things that people do to purchase them at prices artificially inflated by their illegality and with the avoidable absence of quality controls that arises from illegality.[8] In the second place, scientists are far from agreed on the physiological and neurological harms caused by different substances. In 2003, the UK government downgraded the classification of cannabis possession, in line with expert advice. Yet quite apart from the confusion that some British police and public currently experience about the criminal status of cannabis today, some psychiatric specialists made objections. They suggested that the scientific basis for this downgrading is mistaken and have pointed to the apparently raised incidence of psychosis among *some* high-volume cannabis users (i.e. those who have been identified as highly disturbed). Conversely, in the case of ecstasy, it appeared (September 2003) that the cerebral damage caused by ecstasy has been overstated. The conclusion about cerebral damage was based on a mistake that was made during the experiments: the wrong substance had been applied to the monkeys, because the labels on two bottles had been changed. The animals did not get MDMA, but methamphetamine, which poisoned them. Such an accident can happen, but in such conditions of scientific uncertainty, what can and should policy makers do next? Granted, some precautionary principle may lead them to conclude that it is better to be safe than sorry. However, if the substance is not strongly addictive, is mainly connected to raves and

6 In the case of cannabis and diseases such as muscular sclerosis, taking substances *for* medication is illegal too.

7 See Police Foundation (2000) for a good discussion of these issues in Britain.

8 An example of this is the tendency to estimate the 'costs of drugs' to include what people spend on drugs and the crimes they commit to buy them, without making it clear that these (high) costs are largely the result of control efforts. In the Netherlands, ecstasy pills have been controlled by health care institutes at the entrance of discos in order to warn users against polluted pills. This harm reduction measure was highly debated, though.

the techno-music scene and is not demonstrably harmful (if not adulterated), what should be the justification for prohibiting MDMA?[9] The same questions have been raised about cannabis products and have been answered by generations of pot smokers, whose habit has not resulted in a significant public health problem overall. One should accept that a minority have actually been adversely affected psychiatrically; that the smoking of cannabis combined with tobacco has had negative health effects for primary and secondary smokers; that it may harm short-term memory; and that using machinery and driving under its influence is as harmful as drunk driving. However, the 'stepping stone' or 'gateway' theory, according to which the use of mild substances is the first step to heavier ones and subsequent moral and physical doom can be considered analytically empty. The debate about this 'theory' has gone on for decades in practically all consumer countries (see for example: Von Wolffersdorff-Ehlert, 1982). As a *causal* 'theory' it has as much predictive validity as a 'gateway theory' of beer. Many who use more harmful, stronger substances (hard drugs or spirits) started with cannabis or beer, but that was not the necessary *cause* of that conduct. If the theory were generally true, then a larger proportion of cannabis users would come to use other drugs, and all empirical studies show that most do not. Van Ours (2003) indicates that the overlap between cocaine *and* cannabis use is due to personality traits rather than a causal relationship between the two substances. It raises the question whether concern for public health should result in the present strong-arm penal law policy to keep people from developing and indulging in 'bad habits'. The few positive results of this policy to date reinforce these doubts.

It is interesting to observe that at the level of European policy making, such doubts do not mature into a well-founded alternative policy making. Within the European Union there is substantial disagreement on the form of anti-drug policy, with a few member states advocating a more tolerant policy while many prefer a tougher approach. Despite these differences, the European Commission bureaucracy attempts to formulate a more harmonious European approach. However, according to Boekhout van Solinge (2002) bureaucratic policy makers had little awareness of developments in some member states, particularly at local level, where a more pragmatic policy is pursued, directed at prevention and harm reduction. He assessed the expertise and their familiarity with contemporary academic research as low, which resulted (at least in the late 1990s, before the recent massive expansion

9 Experts are not very clear about the harmful effects of ecstasy, if not diluted and not taken in combination with other drugs or in physically unsuitable circumstances like heat. For an early example, see the EMCDDA report by Griffith *et al.* (1997). There are complaints about depression and lack of concentration and about sleep-pattern distortions following ecstasy use, though it remains difficult to determine to what extent these phenomena should be attributed to poly-use or dilution.

of the Justice and Home Affairs Directorate within the EU) in policy papers with hardly any reference to literature. This results in much ritualistic, repetitive policy formulations, by which the risk-averse participants remain largely oriented towards the clichés and 'conventional wisdom' of supply-side repression instead of the more complicated public health and harm-reduction side. Boekhout van Solinge (2002) quotes one EU civil servant: 'With drugs you can always tell a horrifying story. With that you get immediate support of a lot of high-up people'. Such support implies a tough penal law back-up of the public health threat from drugs.

This is not the setting in which to rehearse traditional debates about drug penalization any further. We find it hard to envisage an open, 'global' society without psychoactive substances and without control differences: legitimately, there will always be cultural differences in control-style preferences of democratic societies, as there are on other policy issues. Differences in control style or policy will invariably entail price differences and therefore trafficking motivations and opportunities' arbitrage. At the end of Chapter 2, we referred to the grisly historical condition in which this ideal of total control was approximated: the Second World War during which the stagnation of trade and vigorous cargo controls halted virtually all illegal traffic. But that happened in a world in which we do not want to live or (subject to terrorism and reactions to it) are likely to live. It should be noted that these observations contradict the pressure towards an international acceptance of an American (organized crime) law enforcement control model (Woodiwiss, 2001). This was unambiguously expressed by Clinton's warning in October 1995: 'Nations should work together to bring their banks and financial systems into conformity with the international money-laundering standards. We will help them to do so. And if they refuse we will consider appropriate sanctions'. He called for an international 'no sanctuary' clause 'so that we could say against organized criminals, terrorists, drug traffickers, and smugglers: You have no place to hide'.[10] Yet such an attempt to turn back the tide of individualization and globalized deregulation looks unlikely to succeed, at least in its totality.

Such a claim as President Clinton's is not mere rhetoric. It implies an imposed single perspective and a corresponding globalization of repression model. Thus, quite apart from the need to 'hold the line' symbolically, the pressure for conformity and international harmonization remains. This was discovered by the UK when criticized by the International Narcotics Control Board for downgrading the classification of cannabis. Within such a model, in practice, less attention is devoted to drug harm prevention, including preventing the invention or discovery of future to-be-forbidden synthetic substances and their subsequent spreading. In general, invention of and

10 President Clinton, quoted in the *Guardian*, 23 October, 1995.

experimentation with psychoactive substances has always taken place in social settings in which people do not behave like recluses, but prefer to share whatever new experience they detect. Through worldwide digital communication channels, new discoveries are soon made globally available, though the physical production processes of drugs may require international movement.[11]

We have to face the fact of being surrounded by drugs as well as by incoherent drug-prohibition regimes. 'Effectiveness' is often ill-defined, but controls have hampered, though nowhere stopped, illegal traffic. Given a sufficiently high demand and a willingness to pay the inflated prices, they created the risk 'price wedge' for the risk-accepting crime-entrepreneurs to fulfil that demand. Thus we return to our initial question: given this state of affairs, what has happened to the accrued drug revenues?

7.3 Drugs and money

If psychoactive substances keep haunting policy makers, so do their related revenues. We cannot know whether the criminalization of drug money-laundering and the widening net of regulated bodies would have been accepted and spread so fast had much lower and almost certainly more accurate estimates of the volume of drug moneys been developed earlier. At any rate, the misinformation contributed effectively to the climate of alarm about money-laundering, just as Hamilton Wright's fictitious addiction numbers seventy years earlier had done. In both cases lower, more accurate figures, known to the commissions, were not published, and this choked off a potential debate that might have generated better evidence-led policy. Naylor (1997) even notes a pronounced disregard as far as the figures on the supposed volume of drug money is concerned: as soon as the policy was accepted, neither accuracy nor the figures themselves mattered any more. Accepting this social-political reality as it is, we have to answer the basic question of what is so special about drug money compared with other forms of unaccountable if not criminal incomes?

Let us compare the crime-economy of the psychoactive substances with the other forms of the criminal underground economy (Naylor, 2002) from the perspective of income levels. As in any other economic segment, we have a skewed distribution of income, of which the middle-level and higher segments are of interest because of their financial potential towards the upperworld. In the drug economy, we have the 'big' earners as described in Chapters 5 and 6 and in the journalistic 'Mr Big'-literature, in addition to the many middle-level earners described by Reuter and Haaga (1989) and

11 During house searches in ecstasy investigations the police found the production manuals downloaded from the internet (Gruppo Abele, 2003).

Pearson and Hobbs (2001). We may also include the thriving freelance indoor cannabis growers (see Chapter 4). In the 'economy of fraud and deceit', business crime, we also have the 'big' earners from activities like organized VAT and excise fraud and investment fraud (Meloen *et al.*, 2003; Van Duyne *et al.*, 2003). Depending on the nature of the distribution of goods, we also find a group of middle-level marketeers.[12] Let us assume that at these levels of income, the actors have a surplus potential beyond their exuberant lifestyle expenditures. What difference does it make whether this surplus derives from drugs or fraud? At first sight there is little really special about drug money, though a difference may be made by the social and economic embeddedness of the crime-entrepreneurs and the related financial opportunities. Aside from facilities of laundering the profits, the outlets for the surplus money of the drug entrepreneur differ from those of the business-crime entrepreneur. The financial point of departure of the latter is a bank account (or a multitude of them). The drug entrepreneur starts usually with cash money. Depending on the nature of the business crime-enterprise, in the case of a legitimate continuing business (rather than a self-liquidating scam), the fraudster can plough back his crime-money into his firm.[13] Despite this 'infiltration' opportunity, only a few fraudsters were observed spending their surplus crime-money in that way, mainly in cases of corporate tax fraud, spending the illegal savings (social security contributions) on 'black' payments for their staff. Most of the organized business crime-entrepreneurs appear to spend their additional income from economic crime on an enhancement of their lifestyle, i.e. licit goods (like real estate) and services, while part of the surplus money is put into a (foreign) bank account or conservatively invested in bonds. In this regard, they do not differ from the vast majority of the middle- and higher-level drug entrepreneurs. One important difference concerns the inclination of British- and Dutch-based drug entrepreneurs to spend part of their surplus on the acquisition of night clubs, pubs and restaurants or real estate. The basis for this economic conduct may be social: these locals are the social network hang-outs, and possessing such a place is a tangible and socially understandable investment. However,

12 Whether or not there are layers of transactions depends on the degree to which the fraudsters are integrated in the legitimate industry and the way they interact with their customers and victims. Investment fraudsters do not need a middle-level market, addressing their customers directly. VAT and excise fraudsters need licit intermediate cover firms in order not to raise suspicions and to interrupt the trail of evidence. These cover firms may be a part of the organization, but may also act on their own.

13 See the differentiation between 'economic nomads', the 'front firm jugglers' and the mixers and their relationship to the legitimate industry (Van Duyne, 1997). The 'economic nomads' (like investment fraudsters) and 'front firm jugglers' (long firm fraud schemes, VAT fraud), will have more difficulty in integrating their moneys in the upperworld than will the 'mixers', blending their business fraud schemes with their legitimate paper work.

the night-time economy is also a place where lifestyle, mixing of illicit and licit profits in hard-to-verify ways, and (defensive or offensive) access to physical protection can be readily combined. Real estate is also preferred, because it requires few managerial skills, the technical details of which can be delegated easily. In addition, in recent years, property has appreciated in value because of the excess of demand over supply, without any investment skills being needed.

When we look at the lower levels of the underground economy, the meaning of the differences of the 'colours' of money – criminal, black or grey – blurs from the moment of spending in the upperworld. Apart from the official moral condemnation of the illegal commodities, it is difficult to discern an economic difference between the drug-generated earnings and the income generated by the 'black labour' hired by legal and illegal labour agencies or the revenues from selling pirated branded products. As is the case at the higher levels of the illegal markets, economically these incomes are just a part of a vast number of unrecorded transactions and untaxed revenues, all adding to the 'black' slice of Gross Domestic Product. If the illegal incomes from illegal drugs are exported, for example to production countries, they contribute to the (hidden) GDP in those jurisdictions. Ironically, as we have seen, much exported capital to poor production countries flows back again, when the 'new rich' want to show off their wealth by importing luxury goods from the industrialized consumer countries. To aggravate the negative economic impact, the import of these goods often follows the same smuggling routes as the exported drugs, evading import taxes, by cunning, corruption or incompetence. In addition the influx of this drug capital can cause inflation, like any increase in the circulation of money exceeding the local productivity. This effect has been observed in Colombia and Morocco (De Mas, 2001; Thoumi, 1995; Strong, 1995), where much capital was spent on farmland and real estate. It affected farmers as well as city dwellers, contributing to rising housing prices, while distracting resources from productivity.

The hidden income of this surplus (criminal) capital may be considered a micro-economic 'mixed blessing'. All these illegal incomes provide a boost to the spending power of the economically legitimate circles licitly servicing the criminal earners. This brings wealth in the same way as do the (illegal) migrant workers, repatriating their meagre savings to their families through money-transmission agencies or (more cheaply) by underground banking (Passas, 2001). (All these hidden financial currents have been driven even further underground by post 9/11 registration requirements.) However, though this does bring individual wealth, it represents an unaccountable money volume on top of the official money volume used for budgetary purposes. This implies that the national budgetary policy becomes based on a smaller money volume than there actually is, which distorts fiscal policy. More public income against lower taxes imposed on a broader group of earners would be obtained if the total volume of money could be addressed. It should be noted that the domestic spending of black incomes within the country mitigates this fiscal distortion. Except in very inefficient or corrupt administrations, 'black' money spent in the upperworld economy generates legitimate taxable income of the sellers of taxed licit goods and services. In the end, though more slowly and indirectly than is intended, all the crime-money is processed through the 'big national laundering machine' of the Inland Revenue (Van Duyne *et al.*, 2001). This does not mean that the annual national accounts would not become seriously distorted, if only for the simple reason that the uncontrollable return flow of money in the economy distorts macro-economic variables (Molefsky, 1982). This may have a negative impact on employment policy, public spending and welfare policy.

Irrespective of the nature of its source, crime-money rather appears to be a problem of economic and budgetary control (Tanzi, 1982). However, this would do no justice to an important social-political effect: the *de-legitimizing* effect of the 'grey' economy in which the crime-moneys circulate, as is observed by Thoumi (1995) in the case of Colombia. Such a de-legitimation may develop its own momentum, growing at the expense of the legitimate economy, as can be observed in Italy, Ukraine (Osyka, 2001; 2003), or the Russian Federation (Varese, 2001).

In this perspective, the drug-money issue in the industrialized nations is economically not particularly special and should be considered at the same level as other illegal incomes. A separate point concerns the export of drug moneys by smugglers to the production countries with which they still have connections or which are still their economic and social homes. As far as we are aware, most of the drug money is exported cash to the drug-exporting countries. The huge movement of cash from the US to the cocaine-exporting countries was presented as one of the major concerns of the US policy makers. This concern was explicitly expressed in the first FATF report of 1990. How special was this threat at that time and is it today? At this point we observed a clear gap between the presented image of a threat and the subsequent activities to penetrate the phenomenon and obtain practical insight. As at the beginning of the 1990s, the volume of this cash export still remains unknown, due to the inability (or unwillingness) of the (Western) banks to monitor the cash flow of 'Western' bank notes according to recommendation 19 of the FATF (Van Duyne, 1998).[14] Monitoring should not be impossible, though it should be stressed that the origin of the cross-border cash flows is very diverse and not always criminal: apart from drugs revenues, many migrant workers prefer to send their savings home in cash rather than through bank remittances. Still, an investigation to shed light on this complex

14 This applies to the cash flows between the industrialized consumer countries as well as to the production countries.

phenomenon would be worthwhile, particularly from the perspective of risk analysis. After all, even if the delay is long, most banknotes eventually repatriate to the country of origin, which could generate a country-to-country trail.[15] How much (drugs) cash leaves the European Union? Given the ongoing thriving drug market in western Europe, there is no recorded evidence that this creates such an imbalance as to attract the attention of the monetary supervisors.

We have already observed that in the production countries, the flow of foreign currency can create economic havoc by boosting inflation and distorting the local licit economy. It should be remarked, that this depends on the relation between volumes of the official and hidden economy and the distribution of illegal income. As far as the drug markets are concerned, most of the added value of the transactions is generated in the consumption countries at the lower wholesale and retail level (Reuter, 2000). This income is spread over numerous participants within a strong and diversified economy. The income generated from the export of contraband is more like a bonanza in the hands of much fewer market players, repatriating their profits to a much frailer economy. However, that is not unique to drug money or even crime-money in general. If the revenues from wholesale drug exports entail a bonanza, usually for the few affluent drug merchants, any other 'bonanza export' (e.g. Russian gas, Angolan and Nigerian oil) may create equally distorting effects in a badly and/or corruptly managed economy.

When we return to industrialized economies, like the EU, the drug-money scare becomes well-nigh impossible to explain from an economic point of view. The fear appears to be fanned more from the *law enforcement* and moral perspective than from an economic angle. When the relatively small group of wholesale trading crime-entrepreneurs succeed in acquiring important real-estate interests, they do represent a 'public order embarrassment', morally and in the realm of public order. The moral embarrassment is clear from the adage 'crime does not pay'. For example, it offends the public feeling of justice when there are strong indications that blocks of apartments belong to criminals, even where those alleged connections cannot be substantiated in court. In the field of town planning, quite apart from corruption to evade planning control, the embarrassment concerns the almost invariable mismanagement by crime-entrepreneurs of their real-estate assets, and the pushing up of prices when the council seeks redevelopment. This is also a demonstration of the local knowledge that such rakes' progress appears to proceed with impunity which undermines the legitimacy of law enforcement and the social principle of compliance to legal standards.

15 Unless they are the official currency in the foreign jurisdiction in which they circulate, as is the case with the US dollar in Panama and the euro in Montenegro.

Nevertheless a few remarks should be made. First, such criminal real-estate owners do not necessarily operate very differently compared to powerful licit real-estate corporations, which equally manipulate and frustrate town and country planning (though morality and legal/reputational risk may inhibit licit firms from direct personal bribery). In the second place, outside some southern European resort towns, there is little evidence about the size of the economic and social 'mass' of these affluent criminal investors to exert a decisive influence on local authorities. This may be related to the third observation concerning the social and economic place of top-level affluent drug-entrepreneurs in western Europe. Despite all rumours and concerns, there is hardly any systematic evidence that drug-entrepreneurs are really interested in obtaining strategic real-estate portfolios as a bridgehead to the upperworld. All that could be observed thus far is that a few top-level west European drug-entrepreneurs have succeeded in obtaining more than just a few villas for themselves and relatives: for example some acquired apartment blocks and shopping malls. However, as far as can be observed, these assets have not been used to create a dominant market position. Usually the drug money went *through* the real-estate branch.[16]

To conclude, economically 'lining up' the small elite of really important drug merchants in the industrialized countries yields much justified indignation about their ill-gotten assets, but little discernable economic impact in the form of economic and political 'clout'. This, we stress, reflects what we currently (and only partially) know about those European countries in which published or publishable research has been conducted. The vulnerability of some south-eastern and eastern European countries may be quite different. When one bears in mind that the drug trade has been thriving for decades, the socio-economic impact of mutant narco-capital continues to be a puzzlement.

7.4 Conclusions

It is a well-established custom that researchers in the field of law enforcement conclude their research with some useful recommendations to further the effectiveness of law enforcement (in addition to suggesting further research for which they personally are best qualified). The usual recommendation list contains: more and better policing, investigation, (international) cooperation and the harmonization of legislation. The last often implies increased and

16 There are always worrying exceptions, though with a reassuring outcome: in the 1990s one crime-entrepreneur, a professional fraudster, actually did acquire a real estate corporation, even registered at the Amsterdam stock exchange. However, his conspicuous economic conduct attracted the attention of the supervising authorities, which put the firm under legal restraint. Criminals are required also to behave themselves in the upperworld!

'harmonized toughness' in the sense of the adaptation of mild legal regimes to more repressive ones. However, such a worn-out list of recommendations cannot be deduced as automatically the most appropriate from our description of the drug markets in Europe. We have recounted the emergence and functioning of an illegal market, which is already surrounded by a high density of repressive attention: policing, legislation and international cooperation. Despite these efforts, the drug markets have proven to be highly law enforcement-resistant. We have depicted the smaller and higher-level players in this field, defying for almost a century international attempts to root out their bad habits and the related commercial opportunities. We have also seen that the law enforcement and policy-making elites developed strong resistance traits of their own to policy shifts. In general they prove to be consistently 'refutation-resistant', which implies the blocking of information falsifying the correctness of the prevalent (political) belief system. This results from a combination of foreign policy pressure and social conformity arising from the *group-think* syndrome (Janis, 1972; Janis and Mann, 1977), which does not imply the existence of a conspiracy, but rather a collective decision-making process in which alternative thinking is closed off. An analysis of the decision-making processes in the UN or EU expert commissions as well as the FATF may well be of research interest in this respect. Some of the observations and descriptions of the UN and EU, such as those of Bruun *et al.* (1975) and Boekhout van Solinge (2002), provide valuable insights, which also indicate that the group-think model may have to be supplemented by other explanatory variables. For example, Boekhout van Solinge records little or no inward pressure against dissenting opinions, which do not (or did not at that time) appear to exist on the level of preparatory EU policy making. Neither does he mention the deliberate exclusion of contradictory information, because such reports or publications simply remain unknown or are rarely taken notice of. (Though since his research, there has been a more significant effort to generate funding for more European research on organized crime and to re-think criminal markets in terms of risks and vulnerabilities.) On the other hand, Bruun *et al.* (1975) documented the long-term social cohesion of the 'gentlemen's club', which was furthered by Anslinger's ballot system, pressuring for the appointment of senior staff sharing his opinions (Bewley-Taylor, 1999). The authors also mention the accusatorial, sometimes harsh language used against wavering members of the various bodies of the League of Nations as well as the UN. This is best illustrated by the debates concerning the prohibition of cannabis before and in the decades after the Second World War. Some officials in the UN appeared to have objections to the prevailing policy, but refrained from expressing them publicly, conduct also observed by Boekhout van Solinge in EU bodies. Some members of the Commission of Narcotic Drugs proved to be rigidly inaccessible to dissident public or scientific opinion, as demonstrated by the French delegate, who commented on the research carried out: 'but such investigations should not be allowed to influence international control measures in any way whatsoever' (Bruun *et al.*, 1975, p. 202). In short, the extent to which non-traditional recommendations or critical findings are likely to influence such well-embedded policies and resource priorities as exist in the drugs field remains doubtful.

Our elaboration, reviewing the history and the present state of the drug markets and the related drug money gives little comfort to the official EU repressive[17] law enforcement policy. Nevertheless, the psychological and social health problems surrounding the consumption of illegal psychoactive substances cannot be lightly brushed aside. As Wigotsky (1986) has argued, we can learn to think beyond the war-like imagery. Risks of addiction are not unique to psychoactive substances. Gambling, for a long time forbidden in the US and the Netherlands[18] and exploited by the traditional gangsters as a part of their 'vice industry', can equally lead to a sort of addiction and the ruin of one's life and family. Yet current policy, especially in the UK, appears to favour liberalization of gaming, though maintaining at the same time 'fit and proper person' licensing controls over who is able to operate such businesses, as well as applying money-laundering regulations there. Obesity, due to over-eating, is also a form of life- and health-endangering addiction. Nevertheless, producers of unhealthy fast fattening junk food are not yet successfully branded as 'merchants of death'. Instead of waging a 'war on calories', health departments try to influence the market by stimulating the demand for healthier food, granted with very limited success to date.

Similarly, instead of broadening and perfecting the state's tools of control over its citizens, we can think of scenarios which take the market perspective as seriously as the public health interests. The repeatedly proclaimed aim of 'taking the profit out of crime' can be achieved, not just by stripping the criminals of their assets, but by using the mechanisms of the market, balanced against the public health interests. Medical dispensation of highly addictive substances is already experimented with in the Netherlands and Switzerland, as it was once in the UK. Less habit-forming products like cannabis products and MDMA (in its undiluted form) may be brought under the same regime as tobacco and alcohol. This does not imply that we consider these substances safe or that public health campaigns against them should not be pursued with vigour.[19] Some prestigious medical figures are seeking

17 In the continental European sense of prosecution-oriented rather than in the ethical evaluative sense more common in the English-speaking world.

18 Until the 1970s gambling was forbidden on religious grounds, based on two principles: the command 'Thou shall not serve Mammon' and the temptation of fate, which is assumed to be in the hands of the Lord (depending on the dogma of predestination, which is strongly subscribed to by the Calvinists). This to illustrate the 'connection' between predestination and organized crime!

19 On the one hand, we accept that criminalization and repressive enforcement may reduce the incidence and prevalence of drugs use, via fear of penal sanctions and by forcing

to prohibit smoking in public spaces in the UK altogether (*The Times*, 25 November 2003). Such a prohibition will certainly reduce morbidity and lengthen many lives. However, there is no logical reason for limiting such a health-based prohibition approach to these unsafe substances: there is plenty of room for casting the prohibition net ever wider and, once started, it obtains its own momentum. Instead of allowing such a momentum to develop, it would be better to balance every suggested new prohibition against the societal costs of a clandestine market with all the ensuing criminal behaviour and resulting underground finances. It may be that the benefits of prohibition sometimes outweigh the disadvantages, but this is a potentially rational debate.

We realize that only part of the psychoactive-substance-related delinquency will be affected by such policy changes. In the first place, a part of the prohibited consumer market is inhabited by law breakers who are not primarily addicted to one or more particular substances. Field research shows that most criminal drug users are embedded in (or are addicted to) a criminal lifestyle in which substance abuse does play an important role (Grapendaal *et al.*, 1991), but that the relationship between drug use and law breaking is far from mono-directional or mono-causal (Rasmussen and Benson, 1994; Hough *et al.*, 2001; and Parker *et al.*, undated, for a Europe-wide qualitative review). This implies that part of what is now considered drug-related crime will continue, perhaps concentrated around alcohol or another stimulant like glue. In the second place, the crime-for-profit problem will not disappear but shift to newly created opportunities, given the desire of the authorities to tax any commodity (including currently illegal drugs, if depenalized) that is consumed for pleasure. The 'price wedge' imposed by excise and VAT has already created a thriving economic crime market for alcohol and tobacco in the EU and in North America.

If one supports the right of the State to control the leisure pursuits of its citizens in relation to psychoactive substances,[20] one should realize that such a concern knows neither boundaries nor restraints, leading to policy imbalances if pursued to its logical conclusion. What is required is a much

some level of availability underground, as well as by raising prices (just as higher taxes affect alcohol and tobacco consumption). On the other hand, however, even full decriminalization may not reduce the social stigma that, in addition to pharmacological effects, is a reason why many of us would not take currently illegal drugs.

20 Though the question of at what minimum age one is entitled to decide for oneself is one of the most heated difficulties for even the most ardent depenalizer to deal with. As with many moral panics about crimes and displacement of economic and social despair onto blame for 'drugs', there is a core rationale in the concern about the vulnerability of 'young people' (a usually undefined term) that makes popular sense, especially to parents and communities blighted by rampant situational opportunities for drugs purchase and consumption, and by fear about the future for their children.

more careful and honest balancing of the social and legal costs and benefits of different aspects of harm control in the drug market. It gives us no particular comfort to end with the argument that our societies know far less about how drug moneys are laundered and about the importance of that laundering to the trade than is generally assumed and that 'commonsense' would dictate. But the acknowledgement of relative ignorance can be the beginning of wisdom. We conclude on a note of cautious pessimism, concerned not just about the gaps in our own understanding of the relationship between the proceeds of drug sales and money-laundering, but also about the extent to which those charged with the national and global governance of crime may be willing to re-evaluate their policies in the light of current and future evidence about the drugs–money connection.

References

Abadinsky, H. (1991) *Organized Crime*. Chicago, Nelson Hall.

Adams, S. and D. Franz (1992) *A Full Service Bank: How BCCI Stole Billions Around the World.* New York, Simon & Schuster.

Adler, P. (1985) *Wheeling and Dealing: An Ethnography of an Upper-level Drug Dealing and Smuggling Community*. New York, Columbia University Press.

Adler, W.M. (1995) *Land of Opportunity: One's Family's Quest for the American Dream in the Age of Crack*. New York, The Atlantic Monthly Press.

Albanese, J.S. (1983) God and the Mafia revisited: from Valachi to Fratianno. In G.P. Waldo (ed.) *Career Criminals*. Beverly Hills, Sage.

Alvarez-Roldán, A., J.F. Gamella and J. Sánchez (1997) Trends and patterns of ecstasy use in Spain. In D. Korf and H. Riper (eds) *Illicit Drugs in Europe*. Amsterdam, University of Amsterdam.

Anderson, A.G. (1979) *The Business of Organized Crime: A Cosa Nostra Family*. Stanford, Stanford University.

Ansprenger, F. (1966) *Die Auflösung der Kolonialreiche*. München, Deutsche Taschenbuch Verlag.

d'Aubert, F. (1993) *L'argent sale: Enquête sur un krach rententissant*. Paris, Plon.

Baigent, M. and R. Leigh (1999) *The Inquisition*. London, Penguin.

Barnes, T., R. Elias and P. Walsh (2000) *Cocky: The Rise and Fall of Curtis Warren, Britain's Biggest Drug Baron.* London. Milo Books.

Bartelink, M. (2001) *Antilliaanse drug koeriers: Over de persoon en zijn baan*. Unpublished master thesis, University of Tilburg.

Beare, M. (2002) Organized corporate criminality – Tobacco smuggling between Canada and the US. *Crime, Law and Social Change*, 3, 225–243.

Becchi, A. (1996) Italy: 'Mafia dominated drug market?' In N. Dorn, J. Jepsen and E. Savona (eds) *European Drug Policies and Treatment*. Houndsmill, Macmillan.

Beeching, J. (1975) *The Chinese Opium Wars.* San Diego, Harcourt Brace Jovanovich.

Bell, D. (1964) *The End of Ideology.* New York, Free Press.

Berridge, V. (1999) *Opium and the People: Opiate Use and Drug Control Policy in Nineteenth and Early Twentieth Century England.* London, Free Association.

Berridge, V. and G. Edwards (1987) *Opium and the People: Opiate Use in Nineteenth-Century England.* New Haven, Yale University Press.

Bewley-Taylor, D.R. (1999) *The United States and International Drug Control, 1909–1997*. London, Pinter.

Bieleman, B., L. Schakel, E. de Bie and J. Snippe (1995) *Wolken boven koffieshops.* Groningen, Intraval.

Blum, H. (1993) *De jacht op John Gotti: hoe de FBI de Mafia een gevoelige slag toebracht.* Amsterdam, Luitingh Sijthoff.

Blumenson, E. and E. Nilsen (1997) *Policing for profit: the drugs war hidden agenda.* Http://www.fear.org/chicago.html

Boekhout van Solinge, T. (1996) *L'héroine, la cocaïne et le crack en France: Trafic, usage et politique.* Amsterdam, CEDRO/UVA.

Boekhout van Solinge, T. (2002) *Drugs and Decision-making in the European Union,* London, Transaction. (Also in Dutch as *De besluitvorming rond drugs in de Europese Unie.* Amsterdam, CEDRO/Mets en Schilt, 2000.)

Bovenkerk, F. (2000) 'Wanted Mafia boss' – Essay on the personology of organized crime. *Crime, Law and Social Change,* vol. 33, 3, 225–242.

Bovenkerk, F. and W.I.M. Hogewind (2003) *Hennepteelt in Nederland: het probleem van criminaliteit en haar bestrijding.* Utrecht, Willem Pompe Instituut.

Bovenkerk, F. and Y. Yezilgöz (1998) *De Mafia van Turkije.* Amsterdam, Meulenhoff.

Browne, D., M. Mason and R. Murphy (2003) Drug supply and trafficking: an overview. *The Howard Journal of Criminal Justice,* 4, 324–334.

Bruun, K., L. Pan and I. Rexed (1975) *The Gentlemen's Club: International Control of Drugs and Alcohol.* Chicago, The University of Chicago Press.

Burlingame, T. (1997) Criminal activity in the Russian banking system. *Transnational Organized Crime,* 3, 46–71.

Caulkins, J.R. and P. Reuter (1998) What price data tell us about drug markets. *Journal of Drug Issues,* 3, 593–612.

Cervantes, J. (1983) *Indoor Marijuana Horticulture.* Portland, Interport.

Chambliss, W.J. (1978) *On the Take: From Petty Crooks to Presidents.* Bloomington, Indiana University Press.

Chambliss, W.J. (1994) State-organized crime defined. In P.A. Adler and P. Adler (eds) *Construction of Deviance: Social Power, Context and Interaction.* Belmont, Wadsworth Publishing Company.

Cornwell, R. (1983) *God's Banker: The Life and Death of Roberto Calvi.* Londen, Unwin.

Courtwright, D.T. (1982) *Dark Paradise: Opiate Addiction in America Before 1940.* Cambridge, Harvard University Press.

Courtwright, D.T. (2001) *Forces of Habit: Drugs and the Making of the Modern World.* Cambridge, Harvard University Press.

Courtwright, D.T. (2002) The road to H: the emergence of the American heroin complex, 1898–1956. In D. Musto (ed.) *One Hundred Years of Heroin.* Westport, Auburn House.

Crandall, R. (2002) *Driven by Drugs: U.S. Policy Toward Colombia.* Boulder, Lynne Rienner Publishers.

Curcione, N. (1997) Suburban snowmen: facilitating factors in the careers of middle-class coke dealers. *Deviant Behavior: An Interdisciplinary Journal.* 18, 233–253.

Curtis, R. and T. Wendel (2000) Towards the development of a typology of illegal drug markets. In M. Natarajan and M. Hough (eds) *Illegal Drug Markets: From Research to Prevention Policy.* Money, NY, Criminal Justice Press.

Daams, C.A. (2002) Niederlande. In M. Kilchling (ed.) Die Praxis de Gewinnabschöpfung in Europa. Freiburg, Max-Planck-Institut für ausländisches und internationals Strafrecht.

Della Porta, D, and A. Vannucci (1997) The resources of corruption: some reflections from the Italian case. *Crime, Law and Social Change*, 3–4, 231–254.

De Mas, P. (2001) De poreuze noordkust van Marokko. *Justitiële Verkenningen*, 5, 72–86.

Desroches, F.J. (2003) Drug trafficking and organized crime in Canada: a study of high-level drug networks. In M. Beare (ed.) *Critical Reflections on Transnational Organized Crime, Money Laundering, and Corruption.* Toronto, University of Toronto Press.

Dijk, J.J.M. van (1993) De gelegenheid maakt de Mafia (ook in Nederland). *Nederlands Juristenblad*, 86, 1337–1342.

Dillard, D. (1967) *Economic Development of the North Atlantic Community*. Englewood Cliff, Prentice-Hall.

Dorn, N., K. Murji and N. South (1992) *Traffickers: Drug Markets and Law Enforcement.* London, Routledge.

Dorn, N., T. Bucke and C. Goulden (2003) Traffick, transit and transaction: a conceptual framework for action against drug supply. *The Howard Journal of Criminal Justice*, 4, 348–365.

Droz, J. (1971) *Europe Between the Revolutions 1815–1848*. London, Collins.

Dunlap, E., B.D. Johnson and A. Manwar (1994) A successful female crack dealer: case study of a deviant career. *Deviant Behavior: An Interdisciplinary Journal*, 15, 1–25.

Duyne, P.C. van (1993) Organized crime and business crime-enterprises in the Netherlands. *Crime, Law and Social Change*, 19, 103–142.

Duyne, P.C. van (1994) Money-laundering: estimates in fog. *The Journal of Asset Protection and Financial Crime*, 19, 103–142.

Duyne, P.C. van (1995) *Het spook en de dreiging van de georganiseerde misdaad.* Den Haag, SDU-uitgeverij.

Duyne, P.C. van (1996a) The phantom and threat of organized crime. *Crime, Law and Social Change*, 24, 341–377.

Duyne, P.C. van (1996b) Definitie en kompaswerking. In C. Fijnaut, F. Bovenkerk, G. Bruinsma and H. van de Bunt (eds) *De georganiseerde criminaliteit in Nederland: Het criminologisch onderzoek voor de parlementaire enquêtecommissie opsporingsmethoden.* Arnhem, Gouda Quint.

Duyne, P.C. van (1997) Organized crime, corruption and power. *Crime, Law and Social Change*, 26, 201–238.

Duyne, P.C. van (1998a) Die Organisation der grenzüberschreitenden Kriminalität in Europa. In G. Wolf (ed.) *Kriminalität im Grenzgebiet.* Berlin, Springer Verlag.

Duyne, P.C. van (1998b) Money-laundering, Pavlov's dog and beyond. *The Howard Journal of Criminal Justice*, 4, 374–395.

Duyne, P.C. van (1999) VAT fraud and the policy of global ignorance. *European Journal of Law Reform*, 1, 425–443.

Duyne, P.C. van (2000) Mobsters are human too: behavioural science and organized crime investigation. *Crime, Law and Social Change*, 34, 369–390.

Duyne, P.C. van (2002) Money-laundering policy: Fears and facts. In P.C. van

Duyne, K. von Lampe and N. Passas (eds) *Upperworld and Underworld in Cross-border Crime*. Nijmegen, Wolf Legal Publishers.

Duyne, P.C. van (2003a) Medieval thinking and organized crime economy. In E. Viano, J. Magallanes and L. Bridel (eds) *Transnational Organized Crime: Myth, Power, and Profit*. Durham, NC, Carolina Academic Press.

Duyne, P.C. van (2003b) Organizing cigarette smuggling and policy making, ending up in smoke. *Crime, Law and Social Change*, 39, 285–317.

Duyne, P.C. van (2004) The creation of a threat image. Media, policy making and organised crime. In P.C. van Duyne, M. Jager, K. von Lampe and J.L. Newell (eds) *Threats and Phantoms of Organised Crime, Corruption and Terrorism*. Nijmegen, Wolf Legal Publishers.

Duyne, P.C. van and H. de Miranda (1999) The emperor's clothes of disclosure: hot money and suspect disclosures. *Crime, Law and Social Change*, 3, 245–271.

Duyne, P.C. van and H. de Miranda (2001) *Report on the Falcone Project Database Harmonization of Suspicious Transactions*. Zoetermeer, NRI.

Duyne, P.C. van, R. Kouwenberg and G. Romeijn (1990) *Misdaadondernemingen. Ondernemende misdadigers in Nederland*. Den Haag, Gouda Quint.

Duyne, P.C. van, M. Pheijffer, H.G. Kuijl, Th.H. van Dijk and G. Bakker (2001) *Financial Investigation of Crime: A Tool of the Integral Law Enforcement Approach*. Leliestad, Koninklijke Vermande.

Duyne, P.C. van, K. von Lampe and J.L. Newell (eds) (2003) *Criminal Finances and Organising Crime in Europe*. Nijmegen, Wolf Legal Publishers.

Eekelen, J. van (2000) De neerstag van het misdaadgeld: Montregen, onweersbui of zondvloed? Tilburg, Universiteit van Tilburg.

Fijnaut, C.J.C.F. (1993) De Maffia in Nederland. *Delikt en Delinkwent*, 7, 617–620.

Fijnaut, C., F. Bovenkerk, G.J.N. Bruinsma and H.G. van de Bunt (1996) *Eindrapport georganiseerde criminaliteit in Nederland*. Bijlage VII, Inzake Opsporing. Enquêtecommissie Opsoringsmethoden. Den Haag, SDU Uitgevers.

Fijnaut, C., F. Bovenkerk, G.J.N. Bruinsma and H.G. van de Bunt (1998) *Organized Crime in the Netherlands*, Den Haag, Kluwer Law International.

Firestone, T.A. (1996) Mafia memoirs: what they tell us about organized crime. In P.J. Ryan and G.E. Rush (eds) *Understanding Organized Crime in a Global Perspective*. Thousand Oaks, Sage.

Flormann, W. and P. Krevert (2001) *In den Fängen der Mafia-Kraken: Organisiertes Verbrechen in Deutschland*. Hamburg, Mittler.

Fox, S. (1989) *Blood and Power: Organized Crime in the Twentieth Century*. New York, William Morrow.

Foucault, M. (1977) *Discipline and Punish: The Birth of the Prison*. London, Penguin.

Frank, M. (1988) *Marijuana Grower's Insider's Guide*. Dutch translation by Woord Noord, Drachten, 1994.

Frank, M. and E. Rosenthal (1978) *Marijuana Grower's Guide*. Dutch translation by Woord Noord, Drachten, 1986.

Freiberg, K. and B.G. Thamm (1992) *Das Mafia-Syndrom. Organisierte Kriminalität: Geschichte – Verbrechen – Bekämpfung*. Hilden/ Rhld, Verlag Deutsche Polizeiliteratur.

Frey, B.S. and W.W. Pommerehne (1982) Measuring the hidden economy: though this be madness, there is method in it. In V. Tanzi, (ed.) *The Underground Economy in the United States and Abroad*. Lexington, Lexington Books.

Friman, H.R. (1996) *Narcodiplomacy: Exporting the US War on Drugs*. Ithaca, Cornell University Press.

Friman, H.R. (1999) Germany and the transformations of cocaine, 1860–1920. In P. Gootenberg (ed.) *Cocaine: Global Histories*. London, Routledge.

Gall, L. (1997) *Bismarck: Der weisse Revolutionär*. Berlin, Propyläen Taschenbuch.

Gambetta, D. (1993) *The Sicilian Mafia: The Business of Private Protection*. Cambridge, Harvard University Press.

Gamella, J.F., A. Alvarez-Roldán and N. Romo (1997) The contents of ecstasy in Spain. In D. Korf and H. Riper (eds) *Illicit Drugs in Europe*. Amsterdam, University of Amsterdam.

Gauldie, E. (1974) *Cruel Habitations: A History of Working-class Housing 1780–1918*. London, Unwin University Books.

Gerritsen, J-W. (1993) *De politieke economie van de roes*. Amsterdam, Universiteitspers.

Gold, M. and M. Levi (1994) *Money-Laundering in the UK: An Appraisal of Suspicion-based Reporting*. London, Police Foundation.

Grapendaal, M., E. Leuw and J.M. Nelen (1991) *De economie van het drugsbestaan: Criminaliteit als expressie van levensstijl en loopbaan*. Arnhem, Gouda Quint.

Green, P. (1996) *Drug Couriers: A New Perspective*. London, Quartet Books.

Griffith, P., L. Vingoe, K. Jansen, J. Sherval, R. Lewis and R. Hartnoll (1997) *New Trends in Synthetic Drugs in the European Union: Epidemiology and Demand Reduction Responses*. Lisbon, EMCDDA.

Gruppo Abele, TNI-IECAH and UNICRI (2003) *Synthetic Drugs Trafficking in Three European Cities: Major Trends and the Involvement of Organized Crime*. Turin.

Gunkelmann, M. (1989) Zur Geschichte des Kokains. In S. Scheerer and I. Vogt (eds) *Drogen und Drogenpolitik: Ein Handbuch*. Frankfurt, Campus Verlag.

Haenen, M. (1999) *Baas Bouterse: de krankzinnige klopjacht op het Surinaamse drugskartel*. Amsterdam, Balans.

Haller, M.H. (1994) The Bruno family of Philadelphia: organized crime as a regulatory agency. In R.J. Kelly, K-L. Chin and R. Schwatzberg (eds) *Handbook of Organized Crime in the United States*. Westport, Greenwood Press.

Hamerov, T.S. (1983) *The Birth of a New Europe: State and Society in the Nineteenth Century*. Chapel Hill, The University of North Carolina Press.

Hammersley, D., F. Kahn and J. Ditton (2002) *Ecstasy and the Rise of the Chemical Generation*. London, Routledge.

Harrison, L. (1997) More cannabis in Europe? Perspectives from the USA. In D.J. Korf and H. Riper (eds) *Illicit Drugs in Europe*. Amsterdam, University of Amsterdam.

Harvey, J. (2003) *Compliance and reporting issues arising for financial institutions from money laundering regulations*. Paper presented at the Stokholm International Symposium on Economic Crime.

Himmelstein, J.L. (1983) *The Strange Career of Marijuana: Politics and Ideology of Drug Control in America*. Westport, Greenwood.

Hobbs, D. (1997) Criminal collaboration. In M. Maguire, R. Morgan and R. Reiner (eds) *The Oxford Handbook of Criminology*. 2nd edition, Oxford, Oxford University Press.

Hobbs, D. and C. Dunnighan (1998) Glocal organized crime: context and pretext.

In V. Ruggiero, N. South and I. Taylor (eds) *The New European Criminology*. London, Routledge.

Hobbs, D., P. Hadfield, S. Lister and S. Winlow (2003) *Bouncers: Violence and Governance in the Night-time Economy*. Oxford, Oxford University Press.

Holm, K. (2003) *Das korrupte Imperium: Ein russisches Panorama*. Munich, Carl Hanser Verlag.

Hoyst, B. (1994) Drugs and crime in Poland. *Eurocriminology*, 141–167

Hough, M., T. McSweeney and P. Turnbull (2001) *Drugs and Crime*. London, Drugscope.

Hughes Hallett, A.J. (1997) Money-laundering and measuring illegal activity: an economic analysis. In E.U. Savona (ed.) *Responding to Money Laundering*. Harwood Academic Publishers, ISPAC.

Human Rights Watch (2000) *Punishment and prejudice: Racial disparities in the War on Drugs*. Http://www.hrw.org/reports/2000/usa.

Huskens, M. (2001) *Charles Z: Ex-autocoureur en drugsbaron*. Amsterdam, Meulenhof.

Huskens, M. and F. Vuijst (2002) *XTC smokkel*. Amsterdam, De Boekerij.

ICPO-Interpol General Secretariat Drug Subdivision (1992) *The Balkan Heroin Route*. Lyon.

IPIT-IRT Noord en Oost-Nederland (1996) *Turkse heroïnesmokkel over de weg*. Nijverdal.

Janis, I.L.J. (1972) *Victims of Groupthink: A Psychological Study of Foreign Policy Decisions and Fiascos*. Boston, Houghton Mifflin.

Janis, I.L.J. and L. Mann (1977) *Decision Making: A Psychological Analysis of Conflict Choice and Commitment*. New York, Free Press.

Kalmanovitz, S. (1991) Die Ökonomie des Drogenhandels in Kolumbien. In G. Krauthausen (ed.) *Koka-Kokain: Repotagen, Analysen und Dokumente aus den Andesländern*. München, Rabenverlag.

Keegan, J. (1979) *Dien-Bien Phu*. Antwerp, Standaard Uitgeverij.

Keh, D.I. (1996) *Drug Money in a Changing World: Economic Reform and Criminal Finance*. Vienna, UNDCP.

Keh, D. and G. Farrell (1997) Trafficking drugs in the global village. *Transnational Organized Crime*, 2, 90–110.

Kemmenies, U.E. (2000) *Umgang mit illegalen Drogen im 'bürgerlichen' Milieu: Bericht zur Pilotphase*. Frankfurt am Main, Johann Wolfgang Goethe-Universität.

Kessler, R. (1996) *The Sins of the Father*. New York, Warner Books.

Kilchling, M. (2002) *Die Praxis der Gewinnabschöpfung in Europa*. Freiburg, Max-Planck-Institut.

Kleemans, E.R., E.A.I.M. van den Berg and H.G. van de Bunt (1998) *Georganiseerde criminaliteit in Nederland: Rapportage op basis van de WODC-monitor*. Den Haag, WODC.

Kleemans, E.R., M.E.I. Brienen and H.G. van de Bunt (2002) *Georganiseerde criminaliteit in Nederland: Tweede rapportage op basis van de WODC-monitor*. Meppel, Boom Juridische Uitgevers.

Klerks, P.P.H.M. (2000) *Groot in de hash: Theorie en praktijk van de georganiseerde criminaliteit*. Antwerp, Samson/Kluwer.

Koch, E.R. (1988) *Grenzenlose Geschäfte: Organisierte Wortschaftskriminalität in Europa*. Munich, Knesebeck & Schuler.

Kohn, M. (1999) Sex, drugs and modernity in London during and after the First World War. In P. Gootenberg (ed.) *Cocaine: Global Histories*. London, Routledge.

Korf, D. (1997) Comparison of different estimation methods in the Netherlands. In G.V. Stimson, M. Hickman, A. Quirk, M. Frischer and C. Taylor (eds) *Estimating the Prevalence of Problem Drug Use in Europe*. Luxemburg, EMCDDA.

Korf, D. and M. de Kort (1990) *Drugshandel en drugsbestrijding*. Amsterdam, Criminologisch Instituut Bonger.

Korf, D. and H. Verbraeck (1993) *Dealers en dienders*. Amsterdam, Criminologisch Instituut Bonger.

Kort, M. de (1999) Doctors, diplomats and businessmen: Conflicting interests in the Netherlands and Dutch East Indies. In P. Gootenberg (ed.) *Cocaine: Global Histories*. London, Routledge

Krabbendam, H. (1995) 'De Natie van de vele Naties': Immigranten in de VS, 1776–1924 In E. van de Bilt and J. Toebes (eds) *Een samenleving op de rails: De Verenigde Staten tussen 1776–1917*. Nijmegen, Sun.

Krajewski, K. (2001) Drug trafficking in Poland. In P.C. van Duyne, V. Ruggiero, M. Scheinost and W. Valkenburg (eds) *Cross-border Crime in a Changing Europe*. Huntington, NY, Nova Science Publishers.

Kraus, L., R. Bauernfeind and G. Bühringer (1998) *Epidemiologie des Drogenkonsums: Ergebnisse aus Bevölkerungssurveys 1990 bis 1996*. Bonn, Bundesministerium für Gesundheit.

Labrousse, A. and L. Laniel (eds) (2001) The world geopolitics of drugs, 1998/1999. *Crime, Law and Social Change*, 1–2.

Lacey, R. (1991) *Little Man: Meyer Lansky and the Gangster Life*. London, Random Century.

Lampe, K. von (2002) The trafficking of untaxed cigarettes in Germany: a case study of social embeddedness of illegal markets. In P.C. van Duyne, K. von Lampe and N. Passas (eds) *Upperworld and Underworld in Cross-border Crime*. Nijmegen, Wolf Legal Publishers.

Lampe, K. von (2003) Organizing the nicotine traffic: Patterns of criminal cooperation in the cigarette black market in Germany. In P.C. van Duyne, K. von Lampe and J.L. Newell (eds) *Criminal Finances and Organising Crime in Europe*. Nijmegen, Wolf Legal Publishers.

Levi, M. (1981) *The Phantom Capitalists: The Organization and Control of Long Firm Fraud*. London, Heinemann.

Levi, M. (1994) White-collar crime and the culture of masculinity. In T. Newburn and E. Stanko (eds) *Just Boys Doing Business*, London, Routledge.

Levi, M. (1997) Evaluating the 'New Policy': attacking the money trail of organized crime. *The Australian and New Zealand Journal on Criminology*, 1, 1–25.

Levi, M. (2002a) The organization of serious crimes. In M. Maguire, R. Morgan and R. Reiner (eds) *The Oxford Handbook of Criminology*, 3rd edn. Oxford, Oxford University Press.

Levi, M. (2002b) Money laundering and its regulation. *Annals of the American Academy of Political and Social Science*, 582: July, 181–194.

Levi, M. (2003a) *Controlling the International Money Trail: A Multi-level Cross-national Public Policy Review*, Final Report. Swindon, Economic and Social Research Council.

Levi, M. (2003b) Following the criminal and terrorist money-trail. In P.C. van Duyne, K. von Lampe and J.L. Newell (eds) *Criminal Finances and Organizing Crime in Europe*. Nijmegen, Wolf Legal Publishers.

Levi, M. and L. Osofsky (1995) *Investigating, Freezing and Confiscating the Proceeds of Crime*. London, Home Office.

Levine, M. (1990) *Deep Cover*. New York, Dell.

Levine, M. (1993) I volunteer to kidnap Oliver North. *Crime, Law and Social Change*, 1, 1–13.

Levy, L. (1996) *A License to Steal: The Forfeiture of Property*. Chapel Hill, NC, University of North Carolina Press.

Lewis, R. (1985) Serious business – the global heroin economy. In A. Henman, R. Lewis and T. Malyon (eds) *Big Deal: The Politics of the Illicit Drugs Business*. London, Pluto Press.

Lewis, R. (1989) European markets in cocaine. *Contemporary Crises: Law, Crime and Social Policy*, 13, 35–52.

Liddick, D.R., Jr (2000) Campaign fund-raising abuses and money laundering in recent US elections: Criminal networks in action. *Crime, Law and Social Change*, 2, 111–157.

Lifschultz, L. (1992) Pakistan: the empire of heroin. In A.W. McCoy and A.A. Block (eds) *War on Drugs: Studies in the Failure of US Narcotics Policy*. Boulder, Westview Press.

Lintner, B. (1992) Heroin and highland: Insurgency and the Golden Triangle. In A.W. McCoy and A.A. Block (eds) *War on Drugs: Studies in the Failure of US Narcotics Policy*. Boulder, Westview Press.

Lupsha, P.A. (1987) La Cosa Nostra in drug trafficking. In T.S. Bynum (ed.) *Organized Crime in America: Concepts and Controversies*. Monsey, NY, Willow Tree Press.

Lyman M.D. and G.W. Potter (2000) *Organized Crime*. New Jersey, Prentice Hall.

Lyng, S. (1990) Edge work: a social psychological analysis of voluntary risk taking. *American Journal of Sociology*, 4, 851–886.

Maalsté, N. (1997) The changing use of cannabis after World War II. In D.J. Korf and H. Riper (eds) *Illicit Drugs in Europe*. Amsterdam, University of Amsterdam.

Maalsté, N., I. Jansen, E. van Fessem and A. Mein (2002) *De Noodvoorzieningen voor drugskoeriers*. Den Haag, ES&E.

MacCoun, R. and P. Reuter (1992) Are the wages of sin $30 per hour? Economic aspects of street-level drug dealing. *Crime and Delinquency*, 4, 477–509.

MacCoun, R. and P. Reuter (2002) The varieties of drug control at the dawn of the 21st century, *The Annals of the American Academy of Political and Social Science*, July, 7–19.

McCoy, A.W. (1992) Heroin as a global commodity: a history of Southeast Asia's opium trade. In A.W. McCoy and A.A. Block (eds) *War on Drugs: Studies in the Failure of US Narcotics Policy*. Boulder, Westview Press.

McCoy, A.W. (2000) Coercion and its unintended consequences: a study of heroin trafficking in Southeast and South West Asia. *Crime, Law and Social Change*, 3, 191–224.

McCoy, A.W. (2003) *The Politics of Heroin; CIA Complicity in the Global Drug Trade* (revised edn). Chicago, Lawrence Hill Books.

Mach, H. and S. Scheerer (1998) Vom 'ehrbaren' Kaufmann zum 'gewissenlosen' Dealer: Zum Wandel der moralischen Bewertung des Drogenhandels in der Geschichte des 19. und 20. Jahrhunderts. In B. Paul and H. Schmidt-Semisch (eds) *Drogendealer: Ansichten eines verrufenen Gewerbes.* Freiburg in Breisgau, Lambertus-Verlag.

Mak, G. (1995) *Een kleine geschiedenis van Amsterdam.* Amsterdam, Uitgeverij Atlas.

Malyon, T. (1985) Love seeds and cash crops – The cannabis commodity market. In A. Henman, R. Lewis and T. Malyon (eds) *Big Deal: The Politics of the Illicit Drugs Business* . London, Pluto Press.

Mann, G. (1995) *Deutsche Geschichte des 19. und 20. Jahrhunderts.* Frankfurt am Main, Fischer Taschenbuch Verlag.

Marshall, J. (1991) CIA assets and the rise of the Guadalajara connection. *Crime, Law and Social Change*, 1, 85–96.

Meloen, J., R. Landman, H. De Miranda, J. van Eekelen and S. van Soest (2003) *Buit en besteding: Een empoirisch onderzoek naar de omvang, de kenmerken en de besteding van misdaadgeld.* 's-Gravenhage, Reed Business Information.

Meyer, K. (2002) From British India to the Taliban: lessons from the history of the heroin market. In D. Musto (ed.) *One Hundred Years of Heroin.* Westport, Auburn House.

Middelburg, B. (1992) *De Dominee: Opkomst en ondergang van Mafiabaas Klaas Bruinsma.* Amsterdam, Uitgeverij L.J. Veen.

Middelburg, B. (2000) *De Godmother: De criminele carrière van Tea Moear, medeoprchter van de Bruinsma-Groep.* Amsterdam, Uitgeverij L.J. Veen.

Middelburg, B. and K. van Es (1996) *Operatie Delta: hoe de drugs Mafia het IRT opblies.* Amsterdam, Uitgeverij L.J. Veen.

Middleton, D. and M. Levi (2003) *Dilemmas facing the legal professions and notaries in their professional relationship with criminal clients: national report for the UK.* Amsterdam, unpublished report for the European Commission.

Molefsky, B. (1982) America's underground economy. In V. Tanzi (ed.) *The Underground Economy in the United States and Abroad.* Lexington, Lexington Books.

Mooney, J. (2001) *Gangster: The Inside Story on John Gilligan, His Drugs Empire and the Murder of the Journalist Veronica Guerin.* Edinburgh, Cutting Edge Press.

Morselli, C. (2000) *Contacts, opportunities and crime: relational foundations of criminal enterprise.* Unpublished Doctoral dissertation, Université de Montreal.

Morselli, C. (2001) Structuring Mr Nice: Entrepreneurial opportunities and brokerage positioning in the cannabis trade. *Crime, Law and Social Change*, 3, 203–244.

Mosse, W.E. (1974) *Liberal Europe: The Age of Bourgeois Realism, 1848–1875.* London, Thames & Hudson.

Murphy, S., D. Waldorf and C. Reinarman (1990) Drifting into dealing: becoming a cocaine seller. *Qualitaitve Sociology*, 4, 321–343.

Musto, D.F. (1973) *The American Disease: Origin of Narcotic Control.* New Haven, Yale University Press.

Nadelmann, E.A. (1993) *Cops Across Borders: The Internationalization of US Criminal Law Enforcement.* Pennsylvania, Pennsylvania State University Press.

Nadelmann, E.A. (1990) Global prohibition regimes: the evolution of norms in international society. *International Organization*, 44, 4, 479–512.

Natarajan, M. (2000) Understanding the structure of a drug trafficking organization: a conversational analysis. In M. Natarajan and M. Hough (eds) *Illegal Drug Markets: From Research to Prevention Policy*. Money, NY, Criminal Justice Press.

Naylor, R.T. (1993) The insurgent economy: black market operations of guerrilla organizations. *Crime, Law and Social Change*, 1, 13–52.

Naylor, R.T. (1997) Mafias, myths and markets: on the theory of and practice of enterprise crime. *Transnational Organized Crime*, 3, 1–45.

Naylor, R.T. (1999) Wash-out: A critique of the follow-the-money methods in crime control policy. *Crime, Law and Social Change*, 1, 1–57.

Naylor, R.T. (2002) *The Wages of Crime*. Ithaca, Cornell University Press.

NCIS (2003) *UK Threat Assessment, 2003*. London, National Criminal Intelligence Service.

Oomen, J. (1991) *Coca, vicieuze cirkel in de Andes: Een rapport over cocaverbouw in Peru en Bolivia*. Copenhagen, Impress.

Oosten, R.N.J. van and C.H.D. Steinmetz (1995) *Softdrugs in Nederland: Consumptie en handel*. Amsterdam, Steinmetz advies en Opleiding.

Osyka, I. (2001) Organised economic crime problems in the Ukraine. In P.C. van Duyne, V. Ruggiero, M. Scheinost and W. Valkenburg (eds) *Cross-border Crime in a Changing Europe*. Huntington, NY, Nova Science Publishers.

Osyka, I. (2003) Anti-corruption policies in the Ukraine. In P.C. van Duyne, K. von Lampe and J.L. Newell (eds) *Criminal Finances and Organizing Crime in Europe*. Nijmegen, Wolf Legal Publishers.

Ours, J. van (2003) Is cannabis a stepping-stone for cocaine? *Journal of Health Economics*, 22, 539–554.

Palmer, R.R. and J. Coltin (1995) *A History of the Modern World*. New York, MacGraw-Hill.

Paoli, L. (1997) Seizure and confiscation measures in Italy: an evaluation of their effectiveness and constitutionality. *European Journal of Crime, Criminal Law and Criminal Justice*, 5/3, 256–272.

Paoli, L. (2002a) Italien. In M. Kilchling (ed.) *Die Praxis der Gewinnabschöpfung in Europa*. Freiburg, Max-Planck-Institut.

Paoli, L. (2002b) Paradoxes of organized crime. *Crime, Law and Social Change*, 1, 51–97.

Paoli, L. (2003) *Mafia Brotherhoods. Organised Crime Italian Style*. Oxford, Oxford University Press.

Paoli, L., N. Güller and S. Palidda (2000) *Pilot Report to Describe and Analyse Local Drug Markets. First Phase Final Report: Illegal Drug Markets in Frankfurt and Milan*. Lisbon, EMCDDA.

Parker, H., P. Blanken, J, Fountain, U. Kemmesies, L. Paoli, and K. Spannow (undated) *Workgroup Review of Qualitative Research On Exploring Relationships Between Illicit Drugs And Crime*, www.qed.org.uk/resources/workgroups/crime/crime.shtml.

Parry, N. and J. Parry (1976) *The Rise of the Medical Profession: A Study of Collective Social Mobility*. London, Croom Helm.

Parssinen, T.M. (1983) *Secret Passions, Secret Remedies: Narcotic Drugs in British Society 1820–1930*. Philadelphia, Institute for the Study of Human Issues.

Passas, N. (2001) Facts and myths about the so-called underground banking. In

P.C. van Duyne, V. Ruggiero, M. Scheinost and W. Valkenburg (eds) *Cross-border Crime in a Changing Europe*. Huntington, NY, Nova Science Publishers.

Passas, N. and R.B. Groskin (2001) Overseeing and overlooking: the US federal authorities' response to money-laundering and other misconduct at BCCI. *Crime, Law and Social Change*, 1–2, 141–175.

Pearson, G. and D. Hobbs (2001) *Middle market drug distribution*. London, Home Office Research Study 227.

Pearson, G. and D. Hobbs (2003) King pin? A case study of a middle market drug dealer. *The Howard Journal of Criminal Justice*, 4, 335–347.

Pearson, J. (1973) *The Profession of Violence: The Rise and Fall of the Kray Twins*. London, Weidenfeld & Nicolson.

Perkins, M.K. and H.R. Gilbert (1987) An economic analysis of the US drug control policy: the impact of the cannabis trade. *Corruption and Reform*, 2, 41–54.

Peterson, V.W. (1983) *The Mob: 200 Years of Organized Crime in New York*. Ottawa, Green Hill Publishers.

Police Foundation (2000) *Report of the Independent Inquiry into the Misuse of Drugs Act 1971*, London, Police Foundation.

Port, M. van der (2001) *Geliquideerd: Criminele afrekeningen in Nederland*. Amsterdam, Meulenhoff.

Rakete, G. and U. Flüsmeier (1997) *Der Konsum von Ecstasy. Empirische Studie zu Mustern und psychosozialen Effekten des Ecstasykonsums. Eine Studie im Auftrag der Bundeszentrale für gesundheitliche Aufklärung*. Hamburg.

Rasmussen, D.W. and B. Benson (1994) *The Economic Anatomy of a Drug War. Criminal Justice in the Commons*. Lanham, Rowman & Littlefield.

Rawlinson, P. (1996) Russian organized crime: A brief history. *Transnational Organized Crime*, 1–3, 28–52.

Rawlinson, P. (1998) Mafia, media and myth: representations of Russian organized crime. *The Howard Journal of Criminal Justice*, 4, 346–358.

Rebscher, E. and W. Vahlenkamp (1988) *Organisierte Kriminalität in der Bundesrepublik Deutschland*. Wiesbaden, BKA-Forschungsreihe.

Reuter, P. (1983) *Disorganized Crime: Illegal Markets and the Mafia*. Cambridge (Mass.), MIT Press.

Reuter, P. (2000) *Transnational crime: drug smuggling*. Paper presented at the conference on Transnational Crime, University of Cambridge, January.

Reuter, P. and V. Greenfield (2001) Measuring global drug markets: How good are the numbers and why should we care about them? *World Economics*, 4, 159–173.

Reuter, P. and J. Haaga (1989) *The Organization of High-level Drug Markets: An Exploratory Study*. Rand Corporation.

Ronderos, J.G. (2003) The wars on drugs and the military: the case of Colombia. In M. Beare (ed.) *Critical Reflections on Transnational Organized Crime, Money Laundering, and Corruption*. Toronto, University of Toronto Press.

Rudé, G. (1970) *Paris and London in the 18th Century: Studies in Popular Protest*. London, Fontana.

Ruggiero, V. (2000) Criminal franchising: Albanians and illicit drugs in Italy. In M. Natarajan and M. Hough (eds) *Illegal Drug Markets: From Research to Prevention Policy*. Money, NY, Criminal Justice Press.

Ruggiero, V. and N. South (1995) *Eurodrugs: Drug Use, Markets and Trafficking in Europe*. London, UCL Press.

Sabbag, R. (2003) *Smokescreen*, London, Canongate (published in the US as *Loaded*, Boston, Little Brown).

Savona, E.U. and F. Manzoni (1999) *European Money Trails*. Amsterdam, Harwood.

Schlosser, E. (2003) *Reefer Madness*, New York, Houghton Mifflin.

Schoenberg, R.J. (1992) *Mr Capone*. New York, William Morrow.

Scott, P.D. (1992) Honduras, the Contra support network and cocaine: how the US government has augmented America's drug crisis. In A.W. McCoy and A.A. Block (eds) *War on Drugs: Studies in the Failure of US Narcotics Policy*. Boulder, Westview Press.

Scott, P.D. and J. Marshall (1998) *Cocaine Politics*. Berkeley, University of California Press.

Selling, P. (1989) Zur Geschichte des Umgangs mit Opiaten. In S. Scheerer and I. Vogt (eds) *Drogen und Drogenpolitik: Eind Handbuch*. Frankfurt, Campus Verlag.

Servadio, G. (1976) *Mafioso*. London, Secker & Warburg.

Shawcross, T. and M. Young (1987) *Men of Honour: The Confessions of Tommasso Buscetta*. London, Collins.

Shephard, S. (2000) *Pickled, Potted and Canned: How the Art and Science of Food Preserving Changed the World*. New York, Simon & Schuster.

Simon, H. (1972) Theories of bounded rationality. In C.B. Radner and R. Radner (eds) *Decision and Organization*. Amsterdam, North-Holland Publishing Co.

Slicher van Bath, B. (1987) *De agrarische geschiedenis van West-Europa*. Utrecht, Uitgeverij Het Spectrum BV.

Sournia, J-C. (1990) *A history of alcoholism*. Oxford, Basil Blackwell.

Springer, A. (1989) *Kokain: Mythos und Realität. Eine kritisch dokumentierte Anthologie*. Vienna, Verlag Christian Brandstätter.

Stearns, P.N. (1975) *European Society in Upheaval: Social History Since 1750*. New York, Macmillan.

Stessens, G. (2000) *Money Laundering: A New International Law Enforcement Model*. Cambridge, Cambridge University Press.

Stessens, G. (2001) The FATF 'black list' of non-cooperative countries and territories. *Leiden Journal of International Law*, 14, 199–208.

Stimson, G.V. and N. Metrebian (2003) *Prescribing Heroin: What is the Evidence?* London, Joseph Rowntree Trust.

Stoop, C. de (1998) *Ik ben makelaar in hasj*. Amsterdam, De Bezige Bij.

Strong, S. (1995) *Whitewash: Pablo Escobar and the Cocaine Wars*. London, Macmillan.

Suendorff, U. (2001) *Geldwäsche: Eine kriminologische Untersuchung*. Neuwied, Luchterhand.

Tanzi, V. (1982) Underground economy and tax evasion in the United States: estimates and implications. In V. Tanzi (ed.) *The Underground Economy in the United States and Abroad*. Lexington, Lexington Books.

Tewksbury, R. (1999) The motives and mechanics of operating an illegal drug enterprise. *Deviant Behavior: An Interdisciplinary Journal*, 30, 57–83.

Thoumi, F.E. (forthcoming) The Numbers' Game: Let's All Guess the Size of the Illegal Drugs Industry.

Thoumi, F.E. (1995) *Political Economy and Illegal Drugs in Colombia*. Boulder, Lynne Rienner Publishers.

Toebes, J. (1995) Voorbij de 'Last Frontier'. De Verenigde Staten, 1861–1917. In E. van de Bilt and J. Toebes (eds) *Een samenleving op de rails: De Verenigde Staten tussen 1776–1917*. Nijmegen, Sun.

Tonry, M. (1997) Forfeiture laws, practices and controversies in the US. *European Journal of Crime, Criminal Law and Criminal Justice*, 5/3, 294–307.

Torre, E.J. van der (1996) *Drugtoeristen en kooplieden: Een onderzoek naar Franse drugtoeristen, Marokkaanse drugsrunners en het beheer van dealpanden in Rotterdam.* Arnhem, Gouda Quint.

Transcrime (2001) *The Seizure and Confiscation of the Proceeds from Crime in the European Union Member States: What Works, What Does Not and What is Promising, Final Report*, Trento, Transcrime.

UNDCP (1997) *Economic and Social Consequences of Drug Abuse and Illicit Trafficking.*

Van Nostrand, L-M. and R. Tewksbury (1999) The motives and mechanics of operating an illegal drug enterprise. *Deviant Behaviour: An Interdisciplinary Journal*, 20, 57–83.

Varese, F. (2001) *The Russian Mafia: Private Protection in a New Market Economy.* Oxford, Oxford University Press.

Verbeek, N. (2001) *De baronnen van de cocaïne*. Amstelveen, Uitgeverij de Zaak Haes.

Vettori, B. (2003) *Tough on Criminal Wealth: Law in the Books, Law in Action. An Exploratory Study into the Practice of Proceeds of Crime Confiscation across the EU Member States*, MSc thesis, Cardiff University.

Visser, C.J. (1991) *De Colombiaanse tragedie: Democratie, geweld en cocaïne.* Amsterdam, Uitgeverij Jan Mets.

Wagstaff, A. and A. Maynard (1988) *Economic Aspects of the Illicit Drug Market and Drug Enforcement Policies in the United Kingdom*. London, Home Office Research Study.

Walter, I. (1989) *Secret Money: The Shadowy World of Tax Evasion, Capital Flight and Fraud* . London, Unwin Paperbacks.

Ward, J. and G. Pearson (1997) Recreational drug use and dealing in London. In D. Korf and H. Riper (eds) *Illicit Drugs in Europe*. Amsterdam, University of Amsterdam.

Weijenburg, R. (1996) *Drugs en drugsbestrijding in Nederland.* 's-Gravenhage, Vuga Uitgeverij.

Weisburd, D., E. Waring and E. Chayet (2001) *White-Collar Crime and Criminal Careers*. Cambridge, Cambridge University Press.

Weschke, E. and K. Heine-Heiß (1990) *Organisierte Kriminalität als Netzstruktur-kriminalität.* Berlin, Fachhochschule für Verwaltung und Rechtspflege Berlin.

Westphal, E.J.A. (2002) *Drugsbeleid en synthetische drugsmarkt: Een onderzoek naar vijf jaar aanbod en opsporing van synthetische drugs*. Unpublished Master thesis, University of Tilburg.

Whitaker, B. (1987) *The Global Connection: The Crisis of Drug Addiction*. London, Jonathan Cape.

Wigotsky, S. (1986) *Breaking the Impasse in the War on Drugs.* New York, Greenwood Press.

Wolffersdorff-Ehlert, C. von (1982) Cannabis – die Einstiegsdroge? In W. Burian and I. Eisenbach-Stangl (eds) *Haschisch: Prohibition oder Legalisierung. Ursachen un Folgen des Cannabisverbots*. Weinheim, Beltz Verlag.

Woodiwiss, M. (2001) *Organized Crime and American Power: A History*. Toronto, University of Toronto Press.

Woodiwiss, M. (2003) Transnational organized crime: the strange career of an American concept. In M. Beare (ed.) *Critical Reflections on Transnational Organized Crime, Money Laundering, and Corruption*. Toronto, University of Toronto Press.

Young, J. (1971) *The Drugtakers: The Social Meaning of Drug Use*. London, Paladin.

Zaitch, D. (2002) *Traquetos: Colombian drug entrepreneurs in the Netherlands*. The Hague, Kluwer Law International.

Zuckerman, M. (1980) Sensation seeking. In H. London and J. Exner (eds) *Dimensions of Personality*. New York, Wiley.

Index